HOW TO
CHOOSE
AND USE
TEMPORARY
SERVICES

HOW TO CHOOSE AND USE TEMPORARY SERVICES

William M. Lewis
Nancy H. Molloy

amacom
AMERICAN MANAGEMENT ASSOCIATION

This publication is designed to provide accurate and authoritative information in regard to the subject matter covered. It is sold with the understanding that the publisher is not engaged in rendering legal, accounting, or other professional service. If legal advice or other expert assistance is required, the services of a competent professional person should be sought.

Library of Congress Cataloging-in-Publication Data

Lewis, William, 1946-
    How to choose and use temporary services / William
Lewis, Nancy H. Molloy.
        p.   cm.
    Includes index.
    ISBN 0-8144-5968-4
    1. Temporary employees.   2. Manpower planning.
I. Molloy, Nancy H.
II. Title.
HD5854.L48   1991   90-53214
658.3'128—dc20   CIP

Printing number

10 9 8 7 6 5 4 3 2 1

For
Adele Lewis,
who started it all.

Contents

Foreword

The temporary service business has become a $16 billion per year industry. A temporary employee can fill short-term needs at low cost on little notice, even in specialized fields. This book provides insight into how companies can best take advantage of this growing source of labor.

The benefits of temporary services apply to employees as well as employers. Both parties can gauge skills and aptitudes and decide whether there may be a match leading to permanent employment. As the last of the baby boomers raise families, flextime and job sharing are a fertile environment for temporary employment. This is one way the career-minded can maintain their skills while raising a family.

The homemaker returning to the work force can also develop confidence and additional skills by this gradual reentry into Corporate America. Students may work on a temporary basis to finance their education and check out potential employers.

Specialty temporaries are the newest niche. The health-care, legal, technical, and data-processing industries have a growing demand for skilled, educated labor in the face of a shrinking labor pool. They can tap these resources on a moment's notice, taking advantage of highly qualified specialists with years of experience.

Whether you are in charge of hiring for a small business in the throes of expansion, or are a human resources professional in a major corporation, you will find this book a valuable guide. Its pages explain why companies use temporary help, and how a changing labor market is creating this shift. It shows you how to spot cyclical employment patterns, understand the demographics of the labor market, and determine the cost savings of temporary versus permanent employees.

Training and testing temporary employees are discussed, as well as how to attract and retain the new hire. A seasoned professional will also discuss how to negotiate temporary rates, how to determine the pay scale of temps, and how to select a temporary service that will work for you.

Together, William Lewis and Nancy Molloy bring the confidence and knowledge of forty years' experience to this book. You will find the lessons they share with you to be a valuable foundation upon which to base your plans to buy and use temporary help services.

Betty Connelly
Headquarters Personnel Manager,
Revlon

Acknowledgments

The authors would like to thank the following people who participated in the preparation of this manuscript.

Sincere thanks to Joseph Molloy, without whose support and endurance this manuscript could not have been completed. And to our children, April and Kate, who seemingly understood this effort and played endlessly together while I wrote. And to Michael, with proof that you can set high goals and reach them.

Also with love and affection to Jane and Kirin Lewis.

Special thanks to Doris Wyatt, whose kindness and gentle manner encouraged these writers, and who took care of the children whenever she was needed.

To dear friends Carrie Fried Sutton and Janet Kane, who gave freely of their time and who learned all about the temporary help industry because of this effort. And to Lynn Cohen, who patiently listened to hours of conversation about this manuscript.

The Career Blazers team, especially Arlene Covney, Sarah Engle, Caroline Rau, and Mary Ellen Graziano, who provided insight and information and whose comments helped to refine this book.

The National Association of Temporary Services, especially Sam Sacco, executive director; Louise Gates Seghers, director of public relations; and Ed Lenz, general counsel.

Thanks to Andrea Pedolsky, our editor at AMACOM, who supported this effort from its inception. And to Michael Sivilli, associate editor, who sought perfection.

Nancy Schuman, whose advice is helpful always.

Tom Greble of Roberts and Finger, New York City, whose expertise in the area of labor and employment law provided insight into the law.

HOW TO CHOOSE AND USE TEMPORARY SERVICES

Introduction

Labor is no longer cheap or plentiful. Corporations that were once fat are developing lean profiles, maintaining a core of permanent workers, and "buying" additional temporary staff as needed. Growing domestic and global competition, volatile financial markets, and changing demographics are forcing managers to rethink staffing strategies and to cut expenses. Employers are turning to the temporary help industry for solutions. As a result, the temporary help industry is one of the fastest growing service industries nationwide.

The National Association of Temporary Services reported in 1989 that American businesses employ one million temporary workers each day and are spending in excess of $16 billion annually to purchase the services of temporary help. If the temporary worker or the temporary service is not used wisely, American businesses could loose a large part of this investment. In fact, businesses do not use the services of a temporary help firm as effectively as they could. Research by Career Blazers indicates that less than one percent of all temporary help service users are employing the service to maximum benefit and less than 2 percent are purchasing temporary help services effectively.

Understanding the system can mean more efficient and cost-effective service.

The growth of the temporary industry is part of a larger pattern of nontraditional working arrangements that is transforming the American workplace. Employment growth in the 1980s was marked by dramatic increases in temporary, part-time, contract, and leased workers. Together, these alternative staffing arrangements are often referred to as the *contingent work force.*

As the United States approaches the year 2000, labor economists and industry experts expect the popularity of nontraditional work relationships to outpace the growth of new job development. It is estimated that 28 million people—a quarter of working Americans—hold jobs that deviate from the traditional model of relatively secure, Monday through Friday, 9 to 5 employment. And their ranks are growing about twice as fast as the overall civilian labor force.

Reorganization, mergers and acquisitions, changing global markets, and volatile domestic markets make it difficult at best to forecast staffing needs. At the same time, companies are striving to maintain the minimum work force necessary to handle their daily workload. Managers have discovered that using temporary help enables them to operate with greater efficiency, minimize their obligation, and maintain greater control over their budgets.

The Rise of the Contingent Work Force

The typical model for this postindustrial work force includes a stable core of permanent workers surrounded by rings of temporary, part-time, contract, and other "no strings attached" workers. These peripheral rings compose a work force that can be expanded, contracted, or redeployed according to the shifting needs of the company. Not unlike the much-heralded "just in time" inventory management, contingent-staffing arrangements let employers respond quickly to short-term changes in product or service demand. This elastic outer ring also buffers regular workers against the shocks of downturn or recession, mergers or acquisitions. The battle-scarred survivors of wholesale cut-backs are understandably leery about the next wave of layoffs. This anxiety can take its toll in employee loyalty and productivity. Managers have come to recognize that the use of a contingent work force not only protects but supports and complements the selected core of permanent workers.

While economic pressures are the driving force behind the emergence of the contingent work force, technological and demographic factors have also contributed to its growth. The pervasive computerization of office work strongly encourages the shift to more transitory labor arrangements. The automation of "back-office" data-processing operations has simplified and routinized these tasks. This standardization minimizes the importance of firm-specific training and long-term employee-employer ties. It makes these tasks conducive to part-time, job-sharing arrangements, and unconventional shifts. In addition, the need to capitalize equipment costs encourages the addition of nighttime or weekend shifts, often filled by part-timers.

Professionals are also joining the ranks of the contingent work force in ever greater numbers. Many companies now hire temporary or contract attorneys, accountants, engineers, purchasing agents, marketing specialists—and even chief financial officers. The rapid spread of stand-alone personal computers and word processors has also fostered a new generation of home-based entrepreneurs.

The impact of temporary help has been felt at all corporate levels and in every job category. Office support and clerical temporary workers remain the largest segment of daily workers, filling 63 percent of all temporary work orders. The largest area of temporary help growth in the last three years is the professional temporary worker—the doctor, lawyer, engineer, accountant, nurse, manager, technical writer, and drafter—accounting for 22 percent of all regular temporary workers. The balance of the temporary work force consists of industrial workers, such as custodians, stock handlers, and shipping and receiving clerks. Industry experts assert that there is hardly a job function that could not be, and probably is, assigned to a competent temporary worker.

In the past, temporary help has been used primarily to fill in for vacationing or ill employees. However, a recent survey by the Administrative Management Society on the main reasons for using temporary help indicates that this traditional use has been replaced by the more sophisticated functions of (1) alleviating an overload of work and (2) assisting with special projects.

This book was born out of a need to inform and advise American businesses on how to (1) purchase temporary help services effectively and (2) maximize the value of temporary help.

Chapter 1, "Why Use Temporary Help?" explores traditional use as well as some innovative ways temporary help can work for you. Also in this chapter, we explore various cost factors that may help to reinforce the use of temporary help. Chapter 2, "How the Temporary Help Service Operates," provides insight into the internal organization of a temporary help service. Understanding how the service recruits, trains, and retains its employees will put into perspective the unique relationship that develops between the service, its employees, and you. Chapter 3, "How to Select the Right Service," simplifies the purchasing decision by providing a step-by-step guide to the most effective way to select the right temporary help service for you. Chapter 4, "Strategies for Negotiating Rates," includes straightforward, no-nonsense talk about negotiating hourly rates. Chapter 5, "How to Use a Temporary," will help you prepare for, and integrate the temporary worker into the regular work force in order to get maximum value for your temporary help dollars. It will tell you how to control costs and what you should do if you are dissatisfied with the temporary worker on the job. Chapter 6, "Hiring Professionals as Temporary Workers," illustrates how the use of temporary help has expanded into all levels of management and all job categories, saving even the most sophisticated buyers hundreds of thousands of dollars a year. Chapter 7, "Alternatives to Outside Temporary Help Services," investigates other staffing strategies including such employee-directed policies as flextime and job sharing. Chapter 8, "Employee Leasing," examines this controversial staffing alternative in order to help you determine if it is right for you. Finally, Chapter 9, "Legal Issues Relative to Temporary Help," by Tom Greble, examines areas of possible legal vulnerability inherent with the use of temporary workers.

For your convenience we have included a glossary of terms most often associated with temporary help use. We have also included the "National Association of Temporary Services Membership Directory, by City and State."

1

Why Use Temporary Help?

To remain competitive in an ever-changing marketplace and to cope with fluctuating economic conditions, many managers are adopting a lean and mean style of personnel resource management. In other words, they are cutting back on staff and restructuring jobs, reducing not only annual salary payments but nonwage personnel costs such as recruiting expenses, training, fringe benefits, payroll taxes, worker's compensation, and unemployment insurance premiums. Management has learned that maintaining a lean, regular workforce does not threaten productivity, but rather, provides job security to its selected core.

Temporary help, which had its roots in fill-in replacements for vacationing or ill employees is now being mobilized to enhance and reinforce this leaner work force. More efficient and cost-effective, temporary personnel is helping to reduce the fixed costs of the company payroll. Budget conscious managers have learned that controlling personnel expenses does not mean being understaffed or overburdened. On the contrary, for 90 percent of all business users, temporary help has provided management with its greatest competitive edge. The flexible nature of temporary help has increased productivity, decreased overtime premiums, and asserted savings across the board. Because of this, managers are reevaluating their departmental budgets and including an expense line for temporary help.

An Effective Management Tool

Temporary help is the alternative of choice for managers today because it provides:

- Work force flexibility
- Lowered fixed costs
- Increased productivity

It also supports the principle of "just in time" work force management. Just-in-time work force management is an alternative labor strategy similar to that first introduced by the Japanese, whereby manufacturers take delivery of inventory as needed rather than warehouse large inventories for future use. Recognizing the advantages of just-in-time management relative to the work force, many companies are choosing to buy the services of temporary workers who can be terminated at any time, without obligation. Further, since these arrangements are short-term and intermittent by design, employers have no legal obligation to provide severance pay or rights to reemployment.

Today, employers in every industry are changing the way they meet their short-term and long-term labor needs by staffing on an as-needed basis. These changes are taking place in part because of changes in the makeup of the work force. Some of the dynamics that are creating this flexible work force include:

- Women entering the work force in unprecedented numbers, often combining work and family responsibilities
- Demographics indicating that fewer people overall are entering the work force and warning us of widespread labor shortages

• Second-income households, that are creating more disposable income and a desire for extended leisure time

These demographics are telling us that not only are businesses needing, seeking, and finding a flexible work force, but that workers at all levels are responding in kind, requiring flexible worklife alternatives. The opportunity created by a temporary work force for businesses to purchase specific skills or expertise on an as-needed basis, and to pay for productive time only, has changed the face of the work force forever.

When to Use a Temp

Utilizing a temporary work force is no longer a question of "Should we?" but rather "When should we?" and "How much?" Companies that have never used temporary help before are finding that temporary help is a solution to many of their employment problems.

The following examples are actual staffing problems described to us by our clients. However, the circumstances are generic enough that it is likely that you will recognize or have encountered a variation of the theme. The solutions that follow each example reveal how and why the temporary help service was able to provide the correct response.

Problem: The boss's secretary calls in sick the morning of a big presentation to the board of directors. You need an expert word-processing operator to complete the report this morning. What do you do?

Solution: A good temporary help service is prepared when a client company calls with an urgent need for an experienced temporary worker with proven skills. The temporary help service tests appropriate skills in order to determine and evaluate expertise. It maintains a roster of work-ready candidates who are prepared to report to an assignment immediately. In order to respond to last-minute emergencies, many temporary services have their best temps standing by in their offices ready to be dispatched at a moment's notice.

X   *Problem:* Your company has been awarded a sought-after contract requiring three months of labor-intensive research. You are responsible for coordinating the staffing needs on this project. Do you hire a dozen researchers and place them on the company payroll?

   Solution: Many companies find that it is too costly to process payroll information or to provide benefits for short-term (six months or less) staffing commitments. The temporary help service can provide prescreened, qualified applicants instantly and only for as long as they are needed. For project-type assignments, using an expandable and expendable work force offers both flexibility and significant cost savings.

X   *Problem:* Your company is on the edge of a major breakthrough. If the government approves your product, your permanent staffing needs will double. Past experience dictates caution, yet your staffing needs are increasing every day. How do you manage the increasing workload and at the same time, keep costs down?

   Solution: Temporary help offers the flexibility to staff up or down in direct response to the workload. Using temporary help is the most efficient and convenient way to respond to unexpected or uncertain changes in the workplace.

X   *Problem:* In a drive for business, your company is sending out a mass mailing. The work is simple enough—typing address labels and stuffing envelopes. You hesitate to pull people away from their regular work to accommodate this project. In addition, you don't have the equipment to create the labels or the available space to lay out the materials. The question is, how do you get this vital project done given the limitations on space, equipment, and personnel?

   Solution: Many temporary help services will complete volume projects like this, on their own premises. They use their own equipment and their own employees. They appoint a temporary supervisor to oversee the work and to provide quality controls. The temporary help service relieves the regular staff of the clerical burden and allows them to function in their usual capacity. For the client company, this eliminates space considerations and is cost-efficient.

In each of the above scenarios, the temporary help service can provide a flexible work force that is responsive and tailor-made. Deadlines are met, there is no interruption of service, and the office continues to operate cost-effectively.

When should you use temporary help? Why? The reasons are indeed many and varied. For example:

- *To meet peak staffing demands without overstaffing during seasonal shifts in the workload.* Additional staff may be needed in order to meet cyclical or seasonal workload demands such as inventory, fiscal closings, or budget preparation. Carrying these workers on the payroll all year may be unnecessary and expensive. Instead, recurring or part-time jobs can be filled by skilled temporary workers who can be hired for a specific position/time without obligation. By utilizing temporary staffing you can eliminate employees whose skills are required only some of the time, reinforcing the concept of minimum staffing.

- *To manage unexpected or emergency situations.* The temporary help industry is designed to respond quickly to a call for help. It can provide one or several workers in an hour or less, or a dozen workers often within twenty-four hours.

- *To provide replacements for vacationing or absent personnel.* Absenteeism can mean losses in productivity, orders, or opportunities. The cost of *not* replacing an absent employee is more likely to adversely effect the bottom line than the expense of replacing that employee with a temporary one. Some companies manage the workload during vacation time or extended absences by reassigning the work to other employees, sometimes in other departments. While this may work well for a day, maybe two, it more than likely will create burn-out and lowered morale among an over-worked regular staff. Increases in error, reduced productivity, and overtime pay are decided disadvantages when the regular work force is expected to do too many jobs. Planning ahead and scheduling replacements for vacationing or absent employees can eliminate the need for emergency fill-ins and ensure a continued work flow. It is even possible to reserve the services of a specific temporary worker on a regular basis.

• *To assist during special projects or in meeting deadlines.* The temporary help service is prepared to provide workers who are skilled and ready to work, whenever and wherever they are needed. Situations such as assembling and mailing annual reports, distributing samples, and mailing monthly statements are ideally suited to the use of temporary help. Some temporary help service firms will even act as a subcontractor for a large project and do the work in their own office, or yours, for an hourly or fixed rate. Planned and systematic use of temporary help provides businesses with fast and easy access to a supplementary and flexible work force that can respond quickly and conveniently whenever additional workers are required.

• *Whenever a unique skill is needed for a finite period of time.* From time to time all businesses require expertise which may not be available internally. The temporary help firm maintains a diverse pool of skilled workers who are available for short-term or long-term projects. Managers agree that it is cost-effective to pay for expert or additional help only for as long as it is needed.

• *To fill-in while hiring a permanent replacement or addition to staff.* It typically takes six to eight weeks to fill a vacant position. Among other burdens, this lag-time creates work backlog. Interim staffing with temporary personnel can help to keep the workload up-to-date, thereby easing the burden of backlog and decreasing the cost of lost time for each day a job goes unfilled.

• *In order to curtail overtime pay, supper money, and after-hours transportation expenses.* Overtime pay, at time and one half, is a profit shrinking factor which can cost the company thousands or even millions of dollars a year. Studies conducted by the Bureau of Labor Statistics suggest that permanent employees who work overtime are less efficient and productive. Temporary help can be brought in without the penalty of overtime premiums or differential pay. Supper money and after hours transportation expenses can be curtailed or eliminated.

• *To save on payroll, benefits, and other administrative costs associated with part-time or contingent workers.* Federal and State governments are supporting the adoption of laws requiring businesses to pay a portion of the health benefits for even part-time employees. Some states already require the company to pay a portion of the medical benefits of a part-time employee after 17½ hours a week. These new regulations increase the financial obligation and decrease the advantages of maintaining attachment to a permanent part-time staff. On the other hand, temporary help is not included in departmental head count and the user pays only a predetermined hourly rate and nothing more.

• *To buy time while evaluating a potential new position.* Temporary help can be used while management validates growth or determines the necessity of adding a staff position.

• *To try out a new employee prior to making a firm commitment to hire.* A direct benefit of utilizing temporary help is "try before you hire." There is no better way to predict the success of a potential employee than to evaluate on-the-job performance. Making an informed decision can eliminate costly or embarrassing hiring mistakes.

• *To staff high turnover, routine, and dead-end positions.* Many departments have a need to staff on an on-going basis routine positions that offer little challenge or opportunity for advancement. Because this type of job is subject to high turnover it presents an ideal situation for using temporary personnel. When productivity and interest levels decrease, someone new and eager is assigned.

• *To protect core employees during business growth or decline.* Although periods of transition and expansion often require the resources of additional workers, uncertainty usually prevails. Permanent staff members may feel threatened and resign at a time when it may be difficult or impossible to get authorization for replacements. On the other hand, temporary workers are not subject to head count, are uneffected by the intricacy of corporate changes, and can provide the skills and assistance a department needs during either growth or decline.

■ *To meet the demand of the "new" office.* Office automation has affected how businesses run their offices. Due to the considerable investments businesses have made in their office equipment, it can be costly to leave equipment down for even a few hours. Temporary help keeps the equipment running and productive at a cost you can bear. During a shift from manual to computer or as businesses upgrade their systems, temporary workers help to start the new equipment operating right away and to cover for permanent staff members who are being trained. Temporary help firms have become a major source of workers with sophisticated automation skills.

In 1989, the Administrative Management Society conducted a survey of its members to determine what type of work was being performed by temporary personnel, the frequency of use, and the average length of each assignment. Clerical and secretarial temporary personnel remain the most widely used group of temporary workers. This group of workers is also the easiest to recruit and train. Overall, survey respondents indicated that they have a regular need for temporary help. The majority utilize temporary help on a weekly basis. Finally, the survey notes that the average assignment lasts from one to four weeks. Figure 1-1 shows the results of their survey.

The following lists the wide range of applications for which temporary staffing can effectively be used. Your temporary help sales representative or account coordinator can help you to evaluate and define your temporary help needs, and can recommend which of these applications will save you money:

- Vacation replacement
- To fill-in during illness or temporary absence of permanent staff members
- To handle seasonal or peak workloads
- To supply a specialized skill
- To assist during special projects requiring increased personnel

Figure 1-1. Results of Administrative Management Society survey.

Regarding the *type of work performed,* most companies bring in temps to handle clerical and secretarial duties. Use for clerical functions has increased slightly over last year, while use for secretarial work decreased. The following shows the functions for which temp workers are used.

	1988	1987
Clerical	80%	77%
Secretarial	56%	63%
Word processing	38%	42%
Accounting	28%	29%
Data processing	25%	27%
Central services	13%	13%
Professional/technical	11%	14%
Other	14%	14%

As to the *frequency of use* of temporary help, the majority use temps every week or every other week on average.

Every week	36%
Twice a month	12%
Once a month	6%
Once every few months	28%
Once a year	7%

The *average length of time* for each assignment ranges between one to four weeks.

1 week or less	12%
1–2 weeks	22%
3–4 weeks	22%
1–2 months	13%
3–6 months	13%
Over 6 months	7%

Reprinted with permission from the Administrative Management Society, *1989 AMS Contract Labor Survey,* Business Trend Series.

- To evaluate a position for permanency
- To reduce personnel overhead expenses
- To meet fluctuating business demands
- After a disaster, flood, fire or bankruptcy
- During transition from manual to computer
- During a merger or acquisition
- To restaff after company relocation
- To accommodate full-time employees who request alternative work schedules
- To retain skilled and knowledgeable employees after retirement
- To reduce turnover and subsequent unemployment claims
- To provide work force flexibility

The Hidden Cost Factor

For many organizations, labor is the single greatest expense. The cost of carrying a full-time staff is awesome when the hidden costs are considered (see Figure 1-2). It is our experience that employers often underestimate these costs. The sobering fact is that the real cost of adding just one permanent staff member to the permanent payroll could approach nearly 50 percent above the annual salary. Idle time during recruiting efforts, company-paid benefits, the cost of record keeping in order to comply with government regulations, mandatory unemployment insurance premiums, worker's compensation, and payroll and administrative costs all represent the hidden cost factor associated with hiring permanent personnel. Additional budgeted items such as the cost of advertising to attract talent, agency fees, and preemployment physicals increase the outlay of these hidden costs. The costs to the company for paid vacations and other time-off are also a part of the employment package often overlooked. A cost analysis of these hidden expenses will reveal the true burden of maintaining permanent attachment. According to the U.S. Chamber of Commerce, employing an individual at a salary of $400.00 per week requires $171.28 per week in additional employer paid expenses. Paid time-off could amount to another 9 percent annually. These hidden costs are absorbed by the client company for each employee. When the real cost of permanent attachment is considered, using a flexible temporary work force becomes an appealing and sensible alternative. There are no hidden costs associated with hiring temporary help. When the job is completed the temporary worker leaves and the financial obligation ends.

The use of temporary help is particularly attractive to companies with high fringe-benefits costs. Many companies are actually reducing basic benefits in order to avoid expensive financial commitments and maintain profit margins. Others are coping with escalating benefits costs by supplementing their regular payroll with contingent workers to whom no benefits are paid. To help put this into perspective, the U.S. Chamber of Commerce reports that the average cost of company paid benefits for a full-time permanent employee is 40 percent above the annual salary, not including the cost of recruiting and training. The fact is, that for jobs of short duration (six months

Figure 1-2. The hidden cost factors of hiring and maintaining each permanent staff member.

- Recruitment
- Interviewer's time
- Reference checking
- Payroll processing and mandatory filing compliance
- Taxes—FICA, federal/state, unemployment, worker's comp
- Vacation pay
- Sick pay
- Holiday pay
- Company paid health and life insurance
- Pension plan contributions
- Training
- Bonus
- Payment for nonproductive time
- Recordkeeping

or less), the cost of temporary help is *always* lower than the transaction costs or hidden costs associated with putting a permanent employee on the payroll.

According to the Chamber's *Employee Benefits 1989 Survey*, the average benefit cost in 1988—in addition to wages—was $10,750 *per employee.* This amount includes such nonproductive costs as paid rest periods; payments for time not worked; payment for, or in lieu of, vacation and holidays; sick leave; and parental leave.

Hiring Speed and Efficiency

By employing a large and diverse pool of skilled and available workers, a temporary help service can respond to the short-term and long-term needs of its client companies at a moment's notice. It would be nearly impossible for a client company to match the speed and efficiency of the temporary help service when it comes to filling a vacant position with a skilled candidate. A company would have to wait while it ran a help-wanted ad. It would have to wait for responses, and it would have to conduct interviews before it could fill a given job. It is virtually impossible for a department supervisor to find five experienced data-entry operators ready to start work tomorrow, or a book publisher to find a dozen proofreaders on short notice.

Quite simply, while it typically takes six to eight weeks for a manager to fill a vacant position; longer for positions requiring special skills, the temporary help service is designed especially to meet these immediate needs. "It takes just one call to us and we can instantly supply you with pretested, prescreened and qualified workers. The beauty is that temporary help is never absent and can be excessed when the job is completed," says Barbara Cohen Farber, vice president for Persona, an international personnel service. In most instances, the convenience of using temporary help combined with the minimum training needed by the right temporary worker is appealing and economical.

Increasing Productivity With Temporary Help

Improved productivity and cost containment are priority human resources issues. It is precisely in these areas that the temporary help industry maintains its effectiveness. Industry experts suggest that simply eliminating idle time or nonproductive hours increases productivity. U.S. Department of Labor statistics suggest that temporary workers are productive 90 percent of the day compared to the productivity level of the regular work force that may be productive only 65 percent of the day. Temporary workers are on the job to do one thing—to complete the job. They are not distracted by the socialization or the politics of the office. They are never absent and they don't take long lunch hours. (Interestingly, the longer temporary workers are on the job, the more likely they are to be distracted by the synergy of the office.) The majority of temporary workers are serious about their commitment and will do a good job.

A temporary worker could be deployed to alleviate a highly paid employee from doing routine or fill-in type tasks, thereby increasing productivity and ensuring the value of the high cost employee. A temporary worker hired as a replacement for an absent employee could further reduce the possibility that work would be dumped onto other staff members who then face the burden of doing two jobs. It is clear that productivity is reduced when employees are expected to do too many jobs.

Productivity can be increased by using temporary workers on an on-going basis in tedious jobs. One manager of a major Texas bank reports that she staffs an entire department with temporary help. She explains that when production levels decrease the temporary worker is replaced without obligation. In this way she has cut down on the high cost of turnover and has improved production. Similarly, where projects are labor intensive (litigation support for example), it is possible that permanent workers will exhibit symptoms of burn-out, and increased error ratios; newly assigned prescreened workers bring enthusiasm to the job, decreasing errors, and increasing productivity with sheer eagerness. The net effect of replacing slower workers with new ones results in increased productivity.

Eliminating Costly Overtime

The overtime issue is a critical one. According to the Bureau of Labor Statistics, an employee arriving at work can be considered 100 percent productive. During the course of an eight hour day, productivity steadily declines until, by the end of the day, it is 50 percent of the first hour. At the same time, the probability of error rises to 40 percent. Permanent employees that work overtime are significantly less effective and productive than temporary workers. After the first hour of overtime, productivity continues to decline and the probability of error continues to increase.

Monetary considerations not withstanding, labor experts and managers need to wonder if paying premium wages for overtime is cost-effective at all. Interviews with managers who have utilized temporary personnel as an alternative to overtime, agree that temporary help is productive 90 to 100 percent of the time they are on the job. By incorporating temporary help into your business plans, overtime expenses can be reduced and production levels can be increased.

Turnover Management

Termination by either staff reduction or turnover is costly to any company. Of particular importance and consideration is the cost of unemployment insurance contributions which are the direct result of separations. High turnover situations and staff reductions will adversely effect unemployment insurance rates. The use of temporary help can limit the risks associated with separation because there is *no commitment* to the temporary worker by the client company. Informed managers recognize the positive impact temporary help can have on reducing turnover rates. They are opting to staff routine and repetitive or dead-end jobs with competent temporary workers in order to limit the expense of hiring, training, and maintaining a staff which turns over every six months. In situations where turnover rates are high, many managers are already using temporary help on an on-going basis.

The temporary help service does not eliminate turnover in these jobs. But because of the provisional nature of its work force, it can absorb and insulate the client company from the cost of turnover. The temporary help service keeps its unemployment claims to a minimum by reassigning available workers on an on-going basis.

The Concept of Minimum Staffing

Minimum staffing is defined by labor experts as the fewest number of individuals needed to run an office or worksite effectively and efficiently. Companies are striving to maintain the minimum work force necessary to handle their minimum daily workload. In other words, managers are employing a core of permanent workers and buying the services of additional workers only when needed. This unattached ring of temporary workers are used as a stabilizing force against competition and changing markets, and to reduce and limit the trauma of staff reductions which may result from changes in the marketplace or economy.

The graph in Figure 1-3 is designed to illustrate the cyclical and usually predictable peaks and valley type workload experienced by most companies throughout the year. It makes sense to limit the head count to the minimum number of permanent employees needed to meet the lowest anticipated staffing needs and to plan and budget for temporary help usage in order to handle those peak periods. This avoids overstaffing and overtime, and is cost-efficient.

Managers have learned that maintaining attachment in order to meet fluctuating workload demand is irresponsible. Instead, they are keeping a tight rein on their personnel-related budgets and choosing to operate their departments slightly understaffed. They have gained an edge by using temporary help on an as-needed basis minimizing the risks associated with permanent staff reductions. And, they have seen production increase, overtime premiums decrease, and profit margins grow.

Figure 1-3. Concept of minimum staffing.

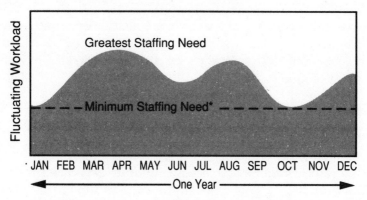

*Staff to this point and supplement staff with temporaries
during periods of increased workload demands.

Advantages vs. Disadvantages of Temporary Staffing

The disadvantages of using temporary help services as well as the advantages must be evaluated (see Figure 1-4). While it is frequently useful for a company to employ a flexible ring, or temporary work force to supplement a core of permanent employees, there are circumstances where management may consider temporary help too costly.

Some people think that when temporary help is needed for a period of six months or more, it is advisable to hire a full-time employee. However, this is not always the case. Work that is tedious, boring, or that offers no opportunity for advancement, often is reflected in constant turnover and high absenteeism. This is the perfect situation for temporary staffing.

It may be less economical to use temporary help for jobs requiring extensive training or supervision, although some temporary help service firms will pretrain and supervise their own employees on the job. Unless the job is company-specific or highly technical, there are probably temporary help services recruiting temporary help workers with the skills you need.

Replacing overtime opportunities for regular employees

Figure 1-4. Advantages and disadvantages of temporary help use.

Advantages	Disadvantages
• Controls or eliminates lay-offs of permanent employees.	• Training and retraining of temporary workers can be an added expense.
• No long-term commitment or financial obligation.	• Low or no attachment or commitment which would encourage quality of work.
• Reduction of turnover statistics for tedious, routine, or dead end jobs.	• Lack of quality control.
• "Try before you hire"—a recruiting source of pretested and prescreened personnel.	• Supervising temporary workers can be more difficult.
• Unsatisfactory temporary workers can be replaced without all the implications of firing permanent employees.	
• Skilled workers are available on short notice, even when a large number are needed.	

with temporary personnel may create a morale problem and result in turnover. However, you can't always get regular employees to work overtime when you need them. Using temporary workers is a quick solution. You should evaluate productivity, availability, and cost relative to overtime premiums, in order to determine if temporary help would be advantageous.

Low attachment could be problematic, yet it is this very feature that makes temporary staffing so attractive to over 90 percent of American businesses. Requesting the services of temporary workers who are already familiar with your office routine, equipment, and even possibly the workload, helps to build a sense of company loyalty with those temporary workers and as a result, improves productivity.

It is possible that regular employees feel burnt out by staff reductions that mean fewer people doing the same amount of work and resentful of temporary help use because of the additional burden it places on them to adjust to changing personnel. Explaining the temp's presence, for example, to provide hands-on assistance during peak workload times or to provide assistance for special projects, can be a real morale booster for the permanent staff.

Managers feel that supervising temporary employees over whom they maintain little control is more difficult. Yet this is an area where a good temporary help company can provide a real service and relieve some of the burden. The temporary help service should give a thorough orientation to each temporary worker that describes what is required by the client on that particular assignment. A good temporary help service will maintain contact throughout the assignment with both the temporary worker and the order placer.

In addition, the application of temporary help to control and eliminate lay-offs due to overstaffing represents real dollar savings on unemployment premiums and severance pay. Overall, you don't want to exchange quality for flexibility so it is important to select a temporary help service that takes applicant screening and quality control seriously.

Common Objections to Utilizing Temporary Help

- *"Temporary help is too expensive."* On the contrary, using temporary help is the cost-conscious alternative. The true cost of labor including, payroll taxes, fringe benefits, hiring costs, and nonproductive time coupled with the fact that when the job is completed the temporary worker is no longer a burden, proves that this obligation-free alternative is the smart choice. We agree, however, that temporary help is too expensive if there is not enough work to keep the temporary busy while on the job or if you are paying for more skill than you need.

- *"Our employees cover whenever someone goes on vacation or is otherwise absent."* Taking an employee from one department to work in another diminishes the productivity of that employee's department. When employees are asked to do too many jobs, morale is affected and productivity is reduced.

- *"The work is too technical or confidential."* The advantages of temporary help can benefit business users at all levels of employment. Technical writers to missile engineers are seeking and finding temporary work. Many temporary workers are bonded and insured. For further protection where confidentiality is an issue, the temporary help service can supply a confidentiality waiver. It is likely that a temporary help company services your specialty.

- *"Temporary workers require too much training."* Temporary workers need a minimum amount of training, because they are skilled in the area that you request and can usually adapt quickly. The worker *will* need a few minutes' orientation, a review of the day's work, and supervision throughout the day.

- *"We keep a list of on-call workers."* The personnel or office manager would have to keep a large and updated list of available workers with a variety of skills in order to meet its needs. Then, he or she would have to make approximately one half dozen calls before filling just one vacancy (the average number of calls the temporary help service makes)—rather time consuming for any manager. Perhaps more important, though, are the high administrative and payroll costs associated with implementing your own temporary pool.

- *"We have been dissatisfied with the temporary help we have used."* This is always unfortunate as the majority of temporary workers are satisfactory. However, if you are dissatisfied with the temporary worker that is assigned, let the service know this immediately and ask for either a replacement or credit. Finding a service that can consistently supply the quality and skilled individuals you require can prove to be an invaluable resource.

2

How the Temporary Help Service Operates

Most temporary help firms are owned and operated by industry professionals. Some have expanded into multinational corporations offering a broad range of personnel services including temporary help, training, and permanent placement services. Some of these are licensees or franchise operations. Others specialize by becoming experts in a particular field and still others are "Mom and Pop" type operations. All act as representatives to both the applicant and the client company. While the temporary help service is satisfying the temporary help needs of its client companies, it must also fulfill the expectations of its workers. Those expectations usually pertain to the type of industry, the location, and the hourly pay the temporary employee is willing to accept. Understanding how the temporary help service operates and learning exactly what services it can provide, will help you to obtain more efficient and cost-effective service.

The temporary help service is the legal employer of the workers it supplies. So that it is capable of filling an important vacant position for a client company—often on short notice, the temporary help service recruits, screens, tests, hires, in some cases trains, and retains a large pool of skilled workers. Because the workers are employed by the temporary help service, the client company is relieved of the burdens and costs associated with hiring. Since the number of temporary workers varies from day to day, this is no small bookkeeping matter. All payroll and bookkeeping responsibilities including Social Security contributions, worker's compensation, state and federal withholding taxes, unemployment insurance premiums, fringe benefits, and all related forms and government reports are paid for and filed by the temporary help service. The temporary help service is also responsible for compliance under the Immigration Reform and Control Act of 1986 (IRCA), Federal EEO/Affirmative Action, OSHA, ERISA, and all other regulatory guidelines outlined by the government.

The temporary worker is employed by, and responsible to the temporary help service. However, as the temporary worker usually reports to work at the premises of the client company, it is the primary responsibility of the client company to plan the workday and supervise the temporary worker on the job. The recipe for successful temporary help deployment depends upon cooperation between the temporary help service and the client company. The division of human resource responsibilities between two organizations challenges even the most adept managers. Open lines of communication and on-going performance tracking by the temporary help service with the cooperation of the client company, will help to ensure the best value for your temporary help dollar. But the implication of separating the employer from the workplace takes on an even greater significance as we discuss the client's legal relationship to the temporary employee assigned to them. This legal relation is discussed in Chapter 9.

How the Temporary Service Attracts and Retains Employees

According to the *Occupational Outlook Handbook,** the forecasted growth in demand for skilled technical and professional help

---

* This is an annual publication of the U.S. Department of Labor, Bureau of Labor Statistics. This forecast is from the 1988–1989 edition.

is significantly greater and will continue to be greater than the growth of the work force as a whole. Every region of the nation has been affected to one degree or another by the growing labor shortage. As a result, competition for skilled temporary workers is challenging the temporary help industry to develop programs to meet and overcome these labor shortages.

Sophisticated and aggressive advertising and recruiting campaigns are part of the strategies developed by the temporary help industry to attract top talent. Recruiting qualified temporary employees is expensive. The help-wanted section of the local newspaper is the number one resource for temporary help workers. But this source alone doesn't come close to supplying the quantity of temporary workers needed in response to client demand. So, the temporary help firm aggressively recruits at job fairs, women's centers (women represent nearly 80 percent of the temporary work force), senior centers, and college campuses.

Retention of the temporary worker is critical to the success of the temporary help service. A service that retains its employees is more likely to have a qualified temporary worker available when you need one. While flexibility remains the calling card for temporary workers, temporary services nationwide are offering liberal benefits packages and free training opportunities in order to attract, encourage, and reward continued service. Some of these perks may include partially paid health benefits, paid vacations, free training seminars, referral and sign-on bonuses, and recognition rewards. As temporary work becomes a way of life for some workers and the temporary help services compete among themselves to retain their temporary staff, social issues such as health insurance protection, portable pensions, paid vacations, and sick pay take on considerable importance. While the proposition of mandatory benefits for temporary workers is a potentially expensive one for the temporary help industry, it seems clear that it is these benefits that ensures the future of the temporary worker. Marty Zobel, President and CEO of Atlanta-based TempWorld, Inc. sums it up this way, "Our benefits package is an important part of our company. It is especially critical to those veteran temps who make temporary employment a long-term lifestyle decision. Today it's justifiably a must do from high quality temporary services."

Tempting Temps

The business community at large recognizes that the use of temporary help is a strategic management tool that can save time and money and increase productivity. At the same time, an expanding temporary work force is recognizing that temporary work is a profitable, credible alternative to a permanent and inflexible work schedule. What makes temporary work such an attractive alternative for nearly one million temporary workers daily? Flexibility. Flexibility. Flexibility.

Acutely aware of the on-going labor shortage, the temporary help industry has tapped into segments of the population which might otherwise not be working. The industry has almost single-handedly created work opportunities for that part of the work force that is either unemployed by choice or circumstance and so might otherwise not be working, such as:

- Parents who want or need to schedule work around the school year
- Students who work during vacation and/or intercession
- Re-entry persons—often housewives and mothers who have made raising a family and homemaking a full-time job and need to refresh or update their skills
- Retirees who have been forced to retire but who don't want to stop working
- Persons pursuing other careers or life-styles such as artists, musicians, writers, or actors
- Job seekers in between jobs
- College graduates who want to test the water before making a commitment
- Persons who have relocated and who want to explore the local market before taking a permanent job

The reasons that temporary workers cite for working temp are as varied as their skills. For instance:

- The temporary worker can accept or reject a work assignment.
- The temporary worker can control the amount of time spent working.
- Temporary work offers the potential for immediate employment and at competitive wages.
- Temporary work offers the opportunity to explore different work environments.
- Temporary work allows for the flexibility and freedom to work without making a permanent commitment.

Training for the Future

As corporate America continues to computerize, there is an increasing need for highly skilled temporary workers. Companies need and expect temporary workers to be skilled in the use of office applications software, including database management, word processing, electronic spreadsheets, and electronic calendaring and messaging. In order to keep pace with this need and to stay competitive, temporary services, large and small, are investing millions of dollars on elaborate and sophisticated in-house training programs. The idea is not just to cross-train temporary workers but to train unskilled applicants and increase the supply of available workers.

Today's temporary workers are better trained and more educated than ever before. They come from all walks of life and bring to the workplace a multitude of experience and skills. Not surprisingly, Mitchell Fromstein, president of Manpower, Inc., reports that nearly 65 percent of the temporary workers employed by his service have some college.

Some services offer free training to all applicants eligible for employment. Others require that the temporary employee work a predetermined number of hours before qualifying for training seminars. In any case, it is clear that on-going training programs provide benefits to all. The temporary worker stands to increase his/her ability and marketability, the temporary help service is able to consistently fill more work orders with better qualified temporary workers, and the client company gets consistently competent temporary workers with state-of-the-art knowledge of the most sophisticated office skills and equipment.

Clearly, on-going training of temporary workers is a major component of the temporary help service. The following temporary help services detail how they provide on-going training for their temporary staff.

Career Blazers has been committed to training and cross-training temporary workers since 1949. It is one of the only temporary help services nationwide that owns and operates a nationally accredited business school. Career Blazers schools are located in key American cities. This affiliation provides an endless source of workers proficient in the skills needed on the equipment most companies use. Academic curriculum is continuously updated and/or newly created to reflect the on-going hardware and software changes of the automated office. Currently students can take courses in a variety of word processing software packages, electronic spreadsheets, database management, desk-top publishing, and old standbys such as typing and shorthand. Career Blazers also takes training one step further by offering customized training to corporate employers, training entire departments at the employer's request.

Kelly Services,® the nation's largest temporary help company, delivers assistance to its customers and temporary employees through the Kelly Service System.* One part of the Kelly Service System is the exclusive Kelly® PC-Pro® training program which offers free hands-on training on twenty-three major word processing and spreadsheet software packages used in business today. Available in every Kelly Temporary Services office, the PC-Pro system utilizes personal computers to provide training for more than 6,000 temporary employees per week. The PC-Pro training programs for each software package lead the temporary employee step-by-step through self-paced, easy-

---

* Kelly Services, PC-Pro, and Kelly are federally registered trademarks of Kelly Services, Inc.

to-follow programs. The Kelly PC-Pro system is designed to teach PC skills to those using PCs for the first time and to transfer skills from one software package to another. The exclusive Kelly Office Automation Hotline provides immediate bilingual assistance to temporary employees on office automation assignments. Kelly also developed quick reference guides for all software packages taught on the Kelly PC-Pro system and supported by its Office Automation Hotline.

Since 1982, Manpower, Inc., has invested $15 million to develop and implement SKILLWARE, its own personal computer software program. This diskette-based training method is a hands-on, step-by-step tutorial, in basic, intermediate, and advanced word processing. The program is self-paced and designed to teach computer skills quickly and effectively. SKILLWARE is currently available in fifteen different software packages and has been translated into seven languages.

These innovative training programs are just a sampling of what temporary services (both large and small) are doing to keep current with clients' needs.

The Temporary Help Service as the Employer

All kinds of workers are welcome to apply for temporary work. The temporary help service is an equal opportunity/affirmative action employer and abides by all laws governing equal opportunity. However, not everyone who applies for temporary work is selected for employment. Industry experts estimate the ratio of applicants hired is about 50 percent of those who apply.

Temporary workers are evaluated and hired based on a combination of appropriate skills testing, an in-person interview, and reference checking. All applicants who want to register for temporary work are required to fill out an application. Each temporary applicant is required to complete and sign a W-4 IRS form authorizing the temporary help service to withhold appropriate taxes. Figure 2-1 is typical of an application given to a temporary worker seeking office work. You will notice that the application requests information relative to employment history and educational background including the name of the supervisor for reference checking. In addition to listing all skills, the application asks about workday availability and location preferences. A record is kept with the application of all temporary assignments. Figure 2-2 is representative of a typical application given to a temporary worker seeking work as a paralegal or other legal-assist type of work.

The application contains the following information:

1. Name, address, and telephone number
2. Social Security number
3. Work day and time availability, and location preferences
4. Record of assignments
5. Test scores and personal evaluation (image, attire, verbal skills, and personality)
6. Employment and education history
7. Detailed skills and experience
8. Contract for employment between the applicant and the temporary help service

Potential employees who register with a temporary help service are administered tests that are designed to be objective and job-related. These tests are used to identify strengths as well as areas where further training may be necessary and/or helpful. Since there is no industry wide standardized testing, each service administers and evaluates its own tests. As a result, there may be great disparity in the level and quality of skills provided by one service over another. As a potential client of the temporary service, you can ask to see copies of job-related tests to determine if the tests reflect the skills you are likely to need. For temporary personnel, good skills testing is the best quality control instrument. At the end of this chapter is a sampling of tests for filing assessment, spelling evaluation, proofreading ability, Multimate and WordPerfect proficiency, Lotus 1-2-3 knowledge, and others. These tests are typical of those administered by the temporary help service in order to evaluate skill level and expertise.

Next, an in-person interview is conducted. The interviewer inquires about the prospective temporary worker's day and
(text continues on page 38)

Figure 2-1. Application for a temporary worker seeking office work.

[front]

[reverse]

FOR OFFICE USE ONLY				
Typing:	Filing:	IM	VS	
Steno:	Spelling:	AT	PERS.	
WP/PC:	Gen Ap:	Remarks		
Math:	Proofrd:			
Stat Typing:	Trans:			
Handwr:	Productn:			Intvr

APPLICANT COMPLETE EMPLOYMENT AND EDUCATION RECORD

Most Recent First	Company Name / Address	Name of Supv. / Telephone	Type of Co. / Position	Salary Start / Salary End	Reason for Leaving	REFER CHECK
From						
To						
From						
To						
From						
To						

	Address	From	To	Grad/Degree	Avg.	Major
High School						
College						
Graduate School						
Special School						

APPLICANT - CHECK BOXES INDICATING YOUR SKILLS AND EXPERIENCE

OFFICE
- ☐ Typing/Electric
  _____ (Models)
- ☐ Memory Typewriter
  _____
  _____ (Systems)
- ☐ Statistical Typing
- ☐ Dict. Eqpmt.
- ☐ Gregg   ☐ Pitman
- ☐ Medical Steno
- ☐ Legal Steno
- ☐ FLH   ☐ Spdwrtg.
- ☐ Reception
- ☐ Switchbd. Model(s)
  _____
- ☐ Filing
- ☐ Collating
- ☐ Photocopying

WORD PROCESSING
- ☐ System(s)
  _____
  _____
  Do you know merge functions? ☐ Y   ☐ N
  PERSONAL COMPUTERS
- ☐ Software
  _____
- ☐ Hardware:
  _____
  EDP
- ☐ CRT Keyboarding
  _____ (Models)
- ☐ Keypunch/No. _____
- ☐ Programming

BKKG/ACCTG
- ☐ A/R   ☐ A/P
- ☐ Full Charge
- ☐ Genl. Ledger
- ☐ Payroll
- ☐ Taxes
- ☐ Bank Recs
- ☐ Computer Sys.
- ☐ Manual Sys.
- ☐ Credit/Coll
- ☐ Figure Clerk
- ☐ Other _____

FOR. LANGUAGE(S)
_____
_____
- ☐ Speak   ☐ Read
- ☐ Write   ☐ Translate
- ☐ Typing   ☐ Steno

SALES/MARKETING
- ☐ Telemktg.
- ☐ Customer Service
- ☐ Trade Shows
- ☐ Demonstrator
- ☐ Pollster
- ☐ Street Distrib.
- ☐ Other _____

ADV/ COMMUNICATIONS
- ☐ Proofreading
- ☐ Proofing With Symbols
- ☐ Editing
- ☐ Copywriting
- ☐ Paste Ups/Mech.
- ☐ Design/Illustration
- ☐ Research
- ☐ Photography
- ☐ Other _____

OFFICE MACHINES
- ☐ FAX   ☐ TELEX
- ☐ Mimeograph
- ☐ Microfiche
- ☐ Videotape/Film
- ☐ Adding Mach.
- ☐ Calculator
- ☐ Copier(s) Model:

MAILRM & LITE INDUSTRIAL
- ☐ Messenger
- ☐ Mailroom
- ☐ Inventory/Stock Clk.
- ☐ Shipping/Receiving
- ☐ Warehouse
- ☐ Assembler
- ☐ Other _____

APPLICANT - PLEASE READ AND SIGN

I understand that Career Blazers' continuing ability to provide work for me and others desiring temporary work, depends upon the quality of service received by clients. As an employee of Career Blazers, I therefore agree to comply with the following:

1. I will be cheerful, courteous, professional and appropriately dressed on all assignments.

2. When I accept any assignment, I will report to work at the scheduled time every day until such assignment is completed.

3. If, for any reason whatsoever, I must be absent or late in reporting for any assignment, I will notify Career Blazers at least two hours before the scheduled starting time. I understand that Career Blazers has a 24 hour telephone answering service.

4. As soon as I know when an assignment is to terminate, I will notify Career Blazers. If I fail to do so, Career Blazers can assume that I am not available for work.

5. If any Career Blazers' client to whom I have been assigned offers me a permanent, temporary, or part-time job within 90 days of the end of such assignment, I will promptly notify Career Blazers and will not accept such offer beforehand.

6. I understand that all matters relating to wages and rates are necessarily confidential and will never discuss same with clients or others.

7. I will discuss any problems I have on assignments with Career Blazers, never with clients.

8. I hereby authorize Career Blazers to check my employment references and educational history.

9. To the best of my knowledge, all information given on this Application is true. I understand that my failure to comply with any provision hereof may be cause for the termination, without notice, of my employment relationship with Career Blazers.

_____

Please sign after completing Application and reading the above.

Reprinted with permission by Career Blazers.

Figure 2-2. Application for a temporary worker seeking work as a paralegal or other legal-assist type work.

[front]

				OFFICE USE ONLY					
☐ PARA ☐ LS	**Career blazers** TEMPORARY PERSONNEL LAW SERVICES DIVISION			Primary Class	Min. Hrly	Typ/Steno	WP/PC	Proof	Mktg. Rating
TODAY'S DATE ___/___/___	EMPLOYMENT APPLICATION Complete all unshaded areas. Abbreviate as necessary. Must be completed even if you have a resume. Please use ballpoint pen only.			Secondary Class					

Name/Last/First/Middle	Home Phone ( )	☐ I-9 ☐ Resume ☐ Notary _____
Address	Business Phone ( )	Soc. Sec. No. ___/___/___
City State Zip	Emergency/Message Phone ( )	Would you consider working in a non-smoking office? ☐ Yes ☐ No

Are you seeking permanent employment?   ☐ Yes ☐ No

Are you collecting unemployment benefits?   ☐ Yes ☐ No   How Long?_____

Available for work beginning _____ Until _____

Days available: ☐ MON ☐ TUE ☐ WED ☐ THUR ☐ FRI ☐ SAT ☐ SUN

Hours available __ to __ __ to __ __ to __ __ to __ __ to __ __ to __ __ to __

Are you presently a student or plan to return to school?   ☐ Yes ☐ No ☐ Maybe

Have you ever been bonded? ☐ Yes ☐ No Ever been refused bond? ☐ Yes ☐ No

Have you ever been convicted of a crime?   ☐ Yes ☐ No

I will usually travel to work by   ☐ Public Transportation ☐ My Car

Public transportation convenient to me (list): _____

In emergency, notify: Name _____ Address _____ Phone _____

Have you worked for other temporary services?   ☐ Yes ☐ No   Which service(s)? _____

Where sent? _____

How did you hear of Career Blazers Temporary? ☐ From Career Blazers Permanent ☐ From Career Blazers School ☐ Reputation

☐ Newspaper Ad (Name)_____ ☐ Radio/TV ☐ Referral ☐ Yellow Pages ☐ Other_____

Why do you wish to work temporary?
_____
_____
_____
_____

New skills I would like to obtain:
☐ Typing ☐ Word Processing/PC ☐ Steno
☐ Increase my earnings capacity in a short time
☐ I want more career/job opportunities open to me
☐ I want opportunity for growth in the future

FOR OFFICE USE ONLY				RECORD OF ASSIGNMENTS								
CLIENT	DEPT.	CONTACT	CLIENT PHONE	TEMP. EXT.	JOB TITLE	ORDER #	PAR	BAR	STRT.	EST. FIN.	ACT. FIN.	PERFORM CHK.

[reverse]

FOR OFFICE USE ONLY

Typing:	Gen Ap:	IM		VS	
Steno:	Proof:	AT		PERS.	
WP/PO:	☐ WITH ☐ W/OUT SYM	Remarks			
Math:	Digest:				
Filing:	Other:				
Spelling:	Other:				Intvr

APPLICANT COMPLETE EMPLOYMENT AND EDUCATION RECORD

Most Recent First	Company Name Address	Name of Supv. Telephone	Type of Co. Position	Salary Start Salary End	Reason for Leaving	REFER CHECK
From						
To						
From						
To						
From						
To						

	Address	From	To	Grad/Degree	Avg.	Major
High School						
College						
Graduate School						
Special School						

APPLICANT - CHECK BOXES INDICATING YOUR SKILLS AND EXPERIENCE

WORK AREAS
- ADMIRALTY
- ANTITRUST
- AVIATION
- BANKING
- CORPORATION
- GCH
- COPYRIGHTS/TRDMKS
- CRIMINAL
- EEO
- ENVIRONMENTAL
- ERISA
- FAMILY
- INSURANCE
- INTERNATIONAL
- LABOR
- LEASING
- LITIGATION
- NATURAL RESOURCES
- NEGLIGENCE
- PATENTS
- PERSONAL INJURY
- PRODUCT LIABILITY
- REAL ESTATE
  - Commercial
  - Residential
  - Co-op/Condo
- REAL PROPERTY
- SECURITIES
- TAXATION
- TRUST & ESTATES
- UCC
- WORKER'S COMPENSATION

OTHER SPECIALIZATIONS

BACKGROUND
- Paralegal Cert
  - School
  - Honors
- JD
  - School
  - State(s)
- Member Bar
  - State(s)
- Notary

LEGAL RESEARCH SKILLS
- Cite Check
- Shepardize
- Auto-Cite Machine
- Research Cases
- Lexis Research Terminal
- Draft Briefs/Memoranda
- Legal Res. Specialties

DOCUMENT CONTROL
- Digest Documents
  - With Dictaphone
  - With Longhand
- Depositions
- Discovery Documents

BACKGROUND CONTINUED
- Keyword Code for Data-Entry
- Lexis Litigation Terminal
- Other Litigation
- Data Machine
- (Which?)
- Work With Computerized Litigation File
- Index Documents
- Organize/Index Document Files
- Proofreading
  - With Symbols
  - Red/Black Lining

GENERAL LITIGATION
- Answer Calendar Call
- Docket
- Serve Papers
- File Papers at Court/With Agencies
- Draft Interrogatories and Responses
- Prepare Trial Exhibits
- Draft Complaints
- Assist Attorney at Trial
- Other

OTHER RESEARCH
- Trademark Search
- Patent Search
- Title Search (Real Estate)
- Title Search (Corporate)
- Blue Sky
- Product Research

- Legislative Research
- Scientific Research
- N Y S E Library
- S E C Library
- N Y Times Info Bank
- N Y C Bar Library
- Other Special Library
- Draft Non-Legal Memoranda (Which?)

DRAFT FORMS
- Tax (Which?)
- Will
- Real Estate Closing Binder
- EEO/AAP
- Corporate Closing
- Corporate Minutes
- Profit Sharing/ Defined Benefit Plans
- Others

FOREIGN LANGUAGES

Language	Read	Speak	Write	Trans-late
French				
German				
Italian				
Spanish				
Japanese				
(Other)				

OFFICE
- Typing Electric
- Memory Typewriter
- Dict Educ
- Gregg
- Pitman
- FLH
- Spdwrtg
- Legal Steno
- Reception
- Switchbd
- Filing/Collating

FILING SYSTEMS
- File Clerk (Law)
- File Management
- File Organization

WORD PROCESSING
- Systems
- Personal Computers
- Fax
- Telex
- Messenger
- Mailroom
- Photocopying

APPLICANT - PLEASE READ AND SIGN

I understand that Career Blazers' continuing ability to provide work for me and others desiring temporary work, depends upon the quality of service received by clients. As an employee of Career Blazers, I therefore agree to comply with the following:

1. I will be cheerful, courteous, professional and appropriately dressed on all assignments.
2. When I accept any assignment, I will report to work at the scheduled time every day until such assignment is completed.
3. If, for any reason whatsoever, I must be absent or late in reporting for any assignment, I will notify Career Blazers at least two hours before the scheduled starting time. I understand that Career Blazers has a 24 hour telephone answering service.
4. As soon as I know when an assignment is to terminate, I will notify Career Blazers. If I fail to do so, Career Blazers can assume that I am not available for work.
5. If any Career Blazers' client to whom I have been assigned offers me a permanent, temporary, or part-time job within 90 days of the end of such assignment, I will promptly notify Career Blazers and will not accept such offer beforehand.

6. I understand that all matters relating to wages and rates are necessarily confidential and will never discuss same with clients or others.
7. I will discuss any problems I have on assignments with Career Blazers, never with clients.
8. I hereby authorize Career Blazers to check my employment references and educational history.
9. To the best of my knowledge, all information given on this Application is true. I understand that my failure to comply with any provision hereof may be cause for the termination, without notice, of my employment relationship with Career Blazers.

Please sign after completing Application and reading the above.

Reprinted with permission by Career Blazers.

hour availability, and records any preferences or limitations regarding location or industry. Details pertaining to educational background and employment history are discussed. Specific or additional skills are noted, as are likes and dislikes. The interviewer is looking for a "can-do" attitude, flexibility, and adaptability—three important personality traits of a successful temporary worker. The temporary help industry recognizes that although skills can be tested, attitude and manner cannot always be accurately assessed upon an initial meeting. This reinforces the importance of feedback from the client company of on-the-job performance of each temporary worker. The temporary help service also recognizes that it is these intangibles that make the difference between a good temporary worker and a great temporary worker—so it keeps an on-going record of performance appraisals. Finally, as references are a good barometer of how the temporary worker will perform on the job, those that are selected for employment are asked for reference information. References *are* checked.

From this information, profiles are developed and recorded so that the temporary worker will closely match your skill requirements and fit into your office environment. The tools that the temporary help service uses to help it make good matches are:

1. Testing
2. Interviewing
3. Evaluating
4. Reference checking

They provide the solid information from which the account coordinator can hope to predict job performance and productivity. Howard W. Scott, Jr., president of CDI Temporary Services, Philadelphia, sums it up, "By providing better trained and tested employees, we are able to greatly increase the level of service to our customers."

In the 1988 Salary and Employment Survey conducted by Tempforce, 60 percent of all respondents (a cross-section of U.S. industries that together employ more than 244,000 employees) were of the opinion that the temporary workers of today are better skilled, trained, educated, experienced, and oriented than they were five years ago. The graph in Figure 2-3 illustrates the percentage of respondents by region.

Meeting the Account Coordinator

When the work order is telephoned into the temporary help service an account coordinator, also known as account representative, account executive, customer service representative, or by some similar title is assigned to service your account. This temporary help staffing specialist acts as an extension of the

Figure 2-3. Percentage of respondents (by region) in the 1988 Salary and Employment Survey conducted by Temp-Force.

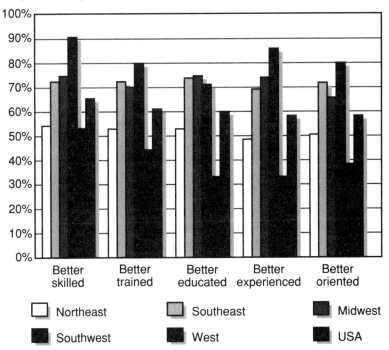

Reprinted with permission by Tempforce, Westbury, N.Y.

client company's personnel department. You should ask how much experience the account coordinator brings to the job. An experienced account coordinator will know how to take a complete work order which will result in better and more consistent matches. He or she will also know how to handle last-minute staffing crises which are characteristic of the need for temporary help. You may also want to know how long the account coordinator has been employed by the temporary help service. Although length of employment is not an assurance of good service, a stable relationship will foster understanding of the client company's temporary needs and help to ensure continuous high quality service.

As most temporary help services use sales personnel in their marketing effort, insist upon meeting with the account coordinator who will be servicing your account. Building a solid relationship with the account coordinator is an effective way to ensure maximum service. As you cannot replace an in-person evaluation of the office environment, standards, and equipment used, it is especially helpful to invite the account coordinator for a tour of your office or worksite. An on-site visit will provide the account coordinator with more information than any verbal description.

Understanding a company's needs goes beyond filling an order. The more information the account coordinator has about the client company, the better he or she can represent the company and the better prepared the temporary workers will be. Getting to know your standards and expectations are part of the account coordinator's job. Pat Galloway, director of human resources for the William Morris Agency says that she, "understands the importance of the account coordinator being tuned into the needs of the William Morris Agency, and therefore likes it when a service asks to see the work environment. It shows that the temporary help service is trying to get a good handle on what I need in order to make good matches."

The account coordinator begins working on an order as soon as it is called into the temporary help service. The order giver should be prepared to supply the account coordinator with a clear and detailed job description and a fair estimate of the length of the assignment. The work order form (Figure

2-4) details the exact information the account coordinator needs to fill your order.

The account coordinator will use the job description you supply to match the requested temporary help needs with the current inventory of available workers in an effort to assign the best applicant to the job based on availability, individual style, personality, and skills. The majority of work orders are placed at least one day in advance but some job orders are for personnel to report immediately or within a few hours. The account coordinator should respond promptly to all work orders. For same day requests, you should expect confirmation in ten to twenty minutes. For next day requests you should expect confirmation in one half hour to two hours. In any case, the account coordinator will call back to provide the name and arrival time of the temporary worker assigned to the job, and to confirm the billing rate. The real test of a good account coordinator comes with how well and how consistently your temporary help needs are met.

Develop a relationship with one or two temporary help services and stick with them. A loyal client can be assured that the order they place will get the attention it deserves. Melodie Fletcher, human resources associate at Canadian Imperial Bank of Commerce told us that she learned the hard way not to get involved with too many services. "You either establish a rapport or you don't. They feel loyal to you, and you feel loyal to them." Donna Mitchell, personnel coordinator for Condé Nast Publications, New York, notes that the relationship you develop with the temporary help service representative can be a turn-on or turn-off. Mitchell says, "Other temporary help services can fill orders but at Condé Nast we need more than order-fillers on the other end. Understanding the different faces of the magazines we publish—the style, the attitude, and the fit, is what separates a good temporary help service from a great temporary help service."

What the Temporary Worker Is Paid

The fact that temporary workers are paid on an hourly basis, and only for actual time worked epitomizes the savings ad-

Figure 2-4. Work order form.

Career blazers®
EXCELLENCE AT WORK

ORDER FORM FOR TEMPORARY PERSONNEL

NY 12848

BRANCH | FIRST ORDER THIS CLIENT | CLIENT INFO CHANGE (CIRCLED) | EMPLOYEE INFO CHANGE (CIRCLED) | SCR?

CLIENT MASTER DATA

CLIENT I.D. NUMBER | CLIENT NAME
NUMBER AND STREET | CITY
STATE | ZIP CODE | MARKETING CONTACT M R/S | COMBINED BILLING? Y or N | TERRITORY
PHONE NUMBER | EXT. | SOURCE | #CLERKS | CREDIT LIMIT | SUPPRESS SKILL CODE? Y or N | CROSS STREETS
FLOOR or ROOM | TYPE OF BUSINESS | CONTACT'S TITLE | BILLING CONTACT IF DIFFERENT M R/S
BILLING ADDRESS IF DIFFERENT: NUMBER AND STREET | CITY
STATE | ZIP CODE | OTHER INFORMATION: _____

THIS JOB ORDER

DEPARTMENT | BILLING INFORMATION | DATE ORDER TAKEN (MONTH DAY YEAR) | TIME TAKEN
SCHEDULED START DATE (MONTH DAY YEAR) | 1ST DAY | EST. DURATION (DAYS WKS MTHS) | SCHED. _____ | #OF TEMPS | J.O. RESPONS.
Job Title _____ Work Description _____
EQUIPMENT
Mfg. _____ Model(s) _____ Reporting Address If Different _____
Report To _____ Fl/Rm _____ Phone Number _____ Work For _____ Title _____
Travel/Other Instructions _____ Order Taken By _____
Requests/ Requirements _____ Thank you. What else can I do for you?

ORDER CHANGE DATA

ACTUAL START DATE (MONTH DAY YEAR) | J.O. RESPONS. | #OF TEMPS | ORDER CANCELLATION | DATE CANCELLED (MONTH DAY YEAR) | TIME CANCELLED | CNCL.CD. | SCR? Y N

EMPLOYEES

EMPLOYEE # | FIRST NAME | LAST NAME | SOCIAL SECURITY NUMBER | SKILL CODE
Confirmed by _____ Date _____ Time _____ With _____ Thank you. What else can I do for you?
PAR | BAR | EMPLOYEE PHONE NO. ( ) | DISPATCHED BY | ARRIVAL REPORT: ON TIME ☐ LATE ☐ CLIENT OK ☐ NO SHOW ☐ TIME ARRIVED _____ CLIENT UPSET ☐ Thank you. What else can I do for you? | PERFORMANCE A B C D F Thank you. What else can I do for you?
COMMENTS ON PERFORMANCE:

EMPLOYEE # | FIRST NAME | LAST NAME | SOCIAL SECURITY NUMBER | SKILL CODE
Confirmed by _____ Date _____ Time _____ With _____ Thank you. What else can I do for you?
PAR | BAR | EMPLOYEE PHONE NO. ( ) | DISPATCHED BY | ARRIVAL REPORT: ON TIME ☐ LATE ☐ CLIENT OK ☐ NO SHOW ☐ TIME ARRIVED _____ CLIENT UPSET ☐ Thank you. What else can I do for you? | PERFORMANCE A B C D F Thank you. What else can I do for you?
COMMENTS ON PERFORMANCE:

NOTES

LAW SVCS. ONLY: CASE/MATTER _____ O.T. AUTH. BY _____

ASSIGNMENT MANAGER

FORM T-201E-

Reprinted with permission by Career Blazers.

vantage of using temporary help. Lunch hours, involuntary lateness, and absences are never included when totaling the temporary worker's hours on the job. Nor does the client company pay for holidays, vacation time, or sick leave. The U.S. Chamber of Commerce confirms that 21 percent of the potential savings from temporary help lies in the elimination of pay for time not worked.

The hourly rate paid to the temporary worker depends upon three factors; the skill and experience of available personnel, the client company's requirements, and the temporary worker's length of service with the temporary help service. Statistics from the Bureau of Labor Statistics, Chamber of Commerce, and other tracking sources may help to factor pay rates. Competition within the industry for qualified applicants helps to keep the hourly pay rate competitive—in some cases paying the temporary worker as well or better than permanent full-time wages for comparable positions.

At all times, the pay rate is negotiated between the temporary worker and the temporary help service, and is of no concern to the client company. (In fact, pay is one of those sensitive issues that might be considered if employer status is challenged. We discuss this further in Chapter 9.) The temporary help service must pay its employees a fair and competitive rate in order to attract and retain quality workers. If you are satisfied with the quality of workers supplied by the temporary help service, you can be sure that they are paying their workers fairly. The temporary employee earns increases that coincide with improved or newly learned skills and that reward continued service.

What the Client Company Is Charged

What determines the hourly rate the client company is billed? The billing rate includes the temporary worker's hourly wage, all required taxes and contributions, administrative expenses plus a small gross profit or mark-up. (Mark-up is the charge to the client company over and above the wages paid to the temporary worker.) At this writing, neither the state or federal government, nor the temporary industry regulates or even monitors the rates charged to client companies. However, the industry is very competitive and in this way regulates itself. Some services charge a predetermined hourly rate based on skill specification and job category; others use a rate range which is determined by the skill level and length of employment of the particular temporary employee assigned to the job. The authors have noticeably excluded lists of specific rate ranges for different categories of temporary personnel from this book, because billing rates vary from city to city. Also because the economy of supply and demand virtually controls the fair market value charged by the temporary help service for a particular skill. You can accurately assess what the going rate is in your area for a particular skill by telephoning several local temporary help services for their hourly rate.

Most temporary help services have a four-hour minimum charge. The minimum charge is in consideration of the temporary worker's time and expense in going to the job, and helps to defray the administrative costs incurred by the temporary help service.

Time Sheets

The time sheet is an exact record of the hours worked by each temporary employee each week. It represents the hours for which the client company will be billed and the number of hours for which the temporary worker will be paid. It should reflect exactly, the starting and stopping time less a lunch hour and any break time allowed. If the client company has a policy requiring the temporary worker to take a lunch hour, make sure the temporary worker is told to take that time off. If the client company does not pay overtime, make sure that the temporary worker is not being asked to put in overtime. (Federal law requires payment of time and one half after forty hours.) The client company should total the hours worked before signing off on each time sheet. Keep a copy of the time sheet for your records so that you can confirm the accuracy of the hours for which you are billed.

Typically, temporary workers are supplied with two time sheets at the time of registration. Thereafter, additional time sheets are supplied with each pay check. It is the responsibility of the temporary worker to supply the time sheet to the client company. It is understood that without a signed time sheet, the temporary worker will not get paid. In the event that no time sheet is available, most temporary help service firms will accept a company letterhead which details the employees name, Social Security number, and the exact number of hours worked, if it bears an authorized signature.

Group time sheets are used for bulk hiring in order to maintain control. For example, a large department store may buy the services of forty or more temporary workers in any given week. It could be confusing to keep track of each temporary worker's hours. Instead, each floor is supplied with a group time sheet. Each temporary worker is required to sign in and sign out on this group time sheet. At the end of the week, the time sheet is picked up by the temporary help service. An invoice is generated from this time sheet. Figure 2-5 shows a sample individual time sheet, and Figure 2-6 shows a group time sheet. The terms and conditions of employment are spelled out on the back of the client's copy which in effect constitutes a contract. (Also see Chapter 9.)

Forged Time Sheets

Forged time sheets do not represent a major problem to the temporary help arrangement. But insofar as the problem does exist, this five-point checklist will (1) help you to know what to look for, and (2) help you to prevent forged time sheets.

1. Make sure that the time sheet is signed in ink at the close of the workday on which the assignment ends.
2. Do not sign a time sheet that contains either erasures

(text continues on page 49)

Figure 2-5. Individual time sheet.

[front]

[reverse]

TERMS AND CONDITIONS

EMPLOYEE: Employee agrees not to accept full time or temporary employment by any client of Career Blazers within 90 days of completing any assignment with such client as a Career Blazers' Employee without written authorization of Career Blazers.

CLIENT: Acknowledging that Career Blazers incurs substantial recruitment, screening, administrative and marketing expenses in connection with Temporary Employee named on the reverse side, Client agrees not to directly employ such Employee within 90 days of Employee's completion if any assignment with Client without first paying Career Blazers liquidated damages which shall be a percent of Employee's agreed upon first year's salary, such percent to be computed by dividing such salary by 1000 and using the result as the applicable percent. Client shall notify Career Blazers before concluding any arrangement with Employee.

With the exception of normal office machines, Client shall not authorize or cause any Career Blazers' Employee to operate machinery or vehicles without first obtaining Career Blazers' written consent. It is understood and agreed that Career Blazers assumes no liability for loss or damage caused by operation of Client's machinery, equipment or vehicles by a Career Blazers' Employee. It is further agreed that if a Career Blazers' Employee operates Client's vehicles, whether owned, borrowed, leased or rented, Client accepts and bears full responsibility for bodily injury, property damage, fire, theft, collision or public liability damage claims. Client warrants that client complies with all OSHA regulations.

Without first obtaining written permission from Career Blazers, Client shall not entrust any Career Blazers' Employee with unattended premises, unsupervised access to telephones, cash, negotiables, jewelry or any other valuables. Career Blazers' fidelity bond or otherwise under any circumstances unless such claims are reported to Career Blazers in writing by the Client within thirty days of the alleged occurrence.

Client shall not advance cash or other valuables to Employee for any reason. Client waives any and all right to offset the amount or value of any such cash or valuables advanced against any money owed to Career Blazers.

Client agrees to comply with Career Blazers' credit terms. Delinquent accounts will be subject to late charges of 1½% monthly (annual rate of 18%) on the unpaid balance. Client agrees to pay any attorney's fees and reasonable court costs required to collect an unpaid balance.

CAREER BLAZERS
Temporary Personnel

Reprinted with permission by Career Blazers.

Figure 2-6. Group time sheet.

[front]

Career blazers
EXCELLENCE AT WORK

GROUP TIME RECORD

CLIENT NUMBER | COMPANY | ADDRESS | CITY/STATE | ZIP CODE

WEEK ENDING DATE

EMPLOYEES: Please cross off all days not worked

EMPLOYEE NAME	SOCIAL SECURITY #	MON			TUES			WED			THURS			FRI			SAT			SUN			TOTAL HOURS WORKED	SIGNATURE
		IN	OUT	Less Lunch	Total Hrs	IN	OUT	Less Lunch	Total Hrs	IN	OUT	Less Lunch	Total Hrs	IN	OUT	Less Lunch	Total Hrs	IN	OUT	Less Lunch	Total Hrs	IN	OUT	Less Lunch	Total Hrs	IN	OUT	Less Lunch	Total Hrs		
1.																															
2.																															
3.																															
4.																															
5.																															
6.																															
7.																															
8.																															
9.																															
10.																															
11.																															
12.																															
13.																															
14.																															
15.																															

IMPORTANT FOR CLIENT: BY EXECUTION OF THIS FORM, CLIENT CERTIFIES THAT; HOURS SHOWN ARE CORRECT; WORK HAS BEEN DONE SATISFACTORILY; AND THAT CLIENT AGREES TO THE TERMS AND CONDITIONS ON THE REVERSE SIDE OF THIS FORM.

CLIENT COMPANY _____ Dept. _____
Authorized Signature _____ Title _____

IMPORTANT FOR EMPLOYEE: BY EXECUTING THIS FORM, EMPLOYEE AGREES TO TERMS AND CONDITIONS ON REVERSE SIDE; CERTIFIES THAT THIS FORM IS TRUE AND ACCURATE; AND THAT NO INJURIES WERE SUFFERED.

HEADQUARTER'S COPY

(continues)

Figure 2-6 (continued)

[reverse]

TERMS AND CONDITIONS

EMPLOYEE: Employee agrees not to accept full time or temporary employment by any client of Career Blazers within 90 days of completing any assignment with such client as a Career Blazers' Employee without written authorization of Career Blazers.

CLIENT: Acknowledging that Career Blazers incurs substantial recruitment, screening, administrative and marketing expenses in connection with Temporary Employee named on the reverse side, Client agrees not to directly employ such Employee within 90 days of Employee's completion if any assignment with Client without first paying Career Blazers liquidated damages which shall be a percent of Employee's agreed upon first year's salary, such percent to be computed by dividing such salary by 1000 and using the result as the applicable percent. Client shall notify Career Blazers before concluding any arrangement with Employee.

With the exception of normal office machines, Client shall not authorize or cause any Career Blazers' Employee to operate machinery or vehicles without first obtaining Career Blazers' written consent. It is understood and agreed that Career Blazers assumes no liability for loss or damage caused by operation of Client's machinery, equipment or vehicles by a Career Blazers' Employee. It is further agreed that if a Career Blazers' Employee operates Client's vehicles, whether owned, borrowed, leased or rented, Client accepts and bears full responsibility for bodily injury, property damage, fire, theft, collision or public liability damage claims. Client warrants that client complies with all OSHA regulations.

Without first obtaining written permission from Career Blazers, Client shall not entrust any Career Blazers' Employee with unattended premises, unsupervised access to telephones, cash, negotiables, jewelry or any other valuables. Career Blazers' fidelity bond or otherwise under any circumstances unless such claims are reported to Career Blazers in writing by the Client within thirty days of the alleged occurrence.

Client shall not advance cash or other valuables to Employee for any reason. Client waives any and all right to offset the amount or value of any such cash or valuables advanced against any money owed to Career Blazers.

Client agrees to comply with Career Blazers' credit terms. Delinquent accounts will be subject to late charges of 1½% monthly (annual rate of 18%) on the unpaid balance. Client agrees to pay any attorney's fees and reasonable court costs required to collect an unpaid balance.

CAREER BLAZERS
Temporary Personnel

Reprinted with permission by Career Blazers.

or cross-outs. If the temporary worker makes a mistake, start a new time sheet.

3. Assign only one person the authority to sign time sheets and be sure that the service knows who it is.
4. Monitor the work time of the temporary worker to confirm hours worked.
5. Some clients prefer to hold on to all time sheets. An authorized person fills in the time worked for each temp and then signs it and mails a copy to the temporary help service at the end of each assignment. The temporary help service could also arrange to pick-up the time sheet from the client company's office.

If the billing invoice you receive at the end of each week or month is inconsistent with your records, request a copy of any time sheet in question. Compare hours. Check signatures. Call the user department to determine if additional hours were worked but not recorded. If a discrepancy persists, expect the temporary help service to adjust your bill.

Quality Control

The quality of the temporary help worker supplied is the number one consideration for measuring the value of temporary help. Therefore quality control is the number one priority for any temporary help service. In order to track performance of its temporary employees, the temporary help service employs sophisticated quality control measures. In addition to the quality control tools discussed above (testing, interviewing, evaluating, and reference checking), the temporary help service relies on the client company for feedback so that it can evaluate on-the-job performance of its temporary personnel. Specifically, the temporary help service wants to know:

1. Did the temporary worker arrive on time?
2. Was he or she prepared for the assignment?
3. Were the skills adequate for the assignment?

4. Was the temporary worker cooperative, reliable, and flexible?
5. Did he or she complete the assignment in a timely manner?
6. Was the overall performance excellent, good, fair, poor?

The ability to closely monitor the performance of the temporary worker on the job enables the temporary help service to determine the types of assignments for which each temporary worker is best suited. (If a temporary worker consistently gets poor performance reviews, he or she is dropped from the roster.) In addition, by hearing what is right or wrong with the temporary worker assigned, the temporary help service can more accurately respond to the needs of its client companies. It is essential to the temporary help service in making future matches that you cooperate with their effort to evaluate each temporary worker assigned to you.

The temporary service will confirm arrival of its temporary worker on the first day of an assignment and then will check in later that same day to affirm satisfaction. For assignments that last one week or more, the account coordinator will follow up weekly to confirm satisfactory performance. However, some clients do not want to be bothered with follow-up calls and that desire, if communicated, can be accommodated too. The office manager at a midwest accounting firm usually tells her services, "Don't call to follow-up. If the temp wasn't doing well, I would call you."

Satisfaction Guaranteed

The cost to the temporary help service of the guarantee is low as the majority of temporary workers are satisfactory. As a result, almost all the temporary services surveyed offered some form of performance guarantee. The best among them offered a 100 percent unconditional guarantee. If the temporary worker is unsatisfactory for any reason, notify the temporary help service immediately. Typically, if you notify the temporary help service within four hours, or in some cases, twenty-four hours, of your dissatisfaction, charges will be cancelled and a replacement will be dispatched immediately. The personnel manager of a large international bank reports that she routinely checks with the department supervisor just shy of the four hour mark to make sure that the temporary worker is satisfactory.

Payrolling

Payrolling or payroll servicing refers to the direct selection of an employee by the client company for a position of limited, but long duration. Then without any intermediation, the temporary help service agrees to carry the person on its payroll assuming all mandatory and discretionary payroll obligations. Payrolling usually involves a charge of 20-25 percent above the wages paid to the employee. Most temporary help services offer payrolling as a convenience to their customers. The National Association of Temporary Services reports that payroll servicing represents "less than 3 percent" of the industry's total revenue.

Companies have used payroll services to reinforce the contingent nature of certain labor commitments. Payrolling may be particularly cost-efficient and effective for hiring casual employees; trying out new employees; retaining retired employees, either part-time or full-time; and rehiring former employees on a part-time basis. It has been used as a mechanism for insulating a company's benefits program against casual or part-time workers and protecting against unemployment insurance and worker's compensation claims.

Not withstanding legal and tax purposes, the relationship between the employee, the client company, and the temporary help service is the same as all other temporary help arrangements—the temporary help service is the employer. A client company may choose to do its own recruiting for a project if a needed skill is peculiar to its company, or if an especially sophisticated skill is desired and the client feels it is in the best position to evaluate expertise. However, the payrolled employee should always be treated in the same manner as any other temporary employee.

Payrolling differs from employee leasing because the workers are temporary and usually employed on large projects for a predetermined period of time. For the employee, being payrolled is simply like being on a long-term temporary assignment. However, this distinction becomes less clear if payrolled employees work largely full-time for more than a year. Whenever contract employees are used it is advisable to consult with legal counsel.

Buying on Credit

A client company that places an order with a temporary help service is making a financial commitment to pay an agreed upon rate for the services of a temporary employee although, *all* work orders are subject to change, confirmation, or cancellation. The temporary help service is extending credit every time it fills a work order. The temporary help service pays its employees each week and then bills the client company for services rendered. The client company may take up to three months to pay even though all invoices are due upon receipt. As the temporary help service wants to limit its risks, new clients may be asked for banking and/or credit references. Be prepared to supply the name of your bank and the name of the bank officer who services your account.

Sampling of Tests

FILING ASSESSMENT

Please file these accounts alphabetically by indicating the proper number (1 though 20) for each in the blank space.

Barney's Menswear	2
Mr. Andrew Abrams	1
Coalmen's Corp.	3

Please begin filing with number 1 and so on.

O'Malley Trucking Co.	_____
Mr. Larry Townsend	_____
Coastal Shipping	_____
Paragon Packaging	_____
Kitty Kat Pet Foods	_____
General Lumber Co.	_____
Field Furniture	_____
Manny's Auto Body	_____
Bayshore Buick	_____
Ms. Susan Walters	_____
Weinberg & Co.	_____
Mr. A.L. Thompson	_____
Mr. & Mrs. Al Zarinski	_____
Jones & Johnson	_____
Menninger TV Service	_____
Victory Market	_____
A.J. Advertising	_____
Mr. David Donaldson	_____
Sharon's Boutique	_____
Chuci's Mexican Kitchen	_____

Name   Score

CAREER BLAZERS KEYBOARDING ASSESSMENT

Career Blazers has been placing qualified applicants in permanent and   3

temporary positions since 1949. Through the years, over one million   6

people have found jobs through Career Blazers and many satisfied job   8

seekers have sent their friends to us. Did you know you will receive a   11

$50 bonus if you refer someone to us whom we place in a new job? You   14

can obtain referral coupons from our reception desk. Career Blazers   17

specializes in helping you find a position which meets your ideal   19

career objectives. We listen to your needs in regard to industry,   22

duties, salary, benefits, title, growth opportunity and whatever else   25

is important to you. Then, we selectively match your needs and skills   28

to our clients. In order to best satisfy our job candidates, we ask   30

that you do a few important things for us: 32

1. Keep in touch and let us know where we can reach you.   34

2. Call us immediately after an interview.   36

3. Dress professionally. Wear appropriate corporate attire.   38

4. If you are working as a ''temp,'' keep us informed of any changes in   41

your assignments ... we want to keep you as busy as you would like to   43

be. By the way, temporary employment is a great way to discover the   46

''hidden job market.'' There are many exciting positions which often go   49

unadvertised, and the only way to know they exist is by being in the   52

right place at the right time.   53

Career Blazers is a recognized expert in the employment marketplace.   56

We are confident that you will benefit from our understanding of   58

interviewing techniques and career strategy. Did you know we are famous 61

for our staff of best-selling authors? Over 19 books have been written   64

by staff members; some of our titles include REVISING YOUR RESUME and   67

FAST TRACK CAREERS. We thank you for visiting us and sincerely hope we   70

are able to help you. Don't forget to tell your friends about us! (If   72

you finish, please begin again.)   74

SPELLING EVALUATION

Please circle the correct spelling:

1. mispel	mispell	misspell	mis-spell
2. neether	niether	nethier	neither
3. commitment	committment	comittment	comitment
4. colatteral	collatteral	collateral	colateral
5. proceedure	procedure	proceedeur	procedur
6. beleive	beleeve	believe	believ
7. interim	intarim	intarum	intirum
8. necesary	necessary	neccesary	neccessary
9. committed	comitted	commited	comited
10. guarentee	garanty	guarantee	guarenty
11. unforseen	unforeseen	unforesene	unforscene
12. relief	releef	releif	reliefe
13. receit	reciept	receipt	receept
14. alluminum	alumminum	allumminum	aluminum
15. complide	complied	compleid	complid
16. availible	avialable	available	avialible
17. judgment	judgement	jugment	jugement
18. privilidge	privalege	privilege	priviledge
19. anticipate	anticapate	antticipate	anticcipate
20. breif	brief	breef	breife

Name   Score

PROOFREADING TEST

Indicate corrections with standard proofreader's marks.

Since 1949 Career Blazers Agency inc. has been placing qualified applicants in permenent and temporary, full-time positions. Over the years more then 100,000 people have found jobs through Career blazers. Often people ask, "what types of jobs do you specialize in." Well, there are certain fields like publishing and fuondations law and entertainement industries, communications and busness in which we do a lot of work. All sorts of people come to our Office. And we do our best to help each one of them.

The people here at Career Blazers have made finding job for you and other qualified applicants thier profession. And such professionalism has not gone unoticed. Career Blazer's founder Adele Lewis has written article on the job market and the applicants' relationsip to it many imgtortant pudlications. She has two books to her credit, one of which FROM COLLEGE TO CAREER (Bobbs Merrill) is used in sevral coleges and universities a a text reference for carrer counceling.

As weare obligated to do our best place you in permaent or temporery work that best mets your requirments, you have an obligation to us and to other seeking employment through us. When reporting for job interviews or temporary assinments, it is your responsibility TO BE WELL groomed and busnesslike.

MATH SKILLS EVALUATION

This is a timed 15-minute skills assessment. Complete as many problems as you can in the allotted time. Use the back for a worksheet.

ADD

1)
$$1 \ \tfrac{3}{4}$$
$$10 \ \tfrac{1}{2}$$
$$\tfrac{7}{8}$$
$$2$$
$$+ \ 8 \ \tfrac{1}{4}$$

2)
$$4,289.48$$
$$9,486.99$$
$$3,371.23$$
$$1,990.46$$
$$+ \ 2,139.77$$

3) $25.00 + $10.50 + $.32 + $5.00 =   _____

MULTIPLY

4) 8 lbs. of apples at $.20 per lb. =   _____
5) 25 cases of beans at $10.00 per case =   _____
6) 1 can of coffee at $6.00 per dozen =   _____

7)
$$53.8$$
$$\times \ \ .24$$

8) 5 × 6 × 10 =   _____
9) ½ × 12 =   _____
10) ¾ × ⅞ =   _____

Subtract

11)
$$4,327.56$$
$$-3,925.68$$

12)
$$8,766.78$$
$$-4,653.34$$

13)
$$977.53$$
$$-892.76$$

14)
$$542.30$$
$$-677.20$$

Divide

15)   356 ⟌ 64,436

16) 5.80 ⟌ 30,943

Percentage

17) 12 is what percent of 60?   _____
18) 30% of 80 is?   _____
19) What is 5% of $50.00? —   _____
20) What percent of 125 is 5?   _____

Name   **Score**

Written Proficiency Test

WordPerfect 5.0

The following set of questions is designed to test your knowledge of WordPerfect 5.0. You will have 10 minutes to work on the test. Please read each question carefully and select the correct answer by circling the appropriate letter. When finished, return the test to the administrator.

1. What function key(s) would you press to retrieve a document?

    a) F7
    b) F3
    c) Shift + F10
    d) F4

2. After completing a fifteen page report, you suddenly notice that a client company name has been misspelled throughout the report. What feature of WordPerfect do you use to quickly replace each misspelling with the correct spelling?

    a) Indent
    b) Spelling
    c) Replace
    d) Pagination

3. How do you insert a paragraph at the beginning of the report you finished yesterday?

    a) Retrieve the document, position the cursor at the beginning of the first paragraph, press the Insert key, and start typing.
    b) Retrieve the document, press the Insert key, and start typing the paragraph.
    c) Retrieve the document, position the cursor at the beginning of the first paragraph, and start typing.
    d) Retrieve the document, press F3, and start typing the paragraph.

4. The easiest way to delete a five character word is to:

    a) Press the Delete key five times.
    b) Block the text, and then press the Delete key.
    c) Press the Space Bar five times.
    d) Press the Control key + the Backspace key.

5. What function key/function key combination would you use to print the document currently on the screen?

   a) Shift + F7
   b) F5
   c) F1
   d) Shift + F8

6. How do you bold a word as you are typing?

   a) Type the word and then press F6.
   b) Press F6 and then type the word.
   c) Press F6, type the word, press F6.
   d) Type the word and then press F9 twice.

7. What function key/function key combination do you press in order to start to copy a single paragraph?

   a) Shift + F4
   b) Control + F4
   c) Control + F8
   d) Control + F10

8. How do you underline a sentence after it has been typed?

   a) Press F8 twice.
   b) Block the sentence and then press F8.
   c) Press F8 then block the sentence.
   d) Press F5.

9. You create a document on Monday. On Tuesday, you retrieve the document and make some editing changes. What must you do now in order to make those changes permanent?

   a) Print the document.
   b) Spell check the document.
   c) Save the document.
   d) Backup the document.

10. How do you access the Spelling feature of WordPerfect 5.0?

   a) Press Control + F2.
   b) Press F1.
   c) Press Shift + F2.
   d) Press Control + F9.

Written Proficiency Test

Lotus 1-2-3

The following set of questions is designed to test your knowledge of Lotus 1-2-3. You have 10 minutes to work on the test. Please read each question carefully and select the correct answer by circling the appropriate letter. When finished, return this test to the administrator.

1. What steps do you take to retrieve a worksheet?

    a) Press the Slash key, F for File, R for Retrieve, type the name of the worksheet, and press the Enter key.
    b) Press F for File, R for Retrieve, type the name of the worksheet, and press the Enter key.
    c) Press the Slash key, W for Worksheet, E for Erase, and Y for Yes.
    d) Press F1.

2. When you input a number into a Lotus spreadsheet, where is it placed in the cell?

    a) In the center of the cell
    b) On the right hand side of the cell
    c) On the left hand side of the cell
    d) One cell to the left

3. Shat do you type in order to center the test entry Sales in the cell A15?

    a) Position the active cell at A15, type "Sales, and press the Enter key.
    b) Position the active cell at A15, type Sales, and press the Enter key.
    c) Position the active cell at A15, type 'Sales, and press the Enter key.
    d) Position the active cell at A15, type Sales, and press the Enter key.

4. What formula do you input in cell A8 in order to add up the values in cells A5, A6, and A7?

   a) A5+A6+A7
   b) +A5+A6+A7
   c) +A5+A6+A7+A8
   d) +A6+A7+A8

5. What commands do you issue to widen all the columns in your worksheet to a width of 18 characters?

   a) Press the Slash key, W for Worksheet, C for Column, S for Set-Width, type 18, and press the Enter key.
   b) Press the Slash key, W for Worksheet, G for Global, C for Column-Width, type 18, and press the Enter key.
   c) Press the Slash key, W for Worksheet, C for Column, type 18, and press the Enter key.
   d) Press the Slash key, W for Worksheet, G for Global, C for Column-Width, and press the Enter key.

6. How do you change the way numbers are displayed on your worksheet, i.e., add dollar signs?

   a) Type in the dollar signs when typing the numbers.
   b) Format the cells in which the numbers are placed.
   c) Widen the columns.
   d) Press the F4 function key.

7. What happens to a formula in Lotus 1-2-3 when you copy it to another location on the worksheet?

   a) The formula does not change.
   b) The cell references in the formula adjust relative to where the copy is located on the worksheet.
   c) The first cell reference in the formula changes.
   d) The copy of the formula has dollar signs in it.

8. What function key is used to move directly to a particular cell location?

   a) F6
   b) F1
   c) F2
   d) F5

9. You have updated a spreadsheet which was created last week. In order to make the changes permanent, what must you do?

   a) Print the spreadsheet.
   b) Erase the worksheet.
   c) Save the spreadsheet.
   d) Backup the spreadsheet.

10. What commands do you issue in order to send the worksheet on the screen to print?

   a) Press the Slash key, P for Print, G for Go.
   b) Press the Slash key, P for Print, A for Align.
   c) Press P for Print and G for Go.
   d) Press the Slash key, P for Print, F for File.

Written Proficiency Test

MultiMate

The following set of questions is designed to test your knowledge of MultiMate. You will have 10 minutes to work on the test. Please read each question carefully and select the correct answer by circling the appropriate letter. When finished, return this test to the administrator.

1. How do you retrieve a document?

    a) Select 1) Edit an Old Document at the Main Menu.
    b) Select 2) Create a New Document at the Main Menu.
    c) Press Shift + F1.
    d) Press the Escape key.

2. After completing a fifteen page report, you suddenly notice that a client company name has been misspelled throughout the report. What feature of Multimate do you use to quickly replace each misspelling with the correct spelling?

    a) Indent
    b) Spelling
    c) Global Search/Replace
    d) Pagination

3. How do you insert a paragraph at the beginning of the report you finished yesterday?

    a) Retrieve the document, position the cursor at the beginning of the first paragraph, press the Insert key, type the paragraph, and press the Insert key a second time.
    b) Retrieve the document, press the Insert key, and start typing the paragraph.
    c) Retrieve the document, position the cursor at the beginning of the first paragraph, and start typing.
    d) Retrieve the document, press F3, and start typing the paragraph.

4. The easiest way to delete a five character word is to:

   a) Press the Delete key five times.
   b) Press the Delete key, highlight the word, press the Delete key again.
   c) Press the Space Bar five times.
   d) Press the Control key + the Delete key.

5. How do you send a document to print from the Main Menu?

   a) Select 4) Printer Control Utilities.
   b) Press Shift + F1.
   c) Select 3) Print Document Utility.
   d) Select 9) Return to DOS.

6. How do you bold a word as you are typing?

   a) Type the word and then press the Alt key + Z
   b) Press the Alt key + Z and then type the word.
   c) Press the Alt key + Z, type the word, press the Alt key + Z.
   d) Type the word and then press Alt + C.

7. What function key/function key combination do you press in order to start to copy a single paragraph?

   a) F8
   b) F7
   c) F9
   d) Shift F10

8. How do you underline a sentence after it has been typed?

   a) Position the cursor at the beginning of the sentence, press the Shift key + Underscore as many times as necessary to underline the sentence.
   b) Press the Shift key + Underscore at the beginning of the sentence.
   c) Position the cursor at the beginning of the sentence and press the Alt key + Underscore.
   d) Press the Alt key + Underscore two times at the beginning of the sentence.

9. You create a document on Monday. On Tuesday, you retrieve the document and make some editing changes. What must you do now in order to make those changes permanent?

   a) Print the document.
   b) Spell check the document.
   c) Save the document.
   d) Backup the document.

10. How do you access the Spelling feature of Multimate from the Main Menu?

   a) Select 6) Document Handling Utilities.
   b) Select 7) Other Utilities.
   c) Select 5) Merge Print Utility.
   d) Select 8) Spell Check a Document.

3

How to Select the Right Service

There are over 7,000 temporary help firms operating nationwide. Selecting the right service can reduce labor costs and increase profits. Contracting with the wrong service can cost a company thousands, or even million of dollars a year. With billions of dollars at stake, it is imperative that selecting a temporary help service be handled systematically and not haphazardly (see Figure 3-1). Whether your temporary help budget is small or large, you must take the buying decision seriously.

Incredibly so, the task of selecting a temporary help service is often entrusted to a receptionist, secretary, or personnel assistant who has no negotiating power and little knowledge of how the temporary service operates. Ordering what you need—not more, not less, takes experience. To this end, we ask, would you give an $18,000 a year data-processing operator the responsibility of purchasing $100,000 of data-processing equipment? The answer is a resounding NO! Rather you should assign a responsible permanent employee to act as coordinator or liaison between the company and the temporary help service. Donna Mitchell, personnel coordinator at Condé Nast Publi-

Figure 3-1. What to consider when selecting a temporary help service.

Considerations:

- Size
- Image
- Responsiveness
- Recruitment
- Retention
- Testing
- Screening

- Training
- Specialization
- Hours of operation
- Quality control
- Services provided
- Local associations
- Member of NATS

Speak directly to the temporary workers. Ask:
- How are you treated?
- What benefits do you receive?
- Are you paid in a timely fashion?

cations, the New York-based magazine empire, is an example of this practice. Mitchell is responsible for coordinating, controlling, and streamlining the temporary help usage at Condé Nast. It is her job to select which services will be used, to negotiate the terms, to develop a relationship, and to maintain good communication with the preselected services in order to effect maximum value for each temporary help dollar spent by Condé Nast.

The temporary help industry is sales-intensive, and to this end, it has developed sophisticated sales and marketing techniques. Most temporary help services employ a highly skilled outside- and inside-sales force. Decision makers like you are contacted daily by sales representatives of competing temporary services soliciting your business. And in fact, the sales person has tremendous influence on the service you choose. This is more often a subjective consideration, because the presentation and marketing effort of the sales person is what will convince you to try his or her service. Although a fancy sales pitch may encourage you to try a temporary help service, actual performance is what builds trust and confidence. The personnel director of a Southern financial organization admits being demanding of the services she uses, ". . . because there are so many services to choose from."

What to Look for When Shopping for a Service

Not all temporary help services are alike, so it is important to shop around. Ask business associates for referrals (try calling your counterpart at an organization of similar size that is likely to use temporary help in the same way as you do), check with the local Chamber of Commerce, or consult the Yellow Pages under Employment Contractors—Temporary Help.

The size of the temporary help service, and whether it is of national or local origin is relative only to the extent that the temporary help service can provide adequate service and meet your company's temporary help needs. Our instincts tell us that if you are a small buyer to a large service, the importance of your business is diminished. If however, you are a big buyer to a small service, and the temporary help service can provide the quality of temporary help you need, you are going to get better service and at the best rates.

The office setting as well as the business style of the temporary help service will greatly affect the quality of workers it attracts and consequently, the quality of temporary help it assigns. In order for the temporary help service to consistently provide superior temporary workers, it must project an image compatible with the type of temporary workers you are likely to need. Select a service that responds to your needs in a timely manner, and with whom you can communicate openly and comfortably (especially when they are unable to fill your order). Rate the temporary help service on the basis of its knowledge, professionalism, interest, and attitude. If you don't feel that the temporary help service is listening, call the next service on your list.

Aggressive recruiting and generous benefits, bonuses and incentives are essential to ensuring a stable work force. A temporary help service that seeks to attract and retain high-quality workers will employ better quality temporary personnel. The temporary help service should screen each applicant for skill level, flexibility, personal presentation, and appearance. Thorough testing and evaluation are what separates the best temporary help services from the mediocre ones. Carefully evaluate and compare the quality of workers employed by the service by requesting that the user supervisor provide an evaluation on each and every temporary worker. Then use this feedback to measure the success of the service(s) you employ. (More on this later.)

As we have already established, training is a critical ingredient for temporary help services today. The best services recognize the changing office and provide on-going skill training for their employees. Some services even offer on- or off-site training for your employees.

Most temporary help services specialize in servicing one aspect of business (i.e., office support, financial services, medical and healthcare). If your temporary needs tend to be clerical then select a service that recruits office support personnel. If your temporary needs are inclined towards financial support or computer operators, then choose a service that specializes in financial or technical support.

Commonly, business hours are 9 A.M. to 5 P.M. In reality, many businesses work some variation of those hours (i.e., 8:30–4:30, 9:30–5:30). You need to query the services you are considering about their hours of operation. They should be able to assure you that they are available during your working hours and that they can accommodate after-hour emergency orders as well.

Quality control is of critical importance. The value of your temporary help dollar is measured in the quality of the worker the temporary help service dispatches. The temporary help service should track on-the-job performance of its temporary workers in order to ensure consistently high caliber temporary workers. (For this, they rely on you.)

In addition, many temporary help services will accommodate the special needs of their clients. Upon request, they will provide off-premises temporary services, conduct special training, and furnish customized billing and invoicing. Seek out those firms that have ties in the community. Look for membership to the local Chamber of Commerce or the Better Business Bureau, the local industry association and/or the National Association of Temporary Services (NATS). Those firms that belong to NATS agree to abide by a code of ethics governing all member temporary help services. While it is not critical that the service you select belong to NATS or to some other temporary association, it does impart that the temporary help service is serious about its business.

Finally, a good barometer of the best temporary help services are the temporary workers themselves. Whenever possible, speak directly to the temporary workers to find out which temporary help services they are most satisfied with.

Getting Maximum Value for Your Temporary Help Dollar

There are eight key steps to selecting a temporary help service.

Step One:	Analyzing your temporary help needs
Step Two:	Preliminary fact finding
Step Three:	Site visit by the client company
Step Four:	Formal proposal presentation
Step Five:	Evaluating the proposal
Step Six:	Negotiating the best contract

Because we recognize the significance of negotiating the most favorable rates, we have devoted a brief, but key chapter (Chapter 4) to strategies for negotiating rates.

Step Seven:	Awarding your business and briefing the service(s) you select
Step Eight:	Tracking performance

Step One: Analyzing Your Temporary Help Needs

Analyzing your temporary help needs will:

- Support your buying decision.

- Give you buying power.
- Control costs.

Before requesting proposals from potential temporary help services it is essential to analyze your temporary help needs. First, define the key employees on your staff. As these people represent the core group of employees, you will want to project what kind of temporary support they will need to maximize their productivity. Next, analyze production schedules and business cycles so that you can anticipate when and why you are most likely to need temporary help. Don't ignore absentee and turnover patterns—and anticipate vacation schedules in an effort to plan your temporary help usage. Developing an understanding of the kinds of temporary help you use, how many, when you will need them, for what length of time, and the quality of temporary workers you require will help you set goals and objectives.

Ask probing questions such as:

- Do you require a source of last-minute help?
- Do you require workers skilled in a particular type of equipment or knowledge about industry procedures?
- Do you require long-term temporary personnel because of continuous and on-going projects?

They will help you to solicit proposals from those temporary help services that can meet your specifications.

Step Two: Preliminary Fact Finding

Select half a dozen firms and telephone those services, paying close attention to their business style. How long does the telephone ring before it is answered? Is the receptionist courteous and professional? Are you put on hold for a long period of time? Is your call forwarded to the right party? The business style of the temporary help service is a good indication of the quality of worker it attracts.

Next, select the two or three firms that make the best impression and request a fact-finding meeting between you or your company's representative and the sales representative. Expect the sales representative to ask a number of questions regarding how your company has used temporary help services in the past. Be prepared to provide information covering the following:

- How often you use temporary help
- What jobs are frequently filled by temporary workers
- What you expect from the temporary worker who is put on assignment at your company

If you aren't given such an interview, you should question the service's qualifications.

You have a right to ask the temporary help service for financial statements to show you how large a service they are. You should ask to see copies of their advertisements to see what kinds of temporary workers they are trying to attract and to learn what benefits or incentives they offer in an effort to retain their staff. (Generally, the more liberal the benefits, the more loyal the staff.)

Once these issues are covered, and you think the service has potential as a source of good temporary help, ask the sales representative to prepare a formal proposal.

Questions to Ask When Shopping for a Temporary Help Service

- *How long has the service been in business?* In order to meet the demands of client companies, the temporary help service must have a large and diverse pool of qualified and available temporary workers. It takes time to build this kind of reservoir.

- *How does the temporary help service recruit and retain its temporary staff?* Temporary help services recruit through the classified employment pages, schools and universities, women's clubs and associations, job fairs and word-of-mouth. Sunday's employment pages can tell you what fringe benefits temporary help services offer in order to attract and retain quality temporary workers. The best temporary help services are aggressive in their recruitment efforts and offer health insurance, paid vacations, and other incentives.

• *How are potential employees screened, tested, and evaluated?* Ask to review the battery of test given to potential employees. Ask what factors are evaluated during in-person interviews.

• *What is the experience of the account coordinator?* It takes an experienced account coordinator to know the "inventory" and to make a good match. Look for a service whose permanent employees are long-term. Stability is important when it comes to consistent service.

• *Does the temporary help service carry worker's compensation, liability insurance, errors and omissions insurance, and/or fidelity bonds? What are the policy limits?* The temporary help service should carry at least a two million dollar liability policy. All other insurance, worker's compensation, errors and omissions, and fidelity bonds are rather standard. The temporary service should be able to provide the buyer with a certificate of insurance. For sensitive assignments, the temporary service should have the worker sign a confidentiality waiver. The above insurance not only protects the temporary help service, more importantly, it protects you!

• *What kind of performance guarantee does the temporary help service offer?* If you are dissatisfied with the services of the temporary worker assigned know what your recourse is. How soon can the worker be replaced? Are charges cancelled or other consideration offered?

• *What if you want to hire the temporary worker on a permanent full-time basis?* Many services bill for "liquidated damages" if you hire one of their workers permanently. You should know up-front what charges, if any, you will incur if you want to hire the temporary worker on a permanent basis. (There is room for negotiation on this issue, especially where high-volume users are concerned.)

• *What references can the service offer?* Ask, the temporary help service to provide references from satisfied customers. When checking these references ask if the same worker usually completes the assignments (frequent turnover increases your cost); if you can rely on the service to respond to last-minute requests or after-hour emergencies; if the service provides prompt confirmation of an order, including the name of the temporary worker.

▪ *What kind of quality control mechanisms are in place?* People and their skills are the stock in trade of the temporary help service. Needless to say, the nature of this inventory is quite variable. Constant on-the-job evaluation is needed to ensure quality control. Expect that the temporary service will first, confirm the temporary worker's arrival and secondly, that it will telephone four hours later to check on the worker's performance. The temporary service may ask for feedback from the user on punctuality, performance, and attitude. Your cooperation will help the service in making subsequent assignments.

Step Three: Site Visit by the Client Company of the Temporary Help Service

An on-site visit to the temporary help service should be standard operating procedure for any consumer of temporary help services. Arrive fifteen minutes to one-half hour earlier than expected. In all probability you will be seated in the reception area which will give you the opportunity to observe:

- Who the applicants are
- How the receptionist relates to the applicants
- How the receptionist handles testing the applicants and if the applicants are being tested thoroughly
- The business environment of the service

Are you seated in nice, pleasant, comfortable surroundings or does the office look as though the company has not upgraded its inside operation for twenty years? This may reflect the type of applicants the service attracts.

During your tour of the premises, try to get a sense of what the employees are like. Do they seem like intelligent, stable, friendly, and warm people? People who care about what they do? Are they professional? All of this will impact on the quality of the workers that the temporary help service attracts and the quality of service you get.

Step Four: **Formal Proposal Presentation**

A formal, in-person presentation should take place. This meeting should focus on a written proposal—a copy of which you should retain.

What should you look for in the proposal? The proposal should include:

- Background information about the temporary help service company and its management team
- A statement about what business the temporary help service is in (i.e., temporary, temporary/permanent)
- The philosophy of the temporary help service covering, how it recruits and retains its employees, the quality of the applicants it employs, and its attitudes toward clients.
- The temporary service's special features: hours of service, testing and evaluation, quality control, reference checking, guarantees, wake-up calls, stand-bys
- A description of how your company's requirements, discussed at the previous meetings, will be handled
- A pricing section that should state the billing rates for skill categories, the time period for which these rates would apply, and details of the service's volume or special rebate schedule
- The service's policy on converting a temporary worker to permanent employment status—liquidated damages

Step Five: **Evaluating the Proposal**

The Office conducts a reader survey every other year on the subject of temporary help services. According to their most recent survey (August 1988)—and not surprisingly—67 percent of all respondents cited quality of personnel as the most important criteria used to evaluate a temporary help service. Other important criteria fell into the following ranking:

1. Quality of personnel	61%
2. Past performance	58%
3. Quality of service	42%
4. Speed in supplying personnel	39%
5. Cost-effectiveness	27%
6. Reputation of service	19%
7. Other	10%

(Reprinted from *The Office*, August 1988, Stamford, Conn.)

On-the-job performance should be valued above all else. Consistent high-quality temporary workers will ensure that you get maximize value for your temporary help dollar. Quality temporary personnel will always get the job done and in a timely manner.

You should ask the temporary service to supply references. From these references you should confirm quality of temporary help and satisfactory service. Also ask your business associates who they use and you will probably hear the names of the same services time and again. The reputation of the temporary help service is its calling card—the best services obviously have the best reputations. Past performance is an accurate yardstick of the service you might expect. If you find a good service, stick with it.

Service is what the temporary help company provides. You should expect your order to be handled promptly and professionally. Quality of service is also reflected in speed of service. The majority of your work orders will be placed at least one day in advance but some work orders will be for personnel to report immediately. It is essential that the service you select maintains an adequate labor pool that can respond to your last-minute staffing emergencies. Ask each service you are considering if it payrolls stand-bys who can be dispatched to your company at a moment's notice.

Cost-effectiveness does not mean lowest price, rather it represents a balance between price and value. Although price is a factor when selecting a temporary help service, it should not be the overriding consideration. It is likely that the temporary help service that comes in with the lowest billing rate is paying their temporary workers the lowest hourly rate. It is reasonable to assume that the most talented and reliable temporary workers are *not* working for minimum wage.

Step Six: Negotiating Favorable Rates

See Chapter 4.

Step Seven: Awarding Your Business and Briefing the Service(s) You Select

Once you select your temporary service of choice, invite the company in; explain that you have accepted their proposal and want to start working with them. At this meeting it is important to spell out what procedures the temporary worker should follow upon arrival to assignments. For example, one company may have a specific check-in procedure or require visitors to obtain a pass; another company might have unusual hours.

Using the services of one or two temporary help firms (first and second choices) makes it easier to control temporary help usage costs. However, it may be unrealistic to assume that one or two services can fill all your temporary needs. Whereas, one service may be the best at providing you with word-processing operators, it may not be set up for providing temporary help at a moment's notice. And so, you should develop a relationship with a third or back-up service who can be called upon when your primary service(s) is unable to meet your needs.

Step Eight: Track Performance

Keeping track of the performance of every temporary worker is the most revealing and critical source for determining quality and value. Yet, we have seen very few companies, in all of our experience, anywhere in the country that track their usage to any measurable extent. *It is critical to track performance.* Once again, if one service is fifty cents more an hour but its success rate is 93.2 percent versus one that is fifty cents less an hour but whose success rate is 68 percent, which is going to be the better value?

You should absolutely keep a centralized list of every temporary worker assigned, even for short-term assignments. In order to track performance you must request feedback about the performance of every temporary worker from the line supervisor. To do this effectively, you will need to develop a uniform rating system. It could be as simple as using the form shown in Figure 3-2.

This form will help you to keep an accounting of which service the temporary worker came from and what kind of position was filled. You will be able to determine:

- What percentage were excellent, good, fair, poor
- What percentage were no shows
- What percentage were tardy

This detailed tracking information will provide the nuts and bolts for objective selection of the best temporary help service. In addition, it will provide information helpful in preparing a budget line for temporary help staffing.

What to Expect From the Service You Select

The following checklist summarizes what services the temporary help service should provide. Expect:

Figure 3-2. Temporary personnel performance rating form.

Date: _____

Position filled: _____

Length of assignment: _____

Name of temporary worker: _____

Employee of which service: _____

	Yes	No
Did the temp arrive on time?	___	___
Was the temp prepared for the assignment?	___	___
Were his/her skills adequate?	___	___
Was he/she cooperative?	___	___
reliable?	___	___
flexible?	___	___
Did the temp complete the assignment in a timely manner?	___	___

Overall performance:

☐ Excellent   ☐ Good   ☐ Fair   ☐ Poor

- All temporary workers to be thoroughly screened and tested.
- References to be checked.
- A detailed interview to determine skills required, starting date, and the anticipated length of the assignment.
- Requests for the name of the supervisor, travel instructions, dress code, and parking regulations.
- A firm rate quote to be made.
- A request for credit information.
- Timely confirmation that the order has been filled.
- The name of the temporary worker assigned.
- Confirmation of arrival of the temp worker and follow-up with quality-control calls.
- A productive and cooperative temporary worker.

4

Strategies for Negotiating Rates

Once you have determined which service(s) can fulfill your needs—which service's image bests suits you, which service(s) you feel comfortable doing business with, and which service(s) are of sufficient size and integrity—you are ready to negotiate for the most favorable rates. But negotiating the best contact doesn't necessarily mean basing your decision on the lowest-priced temporary help. Rather, the *key to buying temporary help is buying value.* You don't want to forfeit **value** for low-cost temporary help. The wrong temporary worker at any price will *not* give you value for your money. In fact, the cost of poor-quality workers will be measured in lost time and mistakes. Therefore:

Value = Quality Workers at the Lowest Price

To illustrate this, consider this example. One temporary worker types 100 envelopes for $10.00 an hour, another types 150 envelopes for $10.50 an hour. Which is the greater value? You can see that (1) value isn't always bought at the lowest price, and (2) value can be measured by performance.

Many of the largest and seemingly most sophisticated consumers of temporary help go through a long and thorough selection process of deciding which temporary services are capable of meeting their demands—as were discussed in the previous chapter. They invite a few select services to submit bids. Then they base the rest of the decision on who submits the lowest bid. Regrettably, this often leads to the self-fulfilling prophecy that all temporary help is marginal to poor. We'll explain why this happens with this example. One of the largest users of temporary help (approximately $20 million in annual volume) is a major East Coast bank. Because of their volume, they use the services of five temporary help services year around. Every two years their contracts with the services expire. At that time, they review the quality of service provided during the preceding two years. They drop the two temporary companies with the worst track records and retain the services of the other three. In order to replace the services that were dropped, they go through the whole selection process again. And once again, they select the services that have submitted the lowest bids.

The local temporary help services know that in order to get the bank's business, it has to put in a low bid. But for various reasons, it may want the business. Unfortunately, no temporary service can deliver a valued product at the rates they have to quote in order to win the bid. In reality, the temporary help service is compromising its profits, so much so, that the best temporary workers are always out-priced from working for this particular client. For the client, the bottom line is that it ends up getting the worst of the temporary workers that the temporary service has available. (The best temporary workers are being assigned to those client companies that are paying fair-market value.) After two years, the quality of service is evaluated again and the nightmare continues.

Finally, the bank resolves that during the last ten years, it has tried twenty different temporary help services and "they are all just as bad." So it determines to continue to select service based on the lowest price.

If you do want to select temporary help services through

competitive bidding, it is essential that the services invited to bid understand that:

- You need good-quality temporary workers.
- You are going to make your selection based on price.
- You are requesting that those services bid at a price that can assure you that they can deliver a valued product.

Remember that negotiating a good billing rate is important but not nearly as important as getting good quality workers when you need them.

Buying Power

The following formula is the key to negotiating the best value for your temporary help dollar.

CENTRALIZED BUYING = BUYING POWER = BEST VALUE

Temporary help service profits are tied directly to volume and based on mark-up: the difference between the hourly rate paid to the temporary worker and the billing rate charged to the client company. This is where you effect the greatest negotiating edge. By centralizing the purchasing of your temporary help usage and assigning your business to a few preselected vendors, you will gain the benefit of buying power. (Even if you favor decentralized ordering, order from a preselected list of services.)

To illustrate this, if you order one secretary, the markup for that one transaction is going to be significantly higher than if you were ordering twenty secretaries. The temporary help service will need to make more money on a one-time transaction than it would on twenty transactions with any one client.

Negotiating hourly rates for temporary help is easier than you think, and more important than you think. A difference of just $.25 an hour represents a significant cost difference over the length of an assignment. For example, if you are paying $12.00 an hour for a secretary for two weeks, the cost is $840.00. If you are paying $12.25 an hour, the cost is $857.50

for a difference of $17.50 for this two-week assignment alone. If your average quarterly expenditure for temporary help is $100,000 and your use is largely clerical, then based on the illustration above, you can begin to calculate the cost difference of just $.25.

The rate of pay (that which constitutes the temp's salary) is not negotiable. What is negotiable is how much mark-up the temporary help service is prepared to work on. For example, if the temporary worker's rate of pay is $8.00 an hour, and the client company is billed for $12.00 an hour, the mark-up is at 50 percent. If the temporary help service agrees to reduce its mark-up by 5 percent (usually based on volume), the client company saves $.20 an hour. Twenty cents an hour is a significant savings as we illustrated above.

Almost all temporary service firms have a rate range for a particular skill category. The range reflects the varying pay rate that the temporary help service may have to pay their temporary employees (based on skill level and length of service). However, if you are a company with sufficient size and volume of use, you should negotiate for a preset rate for those categories where the greatest use is likely to occur. Please note that if you are hiring one or two temporary workers a week this may be an unreasonable request.

We have already established that price is negotiable. What else is negotiable?

- Liquidated damages
- Volume rebates/discounts
- Additional services the temporary help company can provide

Liquidated Damages

Temporary workers can and often do accept permanent staff positions. And while the temporary help service is prohibited by law from charging a permanent placement fee, it is entitled under the law to seek relief and often does, by billing the client for liquidated damages. Liquidated damages are often equal to a percentage of the annual salary or an agreed upon flat rate. High-volume users are in an especially good position to negotiate liquidated damages. Some temporary help services will substantially reduce or even waive these charges for their best customers.

Volume Rebates/Discounts

Volume rebates and discounts on other services (i.e., permanent hires, training courses) are designed as an incentive to encourage and reward the client company for awarding the bulk of its business to one temporary service. A volume-rebate incentive program could actually give dollars back quarterly. Some companies prefer to receive a rebate check while others choose to reduce their bills directly at the end of the quarter.

A rebate program is generally a percentage discount based on the overall volume of use by the client company. The discount is usually determined on a quarterly basis and may be presented this way.

Total Quarterly Billing	Rebate
$0–$74,999	2%
$75,000–$150,000	3%
$150,001+	4%

If your company spends $100,000 every three months for temporary help, you can earn $3,000 cash back just by centralizing your buying effort.

Additional Services the Temporary Help Firm Can Provide

The temporary help service can provide additional services such as:

- Training for internal staff
- A performance tracking system
- Customized billing
- Pick-up and delivery of time sheets and delivery of checks

Based on volume, some temporary help services will provide training for your internal staff at reduced rates or free of charge.

A good temporary help service should be able to provide you with a formal-tracking system for determining the quality of workers it assigns. The more sophisticated services may be able to supply a software package designed to track performance.

Most temporary services will accommodate the billing needs of its client companies. The majority of companies report charging back temporary help usage to the user department and find it helpful to code invoices accordingly. In this way, invoices that should be charged back can be tracked effortlessly.

In addition, the temporary help service can customize invoices to reflect a total sum for weekly use or it can generate individual invoices for each temporary worker. The right temporary help service will not only accommodate your special billing needs, but can show you how to use the invoice to track weekly, monthly, or annual usage and save money.

As a convenience, the temporary help service can arrange pick-up and delivery of time sheets and delivery of pay checks. This will assure that the temporary workers do not lose time from their jobs by having to race across town to drop-off time sheets or pick-up pay checks.

Long-Term Projects—How to Ensure Value

In order to ensure value, continuity, and the lowest rates for long-term projects, charges should be negotiated on a per project basis or whenever possible, by the piece (i.e., mass mailings). Continuity is an issue because turnover of the temporary help during the course of an assignment is expensive. Every time you bring in a new temp, there is time spent on orientation and training, and efficiency suffers.

One sophisticated buyer handles turnover this way. They make it clear to the services they use that turnover will not be tolerated. If a temporary worker is requested for three months or three weeks but does not remain on the assignment for its expected duration—the refilling of the order is never given to that service, but rather to a back-up service. What this communicates to the temporary help service is, don't send us someone you know will be here for only one week or one month, and assume that we will take on another person for the duration.

The temporary help service can assure continuity on long-term projects by building into the agreed upon charge a completion bonus for each temporary worker that stays with the assignment for its duration. For example, the temporary worker is paid $7 an hour but is guaranteed a $1 an hour bonus, retroactive to day one if he/she completes the assignment. The client company should hear from the temporary help service how it is going to ensure continuity. This should be part of the determination of which temporary help service you choose.

5

How to Use a Temporary

Since you pay by the hour for the temporary help you use, it is critical that each hour be used fully and efficiently. Knowing how to place an order, how to put the temporary help to work, and how to control costs will help to ensure the value of the temporary help you buy.

Placing the Order

A qualified and informed member of the permanent staff should be assigned to place all temporary help requests. Some companies prefer to use a single ordering source in order to retain greater control over their temporary help usage and to avoid possible violations of labor laws. These companies believe that a well-coordinated, centralized system will help to maximize cost controls and provide a focal point for quality control. Pat Galloway, director of human resources for the William Morris Agency reports that while temporary help expenses are authorized by each department head, it is the job of her department

87

to place all work orders with the temporary help service. She asserts that in this way she is able to track usage and to contain costs. Other professionals prefer to decentralize, or place the decision-making power and order placing as close as possible to the level of need. They assert that departmental ordering improves communication and cuts through the red tape.

According to *Flexible Staffing and Scheduling in U.S. Corporations*, 57 percent of all firms surveyed indicated that the personnel/human resource department is responsible for placing temporary work orders. Only 16 percent of the firms give individual managers this authority, but limit it by requiring approval. The remaining 27 percent decentralize the ordering process and allow individual managers to place temporary work orders at their discretion.[1]

Placing the order for temporary help is the *pivotal step* to ensuring that a satisfactory temp is assigned to the job. The temporary help service will assign a temporary worker based on the details of the order you place with them. Therefore an accurate and detailed job description is critical to getting what you need on the job.

You will need to tell the temporary help service to whom the temporary worker reports. You will also need to tell them who will be supervising the temporary worker, the scheduled start date of the assignment, and the anticipated hours and length of the assignment. You must present a detailed description of the job responsibilities and the duties that will be performed.

The temporary help request form shown in Figure 5-1 has been designed to provide a simple and direct format for developing a temporary work order. It will help the manager to focus on the information needed to place an accurate and complete work order.

The most common mistake managers make when placing an order for temporary help is that they are not specific enough about the skills they need. When placing an order for temporary help, it is not enough to request a PC operator if what you

---

1. *Flexible Staffing and Scheduling in U.S. Corporations*, Research Bulletin no. 240, published by the Conference Board, 1989.

Figure 5-1. Temporary help request form.

Date: _____

Division/department name: _____

Billing code/cost center number: _____

Reports to: _____   Floor #: _____

Scheduled start date: _____

Length of assignment: From: _____ to _____

Hours: _____ to _____   Lunch hour: _____ to _____

Job title: _____

Job description:

_____

_____

_____

_____

Duties to be performed:

_____

_____

_____

Equipment/machines used: _____

Hardware/software: _____

Foreign language: _____

Special skills required: _____

Dress code: _____

Travel information: _____

Parking information: _____

really need is Lotus 1-2-3. You will be disappointed and probably blame the temporary help service if you placed an order for an accountant but really needed a tax specialist. You may think that placing an order for a secretary is simple enough. Yet, simply requesting a secretary is too vague. You really need to tell the temporary help service if the secretary will be required to type correspondence 70 percent of the day, in which case the services of a secretary that types at least 60 words per minute is required. On the other hand, if the secretary will be handling the telephones for three busy sales executives 70 percent of the day, say so. In that case you may require a lesser skilled secretary and will therefore be billed at a lesser hourly rate. If you told the temporary help service that you needed the temporary worker for two days because you wanted to try him or her out before you made a commitment for two weeks, you may be dismayed to learn that the worker was assigned elsewhere after your two day request was satisfied. The bottom line is that failure to accurately and thoroughly define the job and the skills required could result in an unsatisfactory match and wasted temporary help dollars.

It is effective to state the duties of the job in percentages. For example, 70 percent of the day the temp will be entering data onto the CRT, 30 percent of the day the temp will file. Articulated this way, the account coordinator will know that you need someone proficient on the CRT and someone with experience filing. An order for a typical paralegal temporary might sound like this, "We will be needing a temp for four to six weeks. Sixty percent of the time the temp will be digesting depositions, and 40 percent of the time the temp will be responsible for indexing documents and other general document production." This tells the account coordinator that you need a litigation paralegal with good writing skills. The real advantage to ordering this way is that the account coordinator will be able to ascertain from your description the level of expertise and skill required to successfully complete the job.

How to Avoid Over- and Under-Ordering

It is costly to pay for skills that are not needed. Don't overestimate the level of skills needed to complete an assignment or you will pay for more than you need. Conversely, don't compromise job requirements hoping to get a lower billing rate. Avoid over- or under-ordering by evaluating the work order *before* calling the temporary help service. Linda Cook, special sales/foreign rights manager of the publishing house Taylor and Francis Hemisphere, Bristol, Massachusetts, acknowledges that "temporary help is too costly to use if you are paying for more [skills] than you need." The personnel manager of a major New York newspaper reports that she asks many questions of the ordering supervisor to be sure that the supervisor has a clear need for a temporary worker and that there is enough work to warrant the temporary help. In order to limit abuses of their temporary help support system and control spending, Betty Connelly, personnel manager for Revlon, explains that Revlon recently increased the number of signatures required to complete a requisition for a temporary worker. This is to encourage managers to use internal staffing rather than go to the outside for simple replacement of absent employees.

Ordering what you need—not more, not less—takes experience, and there are steps you can take to ensure that you get the most value for your temporary help dollar.

1. Establish realistic goals and objectives.
2. Know what you need before you call.
3. Define each position by exact responsibilities.
4. Know what type of equipment will be used.
5. Be prepared to estimate as accurately as possible the length of the assignment.
6. Plan ahead—the best temporary workers are promised out first.

What to Expect From a Temporary Worker

The stereotype image of the temporary worker as merely a fill-in for a vacationing employee is obsolete today. The contemporary temporary worker represents a professional, responsible, and integral member of the work force. He or she is quick to adapt to new situations and is serious about the job. Some other characteristics that make a good temporary worker are:

- Motivation
- Punctuality and reliability
- Enthusiasm

- Intelligence

- Timeliness

- Professionalism
- Adaptability and flexibility
- Good skills and resourcefulness
- Agreeable and easygoing personality
- Hardworking

Remember that the temporary worker is not a superhuman. He or she needs and wants the same direction, supervision, encouragement, and appreciation that any regular staff member might require.

What to Do Before the Temporary Worker Arrives

Plan the workload in advance so that the temporary worker can get to work without delay. To eliminate conflicting and confusing directions, assign only one person to supervise both the temporary worker and his/her work output. Arrange for a back-up just in case the designated person is unavailable. Check the work station for supplies. Is the desk stocked with the essentials necessary to complete the job or project? Is the equipment in good-working order? If the temporary worker will answer and route telephone calls, is there a roster of names and extensions on the desk? Is there enough work? Too much work?

Possibly the permanent staff feels threatened or even bothered by "just a temp." Inform permanent staff members of the nature and length of the temporary assignment and if they are required to provide any assistance. If the temporary worker is replacing one individual and is responsible for one individual's workload, make sure the permanent staff doesn't use the temporary worker as a dumping ground. Although all of this may seem simple to you, we are continually surprised at how often the obvious is overlooked or taken for granted.

Proper Management of Temporary Help

Imagine that the personnel manager receives a request for an executive secretary and telephones a preselected temporary help service to place an order. In response, the temporary help service assigns one of its best executive secretaries to the job. She types 70 words per minute, uses the dictaphone, is experienced on the personal computer, and takes shorthand at 90 words per minute.

The temp arrives as scheduled at 9:00 A.M. the next morning and is directed to the vice-president's office. When she arrives there, she is told by another secretary that the vice-president will be in a meeting until 11:30. She is shown to her desk and left alone. The temp is unsure of what to do. She takes an occasional telephone message and shuffles through the papers that were left on the desk. Finally, the vice-president returns around noon. The temp feels as though she has wasted the morning.

After lunch, the vice-president directs the executive secretary to place some calls, do some filing, and type some correspondence from the dictaphone. She is directed to merge documents on the personal computer, but she is unfamiliar with the advanced functions that the job requires. The executive secretary spends the afternoon trying to complete the job.

At 4:00 P.M. the vice-president telephones personnel to complain that the temp is too slow. At the same time, the temp has telephoned the service to complain about the assignment. Dissatisfied, the company cancels the order for the next day and calls the next temporary help service on its list.

What went *right* in the scene above? The personnel manager called a temporary help service from a preselected list of services. Believe it or not, this is all that went right.

What went wrong? First, the personnel manager requested

an executive secretary, but provided few details about the assignment. Nor did the temporary help service probe into what the executive secretary would be expected to do. No hourly rate was discussed. Next, when the temporary worker arrived, there was no one to show her around or to direct her work. In addition, she never used her shorthand, and she was unfamiliar with the advanced functions required to operate the PC package. This no-win situation could have been transformed into a win-win situation if personnel had been specific when ordering, if an alternate supervisor has been arranged, and if the vice-president had left written instructions.

We have already established the importance of designating a permanent staff member to provide orientation and training. This authorized staff member should remain available throughout the day to answer questions, to give directions, and to offer general support. He or she should review the temp's work several times a day so that any error may be corrected without delay.

The temporary worker should always be treated with the same respect and consideration that you would extend to permanent staff members. This will encourage a sense of responsibility and conscientiousness. Overall, you can ensure a satisfying temporary relationship if you maintain a systematic approach to temporary staffing (see Figure 5-2).

Orientation and Training

You can greatly improve your chances of getting satisfactory results from temporary personnel if you work along with the temporary help. By providing a brief orientation and training period of ten to thirty minutes you can open lines of communication, increase productivity, and decrease error.

Orientation including introductions, a review of company policies and procedures, and simple things such as where the coat closet is; where the rest room is located; where the photocopy and fax machines are; where lunch is taken; where the

Figure 5-2. Six-point checklist for putting the temp to work.

1. Arrange to have someone greet the temporary worker upon arrival. Confirm that the temp has the skills you require.
2. Introduce the temporary worker to other employees with whom he/she will need to interact—especially those whose work stations are nearby.
3. Explain office rules, policies and procedures such as smoking regulations, where lunch is taken, personal calls, check-in and sign-out procedures.
4. Describe the assignment and give clear and accurate directions about the work. Explain priorities.
5. Encourage questions. A clear understanding of what to do and how to do it will eliminate costly mistakes.
6. Supervise. Good supervision is essential for all personnel, but especially where temporary workers are concerned. Don't overload the temp or expect the impossible.

water cooler is; and where emergency exits are help to make a temporary worker feel comfortable.

In addition to orientation, training of the temporary worker is necessary and quite simply, a prudent personnel practice. Training, including a hands-on demonstration of the equipment needed to complete the job, will not take up a significant amount of time since it is expected that the temporary worker already possesses the skills you need. Keep in mind that temporary workers who have worked previously for your company help to reduce costs because orientation time and on-the-job training can be eliminated or abbreviated. Plan ahead and reserve the services of a favored temporary worker.

"Temp to Perm" or "Try Before You Hire"

"Temp to perm" conversions provide an excellent opportunity for client company's seeking permanent staff additions. "Temp to perm," also referred to as "try before you hire," is a probationary period of temporary employment prior to a permanent employment commitment. This obligation-free situation provides the employer with the opportunity to experience on-the-job attitude and evaluate performance capabilities of a potential employee. At the same time, a job candidate can gain real insight into the corporate environment and job responsibilities before making a permanent commitment. "Try before you hire" eliminates the time and expense of finding qualified candidates on your own. It also offers a considerable hedge against hiring mistakes by taking the guesswork out of interviewing and the hiring process. There are no hidden or additional costs associated with "try before you hire," it is a by-product and benefit of the temporary help arrangement. However, as the temporary employee is the only asset of the temporary help service, many temporary help companies expect compensation for loss of services if the temporary worker is hired on a permanent basis. This compensation is called liquidated damages and represents the cost of recruiting, interviewing, hiring, and placing the worker on the job. It is advisable to resolve the issue of liquidated damages early on, especially if you are using temporary help to find permanent employees.

What You Should Do If You Are Dissatisfied With the Temporary Worker

Although there are check points along the way to affirm that a qualified temporary worker has been assigned to the job, it is always possible that something will go wrong. If there is a problem, try to determine the cause before taking any action. Conceivably, the work order may not have been specific enough; the signals given to the temporary help service may have been misunderstood; the temporary worker may not be skilled enough; or may be overqualified for the job, in which case you would be paying for more than you need. It may be possible that the supervisor or co-worker(s) are simply not cooperating. Often the department is unprepared for the temporary worker even though a request was made. This in fact, is the most common complaint we hear from temporary workers about their assignments. If the temporary worker appears to have what it takes but the assignment is not going well, consider whether the directions are clear and representative of exactly what you need. Is the supervisor available so that the temporary worker can ask questions? If the difficulty is the attitude of the assigned temporary worker, or if the temporary worker does not have the skills required to complete the job, call the temporary help service immediately for a replacement. This is extremely important, as most temporary help services will offer a free replacement within the first four to twenty-four hours.

In any case, don't put up with an unqualified person—get rid of him/her right away. To this end, it is the responsibility of the employing temporary help service to remove an unsatisfactory temporary worker from an assignment. You need only to call the account coordinator who will speak to, and discharge the temporary worker from the job. If the temporary is being removed because of a sensitive issue or if there is a chance that being cancelled on the job could escalate into an embarrassing situation, the client should ask the service to cancel the temporary worker that evening at home. Recognizing a problem early and taking action swiftly will help you to avoid expensive mistakes.

What You Should Do If the Temporary Worker Is Injured on the Job

As the temporary help service is the legal employer of each temporary worker, all on-the-job injuries are covered under the worker's compensation policy of the temporary help service. This represents an important advantage to your company as any claim made by the temporary worker for worker's compensation is not charged against your company's policy. Still, the client company is fully responsible for providing a reasonably safe workplace and for the maintenance and proper inspection of any equipment the temporary worker may use. In order to protect themselves from spiraling worker's compensation claims, many temporary help services are conducting on-site safety evaluations before committing their workers to a job.

In the event that a temporary worker is injured on the job:

1. Get medical attention at once.
2. Call the temporary help service immediately.
3. Cooperate with both the temporary help service and the insurance carrier in any investigation that may follow.

It is imperative that the client company ask the temporary help service representative about liability and worker's compensation insurance before an accident occurs. Adequate coverage will protect the temporary help service—but more importantly, it will protect you! Ask for a copy of the certificate of both the liability and worker's compensation insurance. If the temporary help service is uncooperative or unable to supply a certificate, take your business elsewhere.

6

Hiring Professionals as Temporary Workers

For years temporary work was the exclusive domain of secretaries and clerical workers, but no longer. The recessions of the 1980s proved that upper- and middle-management jobs were not immune from company downsizing, restructuring, and mergers. As a result of these widespread purges, a new breed of temporary worker was born.

Professional temporary workers represent one of the fastest growing areas in the temporary help industry. Highly trained professionals such as nurses, doctors, physician assistants, pharmacists, psychologists, scientists, accountants, engineers, lawyers, paralegals, graphic artists, computer programmers, technical writers, and data processors are seeking out temporary work. Cost-efficient and productive, professional temporary workers provide labor flexibility for employers who must continually adjust to changing market conditions. According to the National Association of Temporary Services (NATS), they currently represent 21 percent of the temporary work force.

Management recognizes that the very same cost-savings principles that have proven that temporary office support staffing is effective, apply to management-level staffing as well. For this reason, cost-conscious companies are increasing their use of professionals as temporaries to work on special projects, to reduce workloads, and to cover for vacationing employees. Using white-collar temporary workers allows companies to manage the workload without hiring full-time employees and having to lay them off as the business climate changes. It also saves companies personnel and payroll costs which can amount to as much as 50 percent of an employee's wages.

Specialization is in demand and it is predicted that the hiring of temporary professionals will continue to increase as the American economy becomes more and more service oriented. To meet the demands for temporary professionals, the temporary help service industry is developing specialty services that recruit and retain trained professionals who are available on short notice, for finite periods of time, with no strings attached.

The Temporary Healthcare Industry—At Large

In response to the evolving needs within the healthcare community, medical temporary help services have emerged. In the past, nurses have made up the largest part of the medical branch of temporary help. Today, doctors, pharmacists, psychologists, scientists, laboratory technicians, and dentists are members of the temporary healthcare industry.

Increased efficiency and productivity, and decreased paperwork are decided advantages of utilizing temporary healthcare personnel. Healthcare-related temporary workers can provide additional technical skills and expertise for special projects or when workloads are at a peak. (The concept of minimum staffing is alive and well in the healthcare industry.)

The Nursing Shortage—Filling a Void

There is a critical need for registered nurses and licensed practical nurses to supplement hospital staffs and to provide home healthcare. The U.S. Department of Health and Human Services predicted that by 1990 there would be a 40 percent shortage of nurses. Temporary help services specializing in placing nurses on short- and long-term temporary help assignments hope to allay this shortage by recruiting nurses who find flexible hours attractive and who can work at will without the obligation of a full-time commitment. Temporary help services generally hire only registered nurses and licensed practical nurses who have a year or more of work experience in their occupations. While some nurses have chosen to moonlight through temporary help services in order to supplement their incomes, others work to keep their skills up-to-date or simply to have a more flexible work schedule with which they can meet family obligations or pursue personal interests. Assignments may be for as little as one work shift, but usually range from two or three days to several weeks or more. The qualifications of the nurses and the length of their employment will differ according to the assignment.

Traditionally, patients and hospitals have relied on nurses registries and on-call pools to provide private-duty care nurses. Nurses registries initially found assignments for self-employed nurses for a fee. Registered nurses, practical nurses, and nurses aides were considered self-employed independent contractors.

In the mid-1970s, many nurses registries began expanding their roles in the healthcare industry by employing X-ray technicians, laboratory technicians, and other medical workers on a temporary basis. Several services such as Family Care Nurses Registry, Inc., of New York began providing fully screened and tested medical personnel who were bonded, insured, and available twenty-four hours a day.

There are distinct differences between nurses registries and medical temporary help services. According to the National Association of Temporary Services, nurses registries bring together applicants and prospective employers. When applicants of the nurses registry are hired by clients, a fee is paid to the registry. The applicant is not the employee of the Nurses Registry, nor does the registry pay the applicant a salary, contribute to any benefits plan, or make any mandatory contributions or deductions. In contrast, temporary help services that provide medical-related personnel, do indeed employ the worker and as the employer, assume all of the obligations and risks normally incident to all employers. The temporary help service pays wages, withholds mandatory payroll deductions, and provides worker's compensation and unemployment insurance for its employees. Some services provide health and life insurance and other fringe benefits for their healthcare professionals; others offer malpractice insurance and bonding insurance in an effort to retain the service of these valued temps. Today, temporary help services provide alternatives to traditional sources of flexible staffing by providing healthcare personnel for temporary assignments.

The principal users of temporary nursing personnel are hospitals, private households, nursing homes, clinics, and private practices. The use of temporary healthcare workers in hospitals is usually limited to registered nurses, although nursing homes and private households may use both registered nurses and licensed practical nurses. Temporary nurses fill in for permanent staff who are on vacation, ill, or absent for other reasons. An epidemic or disaster would increase the need for temporary personnel. During the summer, the demand for medical temporary personnel is greatest when many regular staff members take vacations and patients schedule elective surgery to coincide with their vacation time. The demand for hospital services in a state like Florida, where the patient load doubles in the winter and drops dramatically in the summer, reinforces the need for flexible staffing.

Future increases in the field of medical temporaries are expected to concentrate in nursing homes and private residences. A contributing factor is the growing number of elderly and disabled people in need of long-term care. In addition, the early discharge of patients from hospitals means more people need medical assistance and supervision while recuperating at home. Changes in private insurance and Medicare coverage make home health care more affordable for patients recovering from acute illnesses. To meet the needs of individuals, temporary help services have developed comprehensive programs for delivering a package of services to the home patient which includes scheduled visits by a registered nurse and basic care by licensed-practical nurses.

According to Anne McCarthy, associate director of patient services for Visiting Nurse Service of New York, the largest home health care service in the United States, there is a growing emphasis on diversified home healthcare involving professional nursing for short and long term care, home health aide service for personal care respiratory therapy, physical therapy, occupational and speech, IV therapy, nutrition counseling, and social work services. Another temporary help service, U.S. Homecare, which has offices in New York, Connecticut, and Florida, is a company growing and diversifying in these areas as well. According to Amy Leshner Thomas, branch director of U.S. Homecare, there is always plenty of temporary work available and not enough employees to meet the daily demands of its clients.

While many medical temporary services are choosing to diversify, some are heading toward specialization. Nurses Connections of Houston, provides only psychiatric medical personnel. Founder Jeanne Parker felt that a specialty profession deserved specialty personnel.

Doctors Too!

The practice of employing temporary physicians is on the rise in this traditionally conservative field. While doctors seldom seek temporary employment to help build their careers they do pursue it as a way to accommodate other interests or to slow down.

KRON Medical Corporation in Chapel Hill, North Carolina, pioneered the practice of utilizing temporary physicians. Dr. Alan Kronhaus, president and chief executive officer of the company, is generally credited with the origin of using temporary physicians or "locum tenens." Having conceived the service to meet the needs of the rural physician, the idea took shape and grew. In addition to rural practices, principal users include hospitals, medical groups, clinics, teaching hospitals, and private practitioners. Similar services are offered throughout the county and include Locum Tenens, Inc., in Atlanta, Relief Network in New Braunfels, Texas, and Comprehensive Health Systems, Inc., in Salt Lake City.

Medical-related situations which have successfully used locum tenens staffing include hospitals in places with seasonal differences in the population, interim coverage while a physician seeks a partner, institutions in the process of recruiting staff, personnel coverage during the start-up or break-up of a practice, and replacement for an ill physician. For the physician wanting more flexibility, desiring to slow down, or wishing to pursue personal interests, the future looks bright because there is an increasing demand for locum tenens in this expanding industry.

Accounting Professionals

If an accountant wants to work full-time for a temporary help service, there are more than enough assignments to keep him or her busy year-round. Experience is valued in a temporary employee who must slip into a high-level job slot and immediately perform up to speed. Early retirees and accountants desiring a change in lifestyle are finding that their services are in demand in today's marketplace. For accounting professionals who want to exercise their essential skills in a more entrepreneurial way, temporary work is an attractive alternative.

According to Walter Murphy, president of Accountant Auditor Temps in New York City, which employs approximately 500 temporary professionals annually, the need for temporary accountants continues to grow. Most of Accountant Auditor Temps' employees are high-level CPAs, although a few are entry-level. It is not unusual for temporary accountants to earn an equivalent of full-time pay on temporary assignments. At times, the pay rate may be higher than full-time wages because there is no benefits package involved. Assignments can range from two weeks to six months or up to several years.

The need for temporary accountants is increasing across the board and includes assignments at private companies, public corporations, restaurants, and art galleries. In addition, many new businesses cannot afford a full-time on-staff accountant, so they use the services of temporary accountants. Hiring a temporary accountant for periodic assignments is the ideal solution for the entrepreneur as well as the company in need of additional accountants. Small to medium-size companies can often buy a level of experience they could not afford on a permanent basis.

Due to the level of responsibility and expertise required for special projects and assignments, temporary accountants must be well educated and be able to adapt to various situations. J. C. Williamson, a partner of Accounting Plus, believes accountants who "temp" become experts in their field. Temporary accountants must learn systems that are flexible and adaptable to a variety of assignments. As a result of being called upon to adapt to different environments, they become very good at solving problems. According to industry experts, the industry has experienced tremendous growth which can be attributed, in part, to the sophistication of specialty temporary help services.

Accountemps, a division of Robert Half and founded by Robert and Maxine Half over forty years ago, was one of the first temporary accounting services in the United States. Accountemps places accountants in companies ranging from small retail operations to major public accounting firms, corporations, and financial institutions. Most assignments are project oriented with finite time frames, enabling the professional to focus on the assignment from beginning to end. Accountemps is the largest temporary accounting service with over 150 offices in the United States and abroad. The three New York offices of Accountemps experience high levels of turnover weekly and, on average, place over 400 temporary accountants per week and over 15,000 annually. On a national level, the company placed over 80,000 temporary accountants in 1989.

To meet critical needs of companies for upper-level accounting professionals, Accountemps also has an upper-level division called Executive Corner where temporary professionals take on positions requiring sophisticated levels of duties and responsibilities. While the concept of using executives on a temporary basis is still relatively new, it has proven cost-effective and has clearly left its imprint on the labor market.

As companies begin to recognize the economic value of hiring temporary accountants, requests for their services will increase. There continues to be a steady demand for accountants to prepare audit schedules, to update and close out the books, and to assist in preparing budgets and forecasts. The emergence of the temporary professional accountant has provided a solution to the corporate dilemma of managing a variable workload in an ever-changing economic environment while containing costs.

Legal Staff

In the legal community, lawyers are joining the ranks of temporary professionals. Women attorneys with young children who want to keep practicing so that they can easily return to the full-time work force in a few years, account for 25 percent of the lawyers who find work through legal temporary help services. The pool of per diem attorneys includes lawyers not yet ready to retire, sole practitioners with cyclical business, lawyers in between permanent positions, recent law school graduates, and individuals seeking flexibility in their work schedules to pursue other interests. The high rate of pay, variety of work, and flexible hours appeal to attorneys who choose the temporary alternative.

Temporary help services employing legal temporary workers have sprung up around the country and include Contract Attorneys, Inc., and Lawsmiths in San Francisco, LAW/Temps in Northfield, Illinois (a suburb of Chicago), Lawyer's Lawyer in Washington, D.C., Lawyer on Call in Detroit, Law Professionals in Atlanta, and Special Counsel in New York. Companies nationwide, attracted by the cost savings and flexibility these services offer, have started using per diem attorneys. According to the Administrative Management Society in 1989, the utilization of temporary help by law firms and legal divisions of corporations is on the rise.

Ethical questions have been raised about temporary lawyers who work for several firms in a short period of time, creating potential conflicts of interest and raising questions regarding confidentiality. To this end, most temporary help services that cater to the legal trade protect themselves and the client company by requesting that all of the temporary workers they assign sign a confidentiality statement. An example of a confidentiality agreement is shown in Figure 6-1.

In New York City, the Bar Association ruled that legal temporary help services must be paid a fixed-hourly rate. In New York, for example, a legal temporary help service would bill a client company an hourly rate for a lawyer's work time. The temporary service would keep 25 percent to 35 percent (considered mark-up which includes overhead expenses, mandatory taxes, benefits, and a profit of two to five percent) and the lawyer would earn the rest. One way temporary lawyer placement services can now be compensated without violating these newer regulations is by formulating a per project charge based on considerations that include the qualifications of the attorney, experience required, and a reasonable prediction of the duration of the temporary assignment.

In addition to dealing with ethical concerns involving temporary help services in the legal profession, the Bar Association, in efforts to support and advance the activities of temporary lawyers, actively engages in programs aimed at promoting the opportunities of temporary or part-time lawyers in their pursuit of professionally rewarding legal work.

For small and medium-size law firms, the use of temporary lawyers gives partners the freedom to take on more work by freeing them of routine tasks and enabling them to increase staffing as the caseload dictates. When the workload eases, the temporary worker is terminated without consequences to the client company. There is no financial commitment—an advantage that personnel and office managers find appealing.

Assignments for lawyers may be for one day or several months. Law firms, corporate counsel, and sole practitioners look to an attorney temporary help service for assistance for a wide range of legal services including trial preparation, research, drafting contracts for real estate transactions, and wills. De-

Figure 6-1. Confidentiality agreement.

CONFIDENTIALITY AGREEMENT

Date _____

As a condition of my employment with the Law Services Division of Career Blazers Temporary Personnel ("Career"), I hereby acknowledge and agree as follows:

I will not disclose or in any way relate or disseminate any information, including any and all information pertaining to Career or any of Career's clients' operating methods and procedures, which may come to my attention or into my possession as a result of this employment, to any person, firm or corporation without the prior written authority of Career and such clients of Career.

I understand that: (i)   I am to make no copies of any documents except as may be specifically authorized by Career or Career's client; and (ii) such documents and any copies thereof are confidential documents to remain in my personal custody until I have completed my assigned duties, whereupon they are to be returned to the party who properly provided me with these documents. Under no circumstances shall I remove documents or copies thereof from the premises in which they reside without specific authorization by Career or Career's client.

I further understand that I shall be responsible for any direct or consequential damages resulting from any violation on my part of this agreement.

IN WITNESS WHEREOF. I have hereunto set my hand and seal the day and year first above written.

_____   _____

         (print name)   (legal signature)

_____
PERMANENT   •   *TEMPORARY*   •   *TRAINING*
590 FIFTH AVENUE ■ *NEW YORK, N.Y. 10036* ■ *212 - 719 - 3232*

Reprinted with permission by Career Blazers.

pending on the individual's area of specialization and experience, an attorney's compensation for temporary work is often comparable to or even greater than an associate's salary.

Paralegals

In addition to hiring temporary lawyers, firms rely heavily on temporary paralegals to meet fluctuating workloads throughout the year. The legal assistance field, which got underway in the 1970s, is one of fastest growing sectors of the temporary work force. Most temporary paralegals are college graduates who have paralegal certificates. Some are law students or new lawyers awaiting test results from the Bar. Still others are actors, actresses, and individuals in pursuit of fulfillment in other areas of their lives. Many have been permanent temporary workers for years because they enjoy the flexibility and project-oriented work. The hourly rates are comparable to full-time workers in the same field. Although the greatest number of assignments tend to be within the areas of litigation and corporate law, temporary paralegals are also needed in the fields of real estate, trusts and estates, labor and employment, and bankruptcy law.

According to the Labor Department's Bureau of Statistics, the number of permanent and temporary paralegals in the marketplace will double to 100,000 by 1995, representing an increase of nearly 100 percent since 1984. Working alongside attorneys, temporary paralegals provide increased efficiency and productivity resulting in profit for the firms that utilize them. The work performed by paralegals relieves the attorney of routine tasks and allows the attorney more time to perform specialized functions such as representing clients in court and giving legal counsel, the two functions a paralegal cannot do. For example, in litigation, a temporary paralegal might interview clients, take depositions, do research and prepare documents. In corporate law, a temporary paralegal might assist in the processing of document filings and closings. In property law or real estate, the temporary paralegal might assist in real estate closings. Services that specialize in the placement of temporary paralegals include Career Blazers Law Services and Planned Staffing in New York, and Legal Assistants Corporation based in Washington, D.C. To protect the confidentiality of clients of law firms, paralegals are usually requested to sign confidentiality statements. Whatever the area of expertise, the need for temporary paralegals and reliance upon them continues to increase in the legal community.

Executives for the Short-Term

Upper-level professional temporary workers are filling a multitude of positions as companies undergo restructuring, establish overseas subsidiaries, or divest. Hesitant to expand permanent staff until business conditions have become more certain, companies are forced to adjust staffing in response to immediate needs. The quick response of the temporary help service in supplying experienced executives is an important attribute of the industry.

The diverse and extensive talent available within the ranks of temporary executives provides a tremendous resource pool for companies that might otherwise be unable to avail themselves of such high-priced expertise. Executive temporary services play an important role in bringing together executives to fill high-level roles for a finite period of time. Companies such as Management Assistance Group of West Hartford, Connecticut, and New York-based Interim Management Co. offer clients top-notch experienced executives for specific projects or situations who leave when the project is completed. These temporary executive help services provide assistance during company takeovers and wholesale downsizing. Companies are increasingly turning to executive temp agencies to provide them with senior executives capable of acting as CEO, CFO, controller, chief-loan officer, marketing director or director of personnel.

Temporary managers are especially valuable for small or growing companies that cannot afford experienced professionals on a full-time basis, need quick-fix executives to help out during expansions, or want additional time to find a permanent replacement. It is easy for business owners to become so pressured by financial details that product sales are neglected. When this occurs, it is wise to find a temporary sales manager who could manage sales and production, relieving the business owner of these responsibilities while he/she addresses financial concerns. Or the other hand, to find a temporary financial manager to step in on an interim basis, bring the accounting records up to date, and help to set the course for future accounting practices within the company. As a company grows, utilizing temporary management help is also an economical way of having an experienced person establish a new function while at the same time limiting obligations and commitments.

The majority of the 200,000 managerial temporary workers in the marketplace today have elected not to hold permanent jobs and prefer to view themselves as independent contractors or consultants. Some top executives, products of widespread managerial lay-offs in recent years, take temporary positions while searching for something permanent. Other executives are parents who find temporary work a suitable alternative for maintaining professional careers while spending more time with their families. Many executives who have taken early retirement are not eager to get back into the day-to-day grind but want to stay alive in the business world. With thirty-five to forty years' experience, retirees bring a wealth of knowledge and expertise to corporate projects and are a vital resource for companies on an interim basis.

One question raised is whether interim executives are less committed to their short-term assignments than staff managers might be. Experience has proven this not to be the case. People who work independently on a temporary-hire basis have loyalty to themselves and to their work. They are committed to their professions and to providing top-notch performances.

The compensation is often comparable to what a permanently hired executive would make. For example, one CFO reported earning $150,000 annually. However, executive perks such as vacations, severance pay, health benefits, stock options and bonuses were not included. A requisite for the high pay is experience. At least ten years of experience is required by the major temporary executive services. The temporary executive is an essential commodity as corporations search to cut costs, and is becoming a permanent fixture in corporate life.

Professional Temporary Help Is Here to Stay

When a company utilizes professional temporary help, it pays only for the actual hours worked, thus avoiding the costs of lunch hours, sick days, and vacation time. In addition, as the temporary worker is an employee of the temporary help service, the client company is relieved of all payroll-related costs. Client companies are also eliminating all the hidden costs of advertising, interviewing, and training. They can avoid hiring permanent people that won't be needed later. Business managers have discovered that employing temporary professionals is a proven solution in cutting costs and avoiding the agony of layoffs.

To find a service that will meet your company's needs, seek referrals through business associates who have used professional temporary services. Although many services are based in specific areas, professional help services send temporary executives out on contracts and assignments all over the country. Most services are listed in the Yellow Pages. If the service you desire is not listed under temporary services, try looking under specialty headings. Professional services also advertise in newspapers and trade journals.

Choosing the right professional temporary help service for your company can mean a difference in performance, cost, and efficiency. Select a few services and ask each representative to make a presentation about its service or make a personal visit to selected companies. Rate the companies on the basis of their knowledge, professionalism, training programs, testing procedures, interest, and attitude.

Flexible staffing is state-of-the-art personnel management and has become one of the more important ways U.S. industry is reordering its priorities in response to demands for greater efficiency and lower labor costs. Utilizing professional temps is not only a good business practice but also an effective and productive management tool.

7

Alternatives to Outside Temporary Help Services

Employment growth in the 1980s was marked by dramatic increases in temporary, part-time, contract, and leased workers. Of course, contingent employment arrangements really are nothing new. Industries such as retail trade and agriculture have long relied on short-term, variable-hour employees. Temporary help services have been active in the United States employment market since the end of World War II. Companies have leased truck drivers and security forces for decades.

What is new about this trend is its pervasiveness. It cuts across a wide range of industries. Not surprisingly, the increase in contingent workers in the last ten years has been greatest in those sectors where computerization has progressed most rapidly such as banking, insurance, retail trade, and food sales. In fact, part-time work in financial services and retail trade is now growing faster than part-time work in construction, the traditional leader. Contingent work patterns are also affecting growth industries such as telecommunications and health care.

Alternative staffing arrangements clearly can no longer be viewed as stopgap responses to transient labor-market problems.

Instead of flagging, the contingent-labor force has grown even larger under post-recession conditions. The demand for a more flexible work force reflects profound structural changes in the way goods and services are produced. As the United States approaches the year 2000, the popularity of nontraditional work relationships should continue to grow.

The Bureau of National Affairs (BNA) conducted a survey of part-time and other alternative staffing practices. Of 223 responding organizations, over 75 percent of the smallest and 85 percent of the largest indicated that they regularly employed part-time workers or bought the services of temporary workers through temporary help services. Over 50 percent of the smallest organizations surveyed reportedly manage in-house temporary pools, while over two-thirds of the largest organizations reported that they maintained in-house temp pools.[1]

Figure 7-1 illustrates the use of alternative staffing practices by type of employer. Note that temporary help use, engaged either directly or through services, represents the largest segment of alternative staffing.

In-House Temp Pools

Some companies that regularly use a large number of temporary workers have created internal-staffing alternatives in order to cut costs. An in-house temp pool eliminates the middleman costs of using a temporary help service. Building a reliable stable of direct-hire temporaries reduces the orientation and training time associated with one-time temporary hires. For workers, on-site placements provide a degree of continuity they can't obtain from the more varied temporary help service assignments. This sense of connection often makes pool members more productive and committed than casual temporary hires. Regular temporary assignments can also provide a proving ground for permanent positions.

There are several ways to set up an in-house temporary

---

1. Bureau of National Affairs, *Bulletin to Management*, (June 23, 1988).

Figure 7-1. Alternative staffing practices (by type of employer).

	Part-Time Schedules	Direct-Hire Temporaries	Agency Temporaries	Outside Contractors
All Companies (223)	81%	59%	84%	57%
By Industry				
Manufacturing (80)	65	54	88	63
Nonmanufacturing (92)	87	54	88	47
Nonbusiness (51)	96	75	73	65
By Size				
Large (111)	87	67	86	60
Small (112)	75	51	83	53
By Union/Nonunion Status				
Union (94)	79	55	84	59
Nonunion (129)	83	61	85	55

Reprinted with permission from *Bulletin to Management* (BNA Policy and Practice series), Vol. 37, No. 25—Part II, pp. 2, 10 (June 23, 1988). Copyright 1988 by The Bureau of National Affairs, Inc.

pool. The most elaborate is a permanent unit of employees who are deployed in temporary assignments throughout the company. Their assignments are coordinated by a unit manager. These "permanent temps" are on the regular payroll and usually receive the same pay and fringe benefits as other workers. They can work full- or part-time hours, or their schedules may be adjusted to meet the employer's projects schedule or seasonal needs.

Extensive recruiting, planning, and supervision is required to maintain a formal internal unit (in-house temp pool) or permanent-floater system. These staffing alternatives are cost-effective only for fairly large organizations. The high fixed costs of guaranteed schedules can only be recouped through the continuous use of these workers. Consequently, the internal pool's size is always smaller than the company's peak demand for temporary workers. Thus, it must often be supplemented with temporary help service hires and other outside sources.

Some high-volume users of temporary help warrant the set up of an in-house temporary service, staffed by representatives of the temporary help company. The service representatives coordinate and organize the temporary help use right along with the client-company representative.

One such set-up is an in-house temporary service at the Coca-Cola Company. Prior to July 1, 1988, Coca-Cola was using twenty-five different services to secure temporary help. A task force was formed by Coca-Cola to simplify/improve this out-of-control situation. It was decided by this task force that the top ten services would be studied, and the best chosen to start an in-house temporary operation at Coca-Cola. The in-house temporary service supervisor describes the operation in this way. The in-house service screens, tests, interviews, and trains its pool of temporary workers on-site. A project manager or supervisor makes a request to the in-house service for a temporary worker. The in-house staff matches the department's need to its pool of temporary workers. If a temporary worker is not found, then one of five back-up services is called. As a result of their in-house service, Coca-Cola has greatly reduced its reliance on outside temporary service companies. Further, it has improved the quality of service and production from its temporary staff because the in-house temporary workers are familiar with Coca-Cola's policies, procedures, and in some cases, jobs.

For a company with substantial on-going needs for temporary help, an internal unit can justify the investment in administrative time and payroll costs. "Permanent temps" have the chance to develop more sophisticated company-specific skills than other temporary hires. The pool can also be a way station to a permanent position or an exit port for employees preparing to retire or reduce their work hours.

Internal pools range in skill from mailroom workers and messengers to legal secretaries, bank loan clerks, and even branch managers. The most common occupations are clerical positions such as secretaries, file clerks, word processors, and data-entry operators.

Using On-Call/Direct-Hire Temporary Workers

A less formal, and more popular, arrangement than a permanent internal unit of temporary workers is an "on-call pool" or direct-hire temps. These workers are usually on the company payroll, but are only called in, and paid, as needed for temporary assignments. An on-call roster eliminates the continuous payroll costs of an internal unit, but the costs of such an operation are not negligible. Recruiting and deploying a corps of reliable workers requires a sizable commitment of administrative time and energy. The employer must also manage the payroll and all the other personnel functions normally assumed by the temporary help service.

On-call workers agree to be more or less available for temporary jobs as needed. Unlike "permanent temps," however, they have the right to turn down assignments. In fact, this freedom is usually precious to the worker who has chosen a "temping" lifestyle. The wild card worker availability complicates the scheduling challenges of the on-call operation. Locating a temporary worker who is willing and ready to accept a particular job becomes the pool administrator's headache, instead of the temporary help service's.

Recruiting and maintaining loyal on-call temporary workers also puts the employer in direct competition with the temporary help services. This creates some formidable tactical and policy dilemmas. The larger temporary help services offer its temporary workers benefits such as paid holidays and vacation, group life and health insurance, and possibly a system of bonuses. The employer must decide whether to offer a comparable benefits package or a benefits package at all. The temporary help services can also promise reliable workers an almost constant stream of job assignments. A number of in-house pools started up with great fanfare only to be disbanded as pool members drifted away because of infrequent work opportunities.

In fact, on-call pools exhibit varying degrees of commitment. One electronics firm guaranteed its on-call workers six months of full-time work per year, with substantial fringe benefits. Some companies offer no guarantees and provide diminished benefits, if any.

The Bank of America's on-call pool is frequently cited as a successful example of this type of temporary program. Several factors have contributed to the San Francisco based bank's ability to attract and retain quality workers. The company pays its temps slightly more than the temporary help services and has devised a system of merit-based pay increases, although it provides no fringe benefits. An additional incentive is the high ratio of temporary workers who become permanent employees—more than 20 percent. For the majority of pool members, the bank's on-call system represents a happy medium between the relative anonymity of temporary help service assignments and the binding ties of a permanent job. The special ambience of the Bay Area is also conducive to supplying an unusual wealth of qualified applicants. Many of the bank's temps are aspiring actors and artists who support themselves with word processing and other marketable office skills.

Although employers can learn from the Bank of America example, its on-call program offers no failsafe blueprint for success. The bank's experience instead illustrates that companies must assess the forces at work in their own labor markets in addition to evaluating their own resources. The net cost of operating an in-house pool must be measured carefully against the hourly rate charged by a temporary help service. The administrative, legal, and tax implications require considerable attention. For example, unemployment laws in most states require employers to promptly notify a temporary employee that he or she is being removed from active status when work is not available. Otherwise, the employee accrues time toward eligibility for unemployment compensation benefits.

Companies that enjoy extensive administrative resources can more easily absorb the costs and handle the logistics of an on-call temporary pool. The Bank of America effort, for example, was supported by a sophisticated computer system, expert legal and tax staff, compensation specialists, and a human resources staff that eagerly greeted this new challenge. While on-call programs are not the exclusive province of large corporations, these support systems clearly give them a headstart over smaller businesses.

Independent Contractors/Freelancers

Independent contractors, also known as freelancers, are the elite corps of temporary workers. These individuals typically provide specialized, professional, or technical services on an ad hoc basis. Independent contractors are generally called in on a project basis, although they can also be hired for a specified period of time. Freelancers represent virtually every profession, including systems analysts, programmers, engineers, researchers, writers, designers, and graphic artists.

The independent contractor is a self-employed individual who is not attached to the company's payroll. Thus, no withholding taxes are deducted from his or her paycheck. The employer also makes no contributions for Social Security, unemployment, retirement, health plans, or other benefits. In some cases, a company may pay the independent contractor a higher rate than a salaried employee in recognition of the loss of such fringe benefits. Even so, the savings on benefits, taxes, and administrative time often more than offset these increased wage costs.

Figure 7-2. Percentage of companies that use contractors.

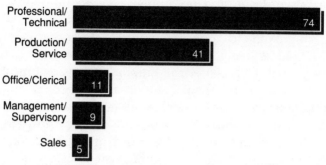

Reprinted with permission from the Bureau of National Affairs, Washington, D.C.

In addition to the lure of higher income, many people pursue freelance work for the greater autonomy, control, and flexibility it offers as compared to more traditional salaried positions. Successful freelancers or independent contractors can parley the demand for their skills into a satisfying and lucrative worklife. In addition, independent contractors and freelancers enjoy the status of sole proprietors of a business, allowing them to claim tax deductions not available to regular employees.

Hiring freelancers can be a way of attracting highly skilled workers who have no interest in becoming employees. Free-lancers are often called in for technical support when a company secures a major contract or to provide expertise that is not available internally. Depending on the nature of the project, the work may be performed on the company's premises or at the freelancer's home or office. A systems analyst, for example, would have to be on-site to diagnose and solve a problem. A technical writer, by contrast, could complete an assignment at home.

According to a BNA (Bureau of National Affairs) survey, nearly three-quarters of the firms that hired independent contractors do so for professional and technical work.[2] The graph in Figure 7-2 illustrates the percentage of companies that use contractors, and the kind of work they are hired to do.

2. Bureau of National Affairs, *Bulletin to Management*, June 23, 1988.

Despite its advantages, the contractor relationship is something of a risk for the employer. Often the quality of the freelancer's work is a relative unknown when he or she is first hired. Gambling on his or her ability to perform the work effectively can be costly, especially when the employer is paying premium rates for valuable expertise. To minimize these risks, you should tap business contacts, trade associations, and professional networks for recommendations. Insist that candidates provide references and, where possible, work samples.

Independent contracting can be a mutually beneficial relationship for both client companies and the individuals who choose to market their specialized skill in this way. But the practice also provides a wide latitude for abuse. To be truly an independent contractor, the worker must exercise control over the execution, pacing, and timing of work, and have the opportunity to gain or suffer losses from his or her efforts. There can be no enduring relationship or permanent attachment with the employer.

The converse is also true. By the common law test, a worker whose hours and working conditions are dictated by an employer and who maintains a continuing relationship with a company is an employee. Many economists and labor analysts see a disturbing trend among employers to use the guise of independent contracting to avoid paying workers either discretionary company benefits or contributing to their Federal benefits such as Social Security, worker's compensation, and unemployment coverage.

Contract labor practices are most suspect when applied to lower-wage skills, such as clerical, janitorial, and maintenance occupations. In sharp contrast to the relatively privileged class of self-employed professionals, these workers have limited leverage or opportunity in the marketplace. These involuntary contractors are often penalized financially for their status.

The apparent abuse of independent contracting has prompted increased IRS scrutiny and spurred demands for tighter regulation. The safe-haven clause in the tax code that exempts employers from having to hire workers as employees even when their status meets the common law definition of employee has come under increasing attack. In 1986 the Repeal of Section 1706 of the IRS tax code removed the exemption in respect to computer specialists and the Congressional Subcommittee on Employment and Housing has called for further weakening of the safe-haven clause. The subcommittee's recommendation was issued in a report on clerical home-based work that concluded that fraudulent use of independent contracting was leading to financial exploitation of home-based clerical workers.[3]

Job Shops

Instead of hiring freelancers directly, an employer can also go through a job shop. These are actually temporary help services that specialize in supplying professional and, especially, technical personnel. Job shops provide companies with engineers, draftsmen, designers, programmers, and technical writers, among other occupations. As a temporary help service, the job shop is the legal employer of the worker but has no formal tie to them when they are not on assignment.

Unlike temporary help services, job shops typically forward several resumes to the client company, who then selects the person to be assigned. Another way in which job shops differ from other temporary services is by placing workers throughout the country and at times around the world, rather than focusing on local markets. While geographically mobile "road" job shoppers are willing to relocate to other areas, "freeway" or "subway" job shoppers go from one assignment to another in the same metropolitan area. If the employee has relocated in order to work on the client's project, the client company may pay a per diem as reimbursement for food and lodging, in addition to the agreed upon hourly rate. Like the temporary help service, job shops will perform the client's work on its own premises or on-site at the client's offices.

---

3. Kathleen Christensen, Ph.D., "Independent Contracting," in *Flexible Workstyles: A Look at Contingent Labor*, Conference Summary, published by U.S. Department of Labor, Women's Bureau, 1988.

Part-Time Workers

Perhaps no trend reflects the changing dynamics of staffing arrangements more dramatically than the unprecedented growth of the part-time work force. An estimated 20 million Americans, nearly one out of five workers, regularly work less than thirty-five hours per week (the accepted benchmark for full-time work). This segment of the contingent work force witnessed its sharpest increases during the recessions of the early 1980s, when the number of employed individuals forced to settle for part-time positions nearly doubled. But the part-time work force continued to expand even as these cyclical factors receded.

The persistent increases in part-time jobs testify to the determination of recession-scarred and competition-toughened employers to coordinate their deployment of labor resources more closely with fluctuations in demand. They also reflect structural changes in the economy and, to a lesser extent, demographic shifts and worker preferences.

The rapid growth of part-time work mimics the unparalleled expansion of the service sector of the American economy. Nearly 80 percent of nonfarm part-time jobs are in service industries such as finance, business, health services, and in the retail trade—especially food stores and drinking and eating establishments.

The concentration of part-time workers in these industries reflects the need to serve customers during evenings, weekends, and other times not easily staffed by full-timers. Part-time positions also help employers to match staffing levels more closely to the characteristic ebb and flow of customer traffic. A third of the wage and salary workers in retail trade, and a fifth of those in the service industry are part-timers.

The occupational distribution of part-time jobs mirrors the growing dominance of the service economy. The common job-holders are sales clerks, bank tellers, clerk typists, data entry clerks, and other office workers. Less than one-fifth of part-time jobs are managerial, professional, and technical positions.

The most prevalent reasons cited by employers for hiring part-time workers are cost related. The guiding impulse is usually the desire to more closely tailor work schedules to periods of high demand. This results in a more efficient staffing pattern with inherent savings.

Despite the permanence of part-time staffing patterns, many employers regard part-timers as temporary workers—or being outside of the corporate working family. Their adjunct status can be a rationale for restricting employee benefits. While hourly wages of part-timers are generally comparable to those of full-time employees with similar skills, according to a BNA report, benefits provisions are much less likely to be so.[4] Less than half of the companies surveyed (44 percent) offered health or life insurance coverage to their part-time employees. The incidence of paid holidays, vacations, and pension programs were higher. Some companies may provide merchandise discounts or better rates of pay to help offset this disadvantage.

The rising concern about the vast numbers of working Americans who are not covered by health-care insurance has prompted several legislative initiatives that would extend such coverage to part-time workers. The Tax Reform Act of 1986 prohibits employers from discriminating in favor of highly compensated employees when offering health and welfare benefits. This provision, which became effective in 1989, could mandate coverage for more of the part-time work force. However, companies that provide no benefits at all are not affected. A Senate proposal, by contrast, would require employers to provide a minimum level of health coverage to all employees who work more than 17.5 hours a week.

In addition to the cost benefits, part-time schedules may be more suitable for stressful jobs or repetitive tasks where full-time hours would lead to employee burnout or carelessness. Such arrangement can help employers retain skilled employees who need more flexibility.

The Administrative Management Society, which has been surveying the employment practices of American businesses for over a decade, reveals that 80–88 percent of all employers with over one hundred employees make use of part-time help. Figure

---

4. Bureau of National Affairs, *Bulletin to Management*, June 23, 1988.

7-3 shows an overview of the trends in part-time employee use from the *1989 AMS Flexible Work Survey.*

Demographics of Part-Time Workers

Not surprisingly, women represent the largest segment (estimates range from one-third to two-thirds) of the part-time labor force. A reduced work schedule can help women juggle family responsibilities and career demands. Part-time work may also be a way to gradually reenter the labor market after a prolonged absence for child-rearing. Younger and older workers also account for a high proportion of the part-time work force. Many young people work part-time while attending school, and part-time work also appeals to older workers as a way to supplement Social Security and pension income. For older employees, a reduced work schedule can ease the transition to retirement.

Although the rise in part-time work has been largely driven by employer demands, it is also a reaction to a more radical, albeit subtle, shift in work-force demographics. The increased participation of women in the labor force has been accompanied by a growing diversity in family structures and lifestyles and a tightening of the labor market as the baby boom generation approaches middle age.

These demographic shifts have fostered reassessments of the way work, family, and leisure time activities relate to each other. This is evidenced by the small, but growing number of highly skilled, well-educated professionals who choose to work part-time. Although it is true that women with child-rearing responsibilities represent the highest percentage of part-time professionals, their ranks are expanding slowly to include professional males who want more flexible work schedules in order to devote more attention to family, avocational interests, or continuing education.

The changing lifestyles, expectations, and household situations of American employees are also prompting a number of more formal workplace initiatives. The effort to accommodate employee demands for more flexible scheduling includes a number of programs that expand the part-time concept and raise the status of what traditionally have been second-rate jobs. These innovations include voluntary-reduced worktime programs, phased retirement options, flextime, and job sharing.

Figure 7-3. Part-time employee wage by company employee size (1987–1989).

In terms of company size, a majority of the large corporations surveyed, three-fifths, use part-time employees.

1–100 employees	62%
101–1,000 employees	82%
1,001–10,000 employees	88%
10,000+ employees	80%

Seventy-eight percent of the responding companies indicate that they use part-time help, up from 71 percent reported in 1988. The majority of companies with part-timers report that these employees comprise between 1 and 5 percent of their overall work forces, as shown in the following:

	1989	1988	1987
1–5% part-time	50%	49%	N.A.
6–10% part-time	12%	9%	N.A.
11–20% part-time	7%	5%	N.A.
Over 20% part-time	9%	8%	N.A.
Total part-time	78%	71%	78%

Among those companies employing part-time help, more of them experience an increase in use over the past year than in the previous years, as shown in the following:

	1989	1988	1987
Increased	29%	31%	22%
Decreased	10%	6%	9%
Stayed same	59%	63%	69%

Regarding functions performed by part-time employees, most companies use them for clerical help, as shown below.

	1989	1988	1987
Clerical	81%	75%	73%
Secretarial	37%	32%	32%
Accounting	21%	24%	17%
Data processing	26%	23%	19%
Word processing	19%	18%	18%
Professional/technical	18%	14%	15%
Central services	13%	14%	13%

Regarding benefits, half of the companies with part-time help offer paid vacations and holidays, as shown below.

	1989	1988	1987
Holiday pay	51%	51%	42%
Vacation pay	48%	51%	40%
Health insurance	31%	37%	33%
Sick pay	26%	31%	30%
Pension/retirement benefits	28%	30%	28%

Reprinted from the *1989 AMS Flexible Work Survey* with permission of AMS, Trevose, Penn. 19047.

Flextime

Flextime is an alternative staffing arrangement that permits employees to choose the starting and ending times of their work shifts within perimeters preset by their employer. These flexible starting and finishing times are usually set up around core hours during which time all employees must be at work.

Companies such as Hewlett Packard, Control Data, Conoco of Houston, and Met Life of New York have been using flextime successfully for years. By accommodating the needs of its employees, these companies and many like them have experienced significant increases in employee morale and measurable decreases in tardiness, absenteeism, and turnover. Some companies reportedly use flextime to cut down on overtime payments and supplemental staffing.

According to the 1989 AMS Flexible Work Survey (see Figure 7-4), flextime has demonstrably decreased tardiness, absenteeism, and turnover.

Flextime is not without its critics who assert that it is difficult to arrange for supervision during staggered hours and that at times, key people may be unavailable when needed. While these stated disadvantages do present challenges to management, managers recognize that they must continue to find ways to retain and attract personnel that reflects the demographic changes of the work force today.

The Administrative Management Society reveals that 30 percent of the companies surveyed for its 1989 Flexible Work Survey report using the flextime alternative. Figure 7-5 (from the same survey) illustrates the progression of flextime use over the past twelve years.

Figure 7-6 analyzes further the patterns of use among various types of businesses.

Figure 7-7 shows that over 40 percent of all companies with 1000 or more employees use the flextime alternative.

The use of flextime remains a viable staffing alternative in all regions (see Figure 7-8).

Job Sharing

In the early 1970s, job sharing was introduced into the workplace. The term *job sharing* refers to two people sharing the

Figure 7-4.   Measurable benefits of flextime.

	1989	1988
Tardiness	52%	42%
Absenteeism	27%	17%
Turnover	16%	17%

Reprinted from the *1989 AMS Flexible Work Survey* with permission of AMS, Trevose, Penn. 19047.

Figure 7-5.   Companies' increase in flextime use.

1977	15%
1981	22%
1985	29%
1987	30%
1988	31%
1989	30%

Reprinted from the *1989 AMS Flexible Work Survey* with permission of AMS, Trevose, Penn. 19047.

Figure 7-6.   Flextime by industry.

	1989	*1988*	*1987*
Insurance	51%	52%	45%
Education/government/nonprofit	48%	25%	27%
Utilities/transportation/communication	35%	38%	22%
Manufacturing/processing	25%	34%	16%
Retail/wholesale	24%	4%	30%
Services	23%	32%	41%
Banking/finance	14%	17%	31%

Reprinted from the *1989 AMS Flexible Work Survey* with permission of AMS, Trevose, Penn. 19047.

Figure 7-7.   Flextime by company size.

	1989	*1987*
1–1,000 employees	20%	23%
101–1,000 employees	22%	22%
1,001–10,000 employees	41%	37%
10,000+ employees	45%	54%

Reprinted from the *1989 AMS Flexible Work Survey* with permission of AMS, Trevose, Penn. 19047.

Figure 7-8. Flextime by region.

	1989	1988	1987
Great Lakes	46%	45%	47%
South	32%	27%	30%
West	31%	35%	28%
Midwest	30%	30%	30%
Northeast	26%	23%	15%
Canada	33%	39%	42%

Reprinted from the *1989 AMS Flexible Work Survey* with permission of AMS, Trevose, Penn. 19047.

responsibilities of a full-time job. Job sharers actually divide the work week, the salary, and the benefits on a prorated basis. Job sharing pays the equivalent of a full-time job yet it offers all the advantages of a part-time work week.

The job-sharing alternative at first provided work-time opportunities for women who needed to combine work and family, but it was soon recognized as an alternative work arrangement for older workers who desired to continue to work but needed a limited work schedule. It has also worked well for individuals who want to pursue other interests or avocations, handicapped individuals, and for students who need to arrange their work schedule around classes. In effect, increasing the shrinking labor pool.

According to New Ways to Work, a nonprofit organization located in San Francisco, which promotes alternative work-time arrangements, during the last ten years dozens of job categories have successfully piloted programs for job-sharing couples including personnel administrator, receptionist, medical technologist, computer programmer, anesthesiologist, social worker, executive secretary, and salesperson. The earliest innovators of job sharing were city and county government agencies and school district offices. The positive experiences in the public sector has prompted private business to experiment with job sharing.

The direct costs associated with employing job-sharing

couples includes the cost of administrative paperwork and the cost of providing benefits coverage for two people (although it is customary that job-sharing partners apportion the benefits costs allocated to a full-time job). Job sharing has proved cost effective in reducing time lost to vacations, illness, or other absence, and in retaining the services of a valued employee who would be expensive to replace. Moreover, managers report that the complement of skills from two employees and year around coverage has consistently increased productivity. Less fatigue and burnout were reported by both employers and job-sharing employees.

This "regular part-time" working arrangement could be especially suited where high-pressure job situations exist. Mona Abbate, a placement manager with Career Blazers Personnel in New York, states that she bears only 50 percent of the pressure from this very pressurized sales job because she works only 50 percent of the time. Abbate reports that since she started job sharing after starting a family in 1986, she and her job sharing partners have consistently been among the top producers at the firm. Another job sharer enthusiastically recounts that by mid-week the rest of the staff is dragging, "but my work week is just beginning. This keeps productivity on the desk high and management more than satisfied."

Many of the job-sharing couples we interviewed described their working arrangement as the best of both worlds, providing a satisfying work life and time to pursue outside interests. Experienced job sharers report that developing an effective communication system is key to their success. Keeping each other informed and being available for consultation even during off-hours is essential.

According to the 1989 Administrative Management Society's *Flexible Work Survey*, over 8 percent of respondents had job sharing in place, with 2 percent considering implementing it. It is interesting to note that one out of five of the largest corporations offer job-sharing opportunities as shown in Figure 7-9.

Figure 7-10 reflects the pattern of job sharing in use among various types of businesses.

Companies in the heartland region of the United States—

Figure 7-9. Job sharing by company size.

1–100 employees	7%
101–1,000 employees	7%
1,001–10,000 employees	9%
10,000+ employees	20%

Reprinted from the *1989 AMS Flexible Work Survey* with permission of AMS, Trevose, Penn. 19047.

Figure 7-10. Job sharing by type of business.

	1989	1988
Insurance	15%	10%
Education/government/nonprofit	12%	13%
Business services	11%	6%
Banking/finance	8%	17%
Utilities/transportation/communication	7%	4%
Manufacturing/processing/construction	6%	8%
Retail/wholesale sales and distribution	5%	1%

Reprinted from the *1989 AMS Flexible Work Survey* with permission of AMS, Trevose, Penn. 19047.

the Midwest and the Great Lakes areas—show the greatest adoption of job sharing (see Figure 7-11).

Home-Based Work/Telecommuting

The advent of the stand alone computer and PC hook-ups have created a "third-tier" of at-home workers. At-home workers, also referred to as home-based workers or telecommuters (terms which will be used interchangeably in this chapter) is largely a computer-based phenomenon, although women have been doing work at home for centuries (i.e., piece work, stuffing envelopes, sewing, typing, babysitting). Today, at-home workers include a new breed of sophisticated professionals such as fiber-

Figure 7-11. Job sharing by region.

Midwest	14%
Great Lakes	13%
Northeast	10%
Canada	8%
South	6%
West	6%

Reprinted from the *1989 AMS Flexible Work Survey* with permission of AMS, Trevose, Penn. 19047.

optic specialists, biostatisticians, researchers, sales people, and computer specialists who for various reasons prefer to work at home.

Some of these telecommuters actually work out of satellite centers which are used as a home base. These offices are located in cities outside of company headquarters and are set up for the purpose of being close to available labor resources or, where sales are concerned, closer to accounts. (The trend toward increased use of home-based work is propelled in part by the need for employers to retain the services of valuable employees who might otherwise seek employment closer to home.)

The design for a setup of home-based work requires the definition of clear-cut organizational goals, careful and in-depth planning and on-going administrative coordination.

Deliberate selection of at-home workers and careful selection of in-house supervisors are essential for success. The employee must be a highly motivated, self-starting, self-disciplined, independent worker. The supervisor must be a confident manager who is a good communicator and who is not threatened by the lack of control over employees who work off-site.

Companies may choose to employ home-based workers on a full-time or part-time basis, and on a permanent or temporary basis, depending on projected workload demands. An important factor for success of home-based work is in *not* converting telecommuters to independent or contract status—but, rather maintaining, for the telecommuter, the same level of compensation and benefits as their colleagues at the office.

Pacific Bell Telephone Company, San Francisco, launched a telecommuting program in 1986 and has successfully incorporated this alternative work option into its business plan. Pacific Bell has been able to measure the success of the program by:

- Significantly reduced overhead
- Reduced turnover
- Increased production

Telecommuting works most efficiently if the telecommuter reports at least once a month (sometimes more frequently) for face-to-face meetings at the home office.

At this time, there is little tracking by public policy makers of home-based workers. Critics submit that as a group, home-based workers are not protected under labor laws that were designed to provide a safety net for all workers. Controversial issues center around considerations of equal pay, lack of health-care insurance, inconsistencies in enforcing affirmative action policies, retirement benefits, and liabilities relative to overseeing that OSHA regulations are enforced.

In an effort to limit liabilities where workers compensation is concerned, companies should (1) regulate the hours worked at-home and (2) reserve the right to visit, with notice, the home work-site of any telecommuter. This, as any work contract, should be reviewed by counsel.

Retirees: One of Business's Most Valuable Labor Resources

The ultimate success of alternative staffing arrangements depends on the ability to attract qualified workers to these positions. As many companies have discovered, some of the most willing and able members of the contingent work force are retirees. Hiring older workers for part-time or temporary work is an effective way to leverage their skills and experience. The growing number of employer-initiated programs to retain or recruit older workers bears witness to the value of this labor pool.

The new respect for older workers is partly a function of shifting demographics. The aging of the populace has resulted in an overall shortage of skilled newcomers to the work force. Employers played an unwitting role in fostering this crisis by promoting early-retirement programs targeted at productive employees still in their early- or mid-fifties. The difficulties in finding qualified applicants and the costs of recruiting and training are forcing a reevaluation of traditionally dismissive attitudes toward older workers.

This labor crunch is reverberating through both the permanent core of regular, full-time employees and the peripheral rings of part-time and temporary help. The explosive growth of service and retail businesses, with their large complements of part-time hours, has intensified the shortage of contingent labor. As the youth population has declined, and teenage workers have become harder to attract, a number of employers have launched campaigns to encourage retirees to return to work.

These efforts have been most visible in the fast-food industry, where chains are forced to hire older people because of the notable shortage of teenagers willing to work at these low-paying jobs. The premium placed on older workers transcends the simple supply and demand economics of a shrinking labor. Companies that have hired retirees are usually delighted with their experience; many are expanding their recruitment efforts. With years of experience and a variety of skills, older workers are a wealth of sometimes unappreciated talent. They often relate better to customers, have better attitudes, and are more productive than younger workers. They also provide positive role models for younger workers.

Hiring older workers for contingent positions effects a natural marriage between employer and employee needs. More and more retirees want to stay in the work force for personal or economic reasons. Some find satisfaction in remaining useful members of society, whereas many need to supplement Social Security and pension income. A 1988 survey by the American Association of Retired Persons found that 51 percent of retirees would like to work past age 65. For this group, part-time or temporary work offers greater freedom than full-time work and needn't jeopardize retirement benefits.

The praises of older workers are echoed enthusiastically by major temporary help services, many of which have launched special programs to recruit retirees, homemakers and other mature workers who have left the work force. Older workers are choice candidates, say industry officials, because they frequently are more experienced and have a stronger work ethic than younger workers. Homemakers who are reentering the paid labor force after an extended absence may need to update their skills, but not their sense of responsibility. In the process of raising a family, they have acquired a mature attitude and take pride in the quality of their work.

Retirees who work on a temporary basis generally earn glowing report cards from the clients of temporary help services. Companies find them more dedicated than younger workers, who may be distracted by family responsibilities or impatient with their career prospects. Experienced, mature individuals bring an intuitive grasp of workplace dynamics and adapt quickly to the special demands of varied assignments.

A number of large corporations have developed their own programs to bring back retirees for temporary or part-time work. The most popular arrangement appears to be the on-call pool of former workers to fill temporary slots. In addition to eliminating the hourly rates charged by temporary help services, these in-house programs supply individuals who are fully trained and well-versed in the way the organization operates.

Travelers Corporation established a pool of on-call retirees in 1981, after a company survey found that 80 percent of older workers and retirees were interested in part-time, flexible hours. Today, retirees fill about 70 percent of the temporary job vacancies at the Hartford, Connecticut, headquarters. These eager retirees are filling assignments such as traditional office positions, clerks, secretarial jobs, and data-processing operators. The company usually relies on outside temporary workers for positions in which new technology has bypassed former employees. However, the company also offers paid-training programs for retirees who want to update their skills.

The retiree temp pool at Banker Life and Casualty Company

proved so successful that it entirely wiped out the need for temporary help service hires by the end of its first year. While Johnson & Johnson in New Brunswick, New Jersey still uses the services of the temporary help company, its managers clearly prefer to fill temporary vacancies with former employees.

Johnson & Johnson is one of several companies to devise further innovative programs to retain the expertise of retiring employees past retirement age. As part of its lean staffing policies, the company sometimes parcels out the subsidiary functions of retiring professionals to other employees. The remaining core duties may require only five hours a day, and the pharmaceutical company often will try to recruit the retiring employee to fill this newly created part-time job.

A number of companies hire former managers and administrators for special projects or as contract consultants. The Grumman Corporation's pool of more than 1,000 job shoppers includes about 200 retired engineers and other professionals. Retirees are often called in to conduct training classes or to work with inexperienced engineers. In other cases, a manager requests a particular person to work on a project for several months.

Efforts to retain and recruit older employees will likely expand in the next few years. The continuing labor crunch will compel companies to adopt more innovative work options for these valued employees. Retiree temporary pools, part-time, and on-call professionals are the harbingers of a more sweeping revision of staffing attitudes and policies. A small vanguard of companies have already implemented more far-reaching initiatives, including older-worker hiring programs and phased retirement and training programs. Instead of encouraging older employees to retire, employers will find themselves devising incentives to conserve this valued human resource.

An Overview of Flexible Staffing

The Conference Board published a study, *Flexible Staffing and Scheduling in U.S. Corporations,*[5] that surveyed, among other

5. Kathleen Christensen, *Flexible Staffing and Scheduling in U.S. Corporations,* The Conference Board, Research Bulletin no. 240, 1989.

Figure 7-12. Prevalence of flexible scheduling arrangements.

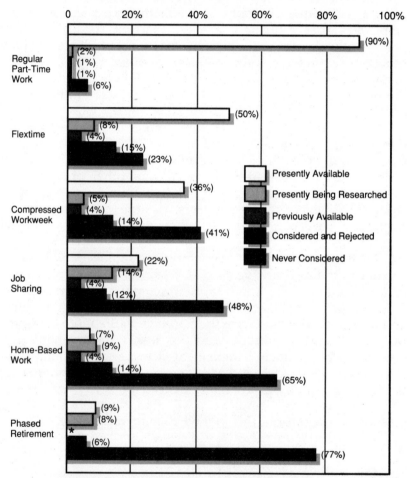

Total responses for each arrangement = 100%

Legend:
- Presently Available
- Presently Being Researched
- Previously Available
- Considered and Rejected
- Never Considered

Regular Part-Time Work
- (90%)
- (2%)
- (1%)
- (1%)
- (6%)

Flextime
- (50%)
- (8%)
- (4%)
- (15%)
- (23%)

Compressed Workweek
- (36%)
- (5%)
- (4%)
- (14%)
- (41%)

Job Sharing
- (22%)
- (14%)
- (4%)
- (12%)
- (48%)

Home-Based Work
- (7%)
- (9%)
- (4%)
- (14%)
- (65%)

Phased Retirement
- (9%)
- (8%)
- *
- (6%)
- (77%)

Note: Number of companies using each arrangement varies.
*Less than 1%

Reprinted with permission by The Conference Board.

issues, the occupational distribution of employees using flexible scheduling. It also surveyed management satisfaction with flexible scheduling.

Figure 7-12 establishes the widespread availability of alternative-staffing arrangements. Ninety percent of all respondents to the survey presently use at least one of the six flexible-scheduling arrangements. Regular part-time work was an overwhelming favorite. Flextime scheduling was the second most employed alternative and represented a three-fold increase in use over a 1979 Conference Board Survey.[6]

Figure 7-13 reveals that professional and managerial employees are more likely to work at-home and less likely to work part-time. Further, it imparts that job sharing and part-time work are the alternatives of choice for clerical and administrative

Figure 7-13. Occupational distribution of employees using flexible schedules.

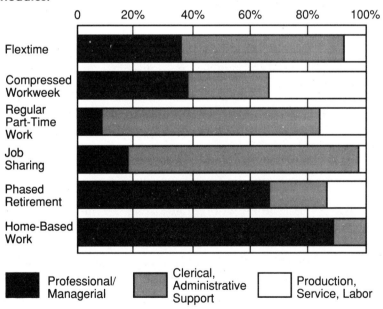

Reprinted with permission by The Conference Board.

---

6. Harriet Gorlin, *Company Experience With Flexible Scheduling,* The Conference Board, Research Bulletin no. 110, 1982.

Figure 7-14.   Management satisfaction with flexible scheduling.

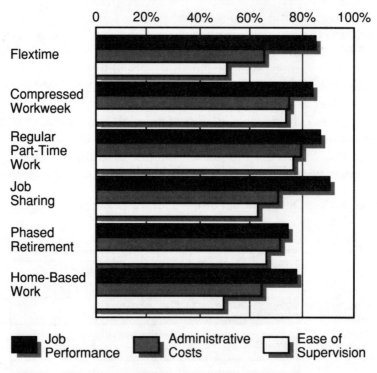

Percentage companies reporting "very satisfactory"
or "satisfactory" in each category

Reprinted with permission by The Conference Board.

support staff. All other work alternatives are used to varying degrees.

Figure 7-14 affirms that respondents to the survey were overwhelmingly satisfied with the job performance of employees engaged in flexible-staffing alternatives. In addition, the survey confirmed that a majority agreed that ease of supervision created their greatest vulnerability.

8

Employee Leasing

The alternative-staffing arrangements that we have been describing are generally used to supplement a core of regular employees. Employee leasing, by contrast, radically transforms the traditional relationship between a company and its permanent staff. It is an arrangement whereby a business formally "fires" its regular employees, who are then hired by a third party—the employee leasing company—and leased back to their original employer. As the employer of record, the leasing company is responsible for hiring, firing, payroll, day-to-day personnel administration, selection and administration of employee benefits, payment of income taxes withheld, worker's compensation, and unemployment insurance premiums.

Employee leasing extends the temporary help service concept into the regular work force of an organization. However, the permanent status of leased employees necessitates a higher degree of involvement in routine human resources management activities. Replacement of an employee due to turnover (or for any other reason) is the direct responsibility of the leasing service as it is the leasing service's employee who is being

141

replaced. Staff leasing services either maintain a pool of pre-screened employees or recruit on behalf of the client company. Supervisory personnel of the client company and, in some cases, its working owners, generally become employees of the leasing service. These administrators generally held supervisory staff positions with the client before the leasing conversion and maintain that status and authority after the conversion. Most services also maintain a staff of field supervisors who call upon the client periodically to conduct performance appraisals and handle employee-related grievances. The disciplining of workers, where appropriate, is also the leasing service's responsibility.

Advantages to Employers

Employee leasing is most effective as a management tool for small businesses. Typically clients include medical and legal practices, real estate firms, retail stores, and consulting firms. The owners or partners of these concerns regard payroll and personnel administration as annoying distractions from their true business of seeing patients, advising clients, or running a retail operation. Employee leasing consolidates these functions and shifts responsibility from the small business owner to a single service company thus, eliminating the headaches of hiring and overseeing accounting, bookkeeping, and other administrative tasks.

For many business owners, the decisive factor is the leasing service's ability to provide substantially better benefits to employees. The economies of scale that govern the cost of health insurance and other coverage enable employee leasing firms to obtain lower rates than small employers. According to benefits experts, companies with less than 200 employees generally do not have the buying power available to employee leasing firms. By pooling employees of its many small clients, the employee leasing service can secure comprehensive, low-cost coverage. Enhanced employee benefits can help to lower turnover, bolster recruitment efforts, and reduce a company's unemployment insurance premiums.

In fact, employee leasing can mean the difference between providing decent employee benefits and none at all. In a 1986 study commissioned by the *Office of Advocacy of the U.S. Small Business Administration,* ten of the twenty-one businesses surveyed provided no medical coverage before the conversion to employee leasing, and none of the twenty-one provided dental coverage. Virtually all those employees received both health and dental benefits after leasing.[1]

Full-service employee leasing companies also provide more sophisticated labor management resources than small businesses can afford on their own. These personnel packages include formal grievance procedures, performance appraisal systems, and outplacement assistance for terminated employees. By assuming a mediator role in work-related conflicts, the leasing service protects the clients against taking precipitous and legally precarious actions against employees. Such intervention can minimize a company's exposure to wrongful-discharge claims, a growing danger in view of the judicial expansion of employee rights.

Many small businesses find that the savings effected in the areas of personnel administration and employee benefits more than offset the cost of the staff leasing company's services. Billing practices and fee structures vary throughout the industry. Some leasing companies charge a fixed percentage of a client's payroll. Others bill for documented costs of employment (payroll, benefits, and payroll taxes), plus a fixed service fee per employee to cover the leasing service's administrative expenses and profit. Some services require an advance deposit from new clients, typically equal to one or two months' net payroll. An alternative practice is a set-up fee of $25 to $30 per employee for new clients. There may also be additional fees for adding new staff or handling turnover.

Less quantifiable is the effect of the leasing arrangement on employee attitudes, an area of considerable debate. Critics assert that imposing an intermediary between employer and employee undermines the entire relationship. Supporters insist

---

1. Office of Advocacy, U.S. Small Business Administration, *Employee Leasing in Small Versus Large Business* (Washington, D.C.: SBA, 1986), p. 57.

that employees actually prefer being leased once they overcome their wariness about terminating their status with a familiar employer. Superior benefits help smooth the road to acceptance. Although statistical evidence in this area is sketchy, the U.S. Small Business Administration sample does confirm a shift from largely negative to largely positive attitudes as employees grow accustomed to the leasing arrangement.

Leasing services see themselves as brokers providing both permanent employment and long-term healthcare and pension benefits. The portability of benefits for leased workers is an attractive safety net, especially for unskilled workers who, in the past, have had little measure of security in maintaining healthcare and pension benefits.

An Industry in Transition

Until recently, employee leasing owed much of its appeal to the safe harbor it provided from normal pension obligations. This exemption was initially based on the legal claim that leased employees were not employees of the client company. A section of the Tax Equity and Fiscal Responsibility Act of 1982 (TEFRA) targeted this perceived abuse of federal pension regulations by doctors and other business owners, who were firing their employees and then leasing them back to avoid covering them under their own generous pension plans. The tax code change required that leased employees who provided services to an organization on a full-time basis must be counted as employees of the organization under IRS rules governing nondiscriminatory pension coverage.

At the same time, however, TEFRA explicitly excused client companies from extending their pension plans to leased employees if the leasing firm covered such employees under a money-purchase pension plan with an employer contribution of at least 7.5 percent of the employee compensation. Ironically, this loophole sanctioned the very abuse that the law was trying to stop, as it left business owners free to establish much richer plans for themselves and their higher paid executives. The leasing industry expanded rapidly after TEFRA's enactment.

The Tax Reform Act of 1986 attacks this loophole more aggressively. It prohibits a company from excluding leased employees from its retirement plan if they comprise more than 20 percent of the company's work force. It also raises the minimum employer contribution to leased employee pension plans from 7.5 percent to 10 percent.

Most industry officials and legal experts agree that the 1986 Act sounds the death knell for safe-harbor leasing, since it virtually eliminates the tax shelter for top-heavy pension plans. Indeed, services that specialized in safe-harbor leasing are either quitting the business or transforming themselves into commercial leasing companies that offer staff leasing services such as personnel administration without the safe-harbor pension feature.

Despite early prediction, the demise of the safe-harbor has not consigned employee leasing to oblivion. Indeed, many industry leaders regard this development as a stimulus, rather than a hindrance, to wider acceptance. Purging its unsavory associations as a tax dodge will permit employee leasing to assert itself purely on its business merits.

There are some indications that nonsafe-harbor leasing is already growing. The number of leased employees jumped to 310,000 in 1987 from 180,000 the previous year, according to an industry consultant. But critics worry that the new leasing arrangements will be less favorable to employees. Without the tax break, it is doubtful whether small employers will adopt leasing arrangements that provide costly pension plans, health benefits, vacations, and personnel management services. A number of leasing companies report that their small clients are not asking for pension coverage because of the cost factor. Some industry leaders envision the growth of a stripped-down version of leasing that will be more affordable to the employer but offer few, if any, benefits to the employee. It is questionable, however, whether such deals will amount to anything more than payroll administration services, contributing little to the employer-employee relationship.

The Legal Minefield

Business owners who assume that employee leasing will release them from all responsibilities as employers may be in for a rude awakening. Unless an employer is willing to surrender day-to-day control of leased employees, he or she risks liability for costly obligations under certain labor and tax laws. This tradeoff may prove unpalatable to many business owners, who would resent having a third party intervening in every aspect of personnel administration from hiring, disciplining, and firing employees to setting their hours and reviewing their time cards.

Furthermore, even the most rigorous leasing contracts don't insulate client companies completely from workplace obligations. They still must comply with the Occupational Safety and Health Administration's regulations. A client may also be found jointly liable with the leasing service for discriminatory hiring practices and other violations of labor laws. In fact, the emerging case law supports the view that the typical staff leasing arrangement establishes a co-employer relationship between leasing service and client company.

Bowing to the prevailing winds of legal opinion, many leasing companies now believe it is best to openly acknowledge this joint responsibility. A contract that clearly defines these mutual obligations, they argue, is infinitely preferable to one that pacifies the putative employer in its zealous defense of the leasing company's claim of employer status. One industry expert has argued that in order to survive a legal challenge the parties must adopt some very stringent practices. For example, the client's former employees must submit to a complete new-hire process with the leasing company, including verification of credentials. In addition, the client cannot pick and choose the benefit package for the workers assigned to it, the leasing service must provide the same benefit package to all its employees.

The co-employer concept may be anathema when client companies discover their status only inadvertently, as part of a court action. But when the duties and responsibilities of each co-employer are spelled out up front, this relationship holds no hidden terrors. With an explicit co-employment contract, a client can also retain a legitimate voice in personnel selection, salaries, job assignments, and promotions. For example, the leasing service might play a supporting role in appraising employee performance and recommending pay increases. The ultimate decision in these matters would reside with the client, however, as would full employer accountability for any adverse consequences.

Implementing the Leasing Decision

Of all the available alternative staffing strategies, employee leasing effects the most sweeping reorganization of workplace relationships. It is clearly not for everyone. A company interested in exploring this option should thoroughly examine its consequences and investigate prospective leasing services. In light of the confusion surrounding the employer-liability question, legal counsel should be sought at an early stage on the critical issue of how much control must be surrendered by management to establish a workable and legitimate leasing contract.

If management decides to proceed, it should solicit competitive bids from several reputable services. The industry has been marred by several major business failures in recent years and the questionable conduct of others. With the modest capital outlay needed to start up shop, staff leasing has attracted its share of underfunded operators who quickly fail, leaving behind a trail of unfunded pension benefits, unpaid taxes, and bounced paychecks. Therefore, each proposal should contain detailed background information about the service, its principals, and, if possible, an audited statement of financial health. The staff leasing service should also agree to furnish at least quarterly verification from a CPA or Public Accounting firm that it has made all withholdings and payments required by law and all employee benefit contributions required by the leasing agreement and/or the Employee Retirement Income Security Act (ERISA).

References should be provided and management should talk personally with other clients of the leasing company, including one or two who have discontinued their services.

The proposal should detail the specific services to be provided and spell out all deposits, fees, start-up costs, and other charges. The leasing company's complete employee benefits package should also be included in this proposal.

In assessing the proposals, management should look closely at the ratio of field supervisors to the number of leased workers on the company's payroll. The leasing service should specify the minimum frequency with which its field supervisor will visit the client site. The client should also establish a rapport with the account representative before an agreement is signed. Of course, any agreement should be thoroughly reviewed by counsel before it is executed.

With detailed proposals in hand, the employer can evaluate the various leasing arrangements against less radical alternatives. Farming out the payrolling functions, adopting a personal computer-based human resources information system, or enrolling in group insurance plans offered through local employer associations may accomplish some of the desired goals. The tangible and psychological costs need to be carefully measured against those of other options.

The psychological impact of the staff leasing decision on employees should also be anticipated and addressed. No assurances can blunt the message to employees that they are being terminated. Although the staff leasing service should assist in easing this transition, the employer must take the initiative in fully explaining the situation and encouraging open discussion of employee's fears.

The Future of Employee Leasing

Proponents of employee leasing assert that the industry is poised for significant growth. Many of the same labor market forces that have given rise to the temporary help service industry should provide momentum for employee leasing. The increased pace of government regulations and the rising cost of employee benefits have certainly made personnel administration costlier, riskier, and more complicated than ever before. The growing emphasis on productivity and competitiveness make the distractions of paperwork and personnel problems even less tolerable to the small-business owner.

There are also indications that employee leasing is making inroads with medium-size and larger businesses. The Southland Corporation completed a pilot program at some of its 7-Eleven stores with National Staff Network, a Van Nuys, California, leasing service. A construction employers' association and several hotel chains are among the larger businesses that have also considered drawing on the labor pools of staff leasing services.

Employee leasing is still in its infancy, relative to the development of the temporary help services industry. However, its most enthusiastic advocates stress its greater potential for growth. The temporary help service industry is restricted to a segment of the contingent work force, they point out, while employee leasing is designed to work with the regular work force. Although this appraisal of the industry's future dimensions may be overly optimistic, it does seem likely that employee leasing will take its place as an increasingly viable alternative to the conventional employment relationship.

9

Legal Issues
Relative to
Temporary Help

Thomas C. Greble, Esq.*

At first blush, the task of summarizing the legal issues with which consumers of temporary help should be familiar did not appear daunting. On further analysis, however, it became apparent that a thorough review of all such legal issues was neither necessary for this book nor a reasonable undertaking.

Instead, this chapter is designed to acquaint you with the key legal considerations arising from the use of temporary help, to provide you with sufficient knowledge to ask the right questions, and to alert client companies to those situations where it would be prudent to obtain specific legal counsel.

While employment laws and judicial decisions govern many aspects of the triangular relationship among temporary worker, temporary help firm, and client company, an often overlooked fact is that the essence of this relationship is contractual in nature. Consequently, the existence and sources of the parties'

---

* Thomas C. Greble is a partner in the New York City-based law firm of Roberts & Finger. Mr. Greble specializes in representing employers in the areas of labor relations, equal employment opportunity, and employment law. In addition, he represents many temporary help firms and is the author of the *NATS Managers Guide to Employment Law.*

own agreements—express and implied—are the logical starting point for the discussion of legal issues arising from that relationship.

Where Is the Contract?

Recent years have seen an increasing number of client companies entering into general contracts with one or more temporary help firms. Typically, large employers or frequent users of temporary help use these contracts to govern virtually all aspects of the entire relationship, including billing rates, methods of payment, overtime, replacement of unsuitable temporary workers, the hiring of temporary workers on a full-time basis, confidentiality of client information, responsibility for damage caused by temporary workers, and numerous other matters. But any company that engages a substantial number of temporary workers would be well-advised to consider developing a general contract with the temporary help firms it uses. Thereafter, when individual departments or managers need temporary workers, they will have access to one or more preselected services for which the terms and conditions of the relationship have been set in advance.

On the other hand, it is often impracticable for small companies or employers that use temporary workers infrequently to secure such a general contract. Nonetheless, most of these companies also enter into a contractual relationship with the temporary help services they use, although they may not be aware of doing so. This is because a representative of the client company must sign and certify as correct a time sheet listing the temporary employee's hours for the week.

In addition, many temporary help services include on the time sheets conditions or promises that often become binding on the client company when it is signed by the client representative. For example, a time sheet may prohibit temporary employees from handling cash, checks, or securities and may insulate the temporary help service from responsibility if a temporary worker absconds with funds to which he or she was entrusted by the client in violation of the (often unread) limitations on the time sheet.

Another typical time sheet provision is a clause that bars the client company from directly hiring the temporary employee for a period of time. These contractual provisions are designed to protect what the temporary help service views as its investment in the temporary worker (i.e., its costs to recruit, identify, train, evaluate, and monitor the performance and behavior of the temporary employee). This investment can only be recouped through frequent or long-term assignments of temporary workers.

To enforce this contractual prohibition, many time sheets provide for "liquidated damages" (damages agreed upon in advance) if a client company should breach the time sheet contract by directly hiring the temporary employee. These liquidated damages provisions are generally enforceable if the amount bears some reasonable relationship to the temporary help service's losses when one of its employees is hired permanently. Because temporary help firms often lack the legal authority to obtain placement fees, the liquidated damages device is a lawful and convenient alternative.

In short, either through a general contract negotiated between the temporary help firm and the client company or by the time sheet contract prepared by the temporary help firm, the parties' own agreement is crucial to understanding a client company's rights and liabilities. Any company that engages temporary help should ensure that only authorized personnel execute the time sheet, and should understand that the time sheet contract contains important terms and conditions.

In addition to these contract issues, client companies should also be aware of the following statutory and regulatory issues that often arise from the use of temporary workers.*

---

* Except where expressly stated, the laws discussed in this section refer to federal laws. Since most states and many municipalities have enacted legislation regarding employers and employees, client companies should confer with counsel to ensure their compliance with such laws and ordinances.

Who is the Employer?
The Service, the Client, or Both?

Many client companies will be surprised to learn that there is even a possibility that they may be viewed as the legal "employer" of temporary help for certain purposes. While the temporary help service is the employer of the temporary employee for many purposes, exceptions and qualifications to this general rule do exist. Identifying the employer of the temporary worker is significant, because it is the employer that is responsible for complying with the myriad laws and rules that regulate the employment relationship or that confer rights upon employees. The following sections briefly discuss who the employer is in the context of the primary employment laws.

1. *Employment Taxes and Payroll Obligations.* The temporary help firm is responsible for paying the temporary worker, withholding taxes, and making mandatory Social Security contributions. The temporary help service is also responsible for keeping required payroll records and complying with federal and state labor laws regulating the frequency, timing, and manner of payment.

In addition, the temporary help service is almost always viewed as the employer for purposes of unemployment compensation laws. A client company is obligated only to pay the temporary service its charges; it has no obligation (and may violate its contract) to make any payments directly to the temporary employee.

2. *Equal Employment Opportunity Laws.* Federal equal employment opportunity (EEO) laws prohibit employers from discriminating against applicants or employees on the basis of their race, color, religion, sex, age, or national origin. Clearly, a temporary help firm cannot segregate, treat adversely, or refuse to employ any person on one or more of these grounds, and it is legally responsible if it does so.

A more difficult question arises when the client company plays a role in the discriminatory act (e.g., requests white secretaries only, refuses older workers, discontinues an assignment of a hispanic accountant). In these situations, it is likely that the temporary help company *and* the client company will be held jointly liable for such unlawful conduct. In legal parlance, the two entities will be deemed to be "joint employers" or "co-employers," and the relative responsibility of each entity will depend on the facts of each situation.

One particular form of unlawful discrimination—sexual harassment in the workplace—merits separate comment. Where a client company creates or knowingly tolerates a sexually abusive work environment or where an employee of a client company conditions job benefits upon sexual favors from a temporary employee, the client company and the temporary help firm share a substantial risk of joint liability.

Accordingly, client companies and temporary help firms would be well-advised to approach sexual harassment complaints in a cooperative manner. In most instances, a complaint of sexual harassment triggers a duty to investigate, followed by an obligation to take prompt, appropriate corrective measures that do not retaliate against the complainant. Where a temporary worker is the complainant, it often happens that the temporary help firm and the client company are each aware of part of the story, so by working together they stand a much better chance of conducting a meaningful investigation leading to an appropriate resolution consistent with their legal obligations.

3. *Workplace Safety and Health Laws.* When a temporary worker suffers a job-related injury or illness while on an assignment to a client company, two sources of employee rights should be assessed—state workers compensation laws and the federal Occupational Safety and Health (OSH) Act. These topics are discussed separately.

a. *Workers Compensation.* Virtually every jurisdiction has enacted some form of workers compensation legislation assigned to (1) protect workers injured on the job and (2) reduce employers' liability for such injuries. Only employees are entitled to workers compensation benefits.

Client companies should be certain that the temporary help service maintains workers compensation insurance coverage to protect its temporary workers. Most reputable temporary help firms have such coverage in force and will not object to supplying a certificate of insurance as proof.

Even if the temporary help firm does maintain workers compensation insurance, however, the workers compensation agency and the courts will still examine the facts of each situation to determine whether the temporary service, the client company, or both will be viewed as the employer of the injured temporary worker for purposes of the workers compensation law.

In many states, the client company is considered the employer of the temporary worker or a joint employer with the temporary help company if (1) it has the right to control the manner in which the employee works, (2) the work being done is essentially that of the client company, and (3) there is an implied or express contract of hire between the employee and client company. The power to control and direct the employee's work is generally the most important factor.

On the other hand, where a temporary service restricts the type of work its temporary employees can do for a client company and retains the right to fire the employee, and the temporary employee is treated differently from the client customer's regular employees (e.g., the temporary worker is required to sign in instead of punching a clock or is given no benefits, identification card, or uniform), the courts are more inclined to find that the temporary service is the sole employer.

Unlike other situations, a client company may prefer to be viewed as a joint employer with the temporary service in the workers compensation context. When a temporary worker is injured while working at a client company's place of business, he or she may file a workers compensation claim against the temporary help company *and* sue the client company in court for negligence. Unless the client company is protected by the shield of workers compensation, it can be subject to a jury verdict for damages to the temporary worker. If the client company is held to be a joint employer with the temporary help firm, then neither entity can be sued for negligence and the temporary worker's exclusive remedy is his or her workers compensation benefits.

b. *The Occupational Safety and Health (OSH) Act.* The Occupational Safety and Health Administration (OSHA) is the agency that enforces the federal OSH Act. OSHA has informally declared that the company which utilizes the services of a temporary employee is the "employer" for purposes of complying with the OSH Act, primarily because the client company controls the workplace and therefore can cure any workplace hazards. In OSHA's jargon, the client company is the "utilizing employer" and must comply with OSHA's requirements. It is unlikely that a temporary help service would be liable for a client company's failure to comply with the OSH Act, even if a temporary employee should suffer an injury due to such violation.

4. *Fair Labor Standards Act: Minimum Wage and Overtime.* Under federal law, employees paid on an hourly basis are entitled to the applicable minimum wage and to time and one-half (premium pay) for every hour worked in excess of forty hours in any workweek. Even if the temporary worker would be treated as exempt from overtime if employed on a full-time basis (e.g., a nurse or accountant), employees who are paid on an hourly basis, including temporaries, must be paid overtime.

The temporary service is legally responsible for paying the overtime. A "shift differential" or "graveyard tour bonus" is not a substitute for premium pay. On the contrary, when a temporary worker earns different hourly rates in the same week, the overtime must be calculated on a weighted average basis, so paying higher rates for certain shifts will actually increase that employee's average hourly rate and thus increase the amount of premium pay to which he or she is entitled.

A temporary employee who works more than forty hours in a workweek for different client companies is still entitled to overtime from the temporary service based on all hours worked in that workweek. A temporary help service may also prohibit an employee from working overtime without advance permission, and may withhold such permission unless the client company agrees to absorb the overtime costs.

It is lawful for a client company to pay the temporary

help firm a higher fee to compensate it for the premium pay it provides temporary workers who work for the client company for more than eight hours in a day or more than forty hours in a week (watch out for those time sheet contracts).

5. *Immigration Reform and Control Act of 1986 (IRCA)*. IRCA requires employers to verify employees' identity and eligibility to work in this country and to complete the now well-known I-9 Form. A temporary help service, not the client company, is legally responsible for complying with IRCA with respect to temporary employees.

A client company has no obligations under IRCA unless it directly hires the temporary employee. In that case, the client company has an independent legal obligation to comply with IRCA and may not rely upon the temporary help firm's assurances that it has obtained a valid and completed I-9 Form.

In sum, determining who is the "employer" of the temporary employee depends on the context in which the question arises. Sometimes the temporary help service is the only employer (e.g., for employment taxes or IRCA); sometimes the service and the client company are treated as joint employers (e.g., EEO laws); occasionally only the client company is viewed as the employer (e.g., the OSH Act); sometimes the question of who is the employer depends upon the terms and conditions of the employment relationship at issue (e.g., state workers compensation laws).

When Does a Temporary Employee Become a Leased Employee?

The concept of leased employees is discussed in Chapter 7. The only additional point to note here is that a temporary employee assigned to the same client company for long periods of time may evolve into a leased employee. Generally, if a temporary worker works for more than 1,500 hours in one year or more than 750 hours in a six-month period, he or she may satisfy the criteria for being denominated a leased employee. There are exceptions to this rule of thumb, but any client company that does engage temporary employees for long periods of time should be familiar with the concept of leased employees and implement controls designed to prevent the inadvertent transformation of temporary employees into that category.

What Is the Distinction Between Independent Contractors and Temporary Employees, and Should Client Companies Care?

Indeed they should. There are substantial distinctions between an employer's obligations towards employees and the same company's obligations towards independent contractors (sometimes referred to as freelancers or consultants). In addition to being obligated to withhold employment taxes from employees' paychecks, employees are entitled to overtime payments, workers compensation, unemployment, statutory disability benefits, and numerous other legal rights.

Some individuals prefer to be denominated as independent contractors, because employment taxes are not withheld and because this status may provide the contractor with tax advantages. As a rule of thumb, and regardless of how the parties characterize their relationship, the degree of control exercised by the employer, the method of payment, and the independent contractor's risk, if any, for profit and loss are the key factors that courts will assess to determine whether a *bona fide* independent contractor relationship exists.

If a putative independent contractor is ultimately held to be an employee, the client company may well be viewed as the employer, with the serious tax and financial consequences. Treating a temporary worker as an independent contractor should not be done solely as an accommodation to the worker, but only after a careful assessment of whether the independent contractor status could be sustained if later challenged.

May—And How May—A Client Company Protect Its Confidential Information and Trade Secrets From Unauthorized Use or Disclosure by a Temporary Employee?

The importance of this issue depends upon the nature of the client company's business and the information to which the temporary employee is given access. Even clerical employees may receive access to confidential information about the client company or confidential information that the client company's customers or others have entrusted to the client company.

One obvious way for a client company to protect its sensitive data is to minimize the nature or amount of information it shares with temporary employees. In situations where this remedy is not viewed as feasible or as sufficient protection, a client company would be prudent to consider entering into an agreement with either or both the temporary employee and the temporary help service. Such an agreement should, among other things, clearly spell out the client company's concerns and impose upon the temporary worker and the temporary help firm joint responsibility for any damages that may arise from the unauthorized use or disclosure of confidential information by the temporary worker. Some client companies insist that the temporary help firm indemnify the client company for any damages it suffers due to disclosure of confidential data, or they require the temporary service to purchase substantial insurance protection running in favor of the client company.

At a minimum, client companies should be alert to this topic, discuss it with their usual temporary help providers, and review the law in their jurisdiction to determine whether contractual protection is desirable or necessary.

This chapter has highlighted the key legal issues that often arise from the use of temporary help. Needless to say, the treatment has not been exhaustive, and particular situations may pose other legal questions beyond the scope of this chapter. But it is hoped that this chapter will alert you to the need to consider and address legal issues, provide sufficient insight to enable you to ask the right questions, and sensitize client companies to the wisdom of obtaining specific legal advice in unusual or risky situations.

National Association of Temporary Services Membership Directory, by City and State

For easy reference, we have included the *National Association of Temporary Services' Membership Directory,* listing its member services by city and state. As members of the National Association of Temporary Services (NATS), these temporary help firms agree to abide by a code of ethics and good practices set forth by the association.

Our intention is that this directory will provide a good source for quality temporary help services in your area. While it is our choice to list members only, we recognize that other credible temporary help services exist that may not be members of the NATS. Clearly, we would encourage you to secure the services of a temporary help firm based only upon its ability to consistently satisfy your temporary help needs.

Kelly Services Inc., Manpower Inc., and The Olsten Corporation are listed in this directory, but only by headquarters location. If you are interested in the national network they may provide, you may write to their corporate headquarters as listed below.

- Kelly Services, Inc.
  999 West Big Beaver Road
  Troy, Michigan 48084
- Manpower, Inc.
  5301 North Ironwood Road
  P.O. Box 2053
  Milwaukee, Wisconsin 53201
- The Olsten Corporation
  1 Merrick Avenue
  Westbury, New York 11590

Although Western Temporary Services and Accountemps are not members of NATS, but because they are nationwide, we offer the addresses of their corporate headquarters, too.

- Western Temporary Services
  301 Lennon Lane
  P.O. Box 9230
  Walnut Creek, California 94596-9280
- Accountemps, Inc.
  111 Pine Street #1500
  San Francisco, California 94111

City, State Membership Listing

ALABAMA

Anniston

Tempforce
Snelling Temporaries

Auburn

Victor Interim Services

Birmingham

Action Temps, Inc.
Adia Personnel Services
Dunhill Temporary Systems
Express Services, Inc.
Legal 'Ees, Inc.
Manpower, Inc.
Personnel Pool
Talent Tree

Tempworld, Inc.
Xtra Helpers

Decatur
Manpower, Inc

Dothan
Manpower, Inc.
Personnel Resources

Edmonton
Victor Interim Services

Eufala
Personnel Resources

Florence
Varner Personnel, Inc.

Gadsden
Con-Temporary Personnel

Gadsen
Tempforce

Hoover
Tempworld, Inc.
Xtra Helpers

Huntsville
Adia Personnel Services
Alabama Temporary & Technical
  Service
Manpower, Inc.
Norrell Services
Snelling Temporaries
Tempforce
Xtra Helpers

Mobile
Manpower, Inc
Multi Personnel Services, Inc.
Multi Service Systems
Snelling Temporaries

Montgomery
Manpower, Inc.
Multi Service Systems
Snelling Temporaries

Tuscaloosa
Talent Tree

ALASKA

Anchorage
Professional Business Services

ARIZONA

Casa Grande
New Concepts Employment

East Phoenix
TAD Temporaries

Glendale
Adia Personnel Services
Manpower, Inc.

Little Rock
Adia Personnel Services

Mesa
Adia Personnel Services
Manpower, Inc.
Norrell Services
Uniforce Temporary Services
Volt Temporary Services

Phoenix
Accent' Human Resource Specialists
Adia Personnel Services
Career Blazers Personnel Svcs.
Data Registry, Inc.
Echales And Associates, Inc.
Goodfriend of Phoenix d/b/a Top
  Talent Temporaries
Manpower, Inc.
Norrell Services
Peakload Services
Personnel Pool
Pro-Tem Service
Professional Nurses Bureau
Snelling Temporaries
Staff Builders
Stivers Temporary Personnel
TAD Temporaries
Talent Tree

Top Temps div. Top Personnel
Tracy Temporaries, Inc.
Uniforce Temporary Services
United Temporary Services, Inc.
Victor Interim Services
Volt Temporary Services

Scottsdale

Norrell Services
Temporary Techs of Arizona, Inc.

Tempe

Adia Personnel Services
Cameron & Company
MSI International d/b/a Temps &
   Co.
Manpower, Inc.
Personnel Pool
Pro-Tem Service
Staff Builders
TAD Temporaries
Victor Interim Services

Tucson

Adia Personnel Services
Alice Campbell Temporaries
CDI Temporary Services, Inc.
Express Services, Inc.
Manpower, Inc.
Norrell Services
Personnel Pool
Pro-Tem Service
Professional Nurses Bureau
Retiree Skills, Inc.
Snelling Temporaries
TAD Temporaries
Temporary Techs of Tucson
Volt Temporary Services

ARKANSAS

Conway

Prostaff Temporary Systems

Fayetteville

Brewer Temporaries

Fort Smith

Express Services, Inc.
Manpower, Inc.
Metro Temporaries, Inc.

PRN
Tempforce

Little Rock

Manpower, Inc.
Personnel Pool
Prostaff Temporary Systems
Quality Temporary Service
Snelling Temporaries
Sunmark Staffing Services, Inc.

North Little Rock

CSI Temporaries
Express Services, Inc.
Manpower, Inc.

Pine Bluff

Express Services, Inc.
Tempforce

Rogers

Brewer Temporaries

Russellville

Express Services, Inc.

Searcy

Prostaff Temporary Systems

Silaom Springs

Express Services, Inc.

Springdale

Express Services, Inc.
Manpower, Inc.

Texarkana

Express Services, Inc.
Temporary Services Unlimited

CALIFORNIA

Alhambra

A & S Services

Anaheim

Adia Personnel Services
Helpmates Personnel Services
Manpower, Inc.
Norrell Services
Office Specialists

Professional Nurses Bureau
Uniforce Temporary Services
United Temporary Services, Inc.
Volt Temporary Services

Arcadia

Courtesy Temporary Service, Inc.
Norrell Services

Aurora

Stivers Temporary Personnel

Bakersfield

Automated Temporary Service
Manpower, Inc.
Norrell Services
Personnel Pool
Volt Temporary Services

Belmont

TemPositions, Inc.

Berkeley

Adia Personnel Services

Beverly Hills

Tempforce
Uniforce Temporary Services

Brea

Abigail Abbott Temporaries, Inc.
Helpmates Personnel Services
Norrell Services
Talent Tree
United Temporary Services, Inc.
Volt Temporary Services

Burbank

Active Personnel
Volt Temporary Services

Burlingame

Accountants Inc
CDI Temporary Services, Inc. d/b/a
    Timesavers
The Mortgage Professionals

Calabasas

Professional Nurses Bureau

Campbell

Certified Personnel Service

Canoga Park

TAD Temporaries
Valley Temps, Inc.
Volt Temporary Services

Capitola

Express Services, Inc.

Carlsbad

Adia Personnel Services
Manpower, Inc.
Volt Temporary Services

Carson

Norrell Services

Cerritos

Abigail Abbott Temporaries, Inc.
Accountants Overload
Adia Personnel Services
Personnel Pool
Volt Temporary Services

Chico

Anderson & Associates, Inc.
Staff Temps, Inc.

Chula Vista

Manpower, Inc.

Citrus Heights

Adia Personnel Services
Cal Temps
Express Services, Inc.
Snelling Temporaries

City of Industry

Accountants Overload
Talent Tree

Colton

Jobs Unlimited

Concord

Manpower, Inc.
Norrell Services
Office Specialists
Pacific Medical Care, Inc.
Temporary Skills Unlimited, Inc.

Corona

Corona Temporaries
Manpower, Inc.

Costa Mesa

Accountants Overload
Adia Personnel Services
Talent Tree
Uniforce Temporary Services
Victor Interim Services
Volt Temporary Services

Covina

Adia Personnel Services
Manpower, Inc.
Olympic Temporary Svcs./Profor
Personnel Pool
Staff Builders
Volt Temporary Services

Culver City

Adia Personnel Services

Cupertino

Adia Personnel Services
Complimate, Inc.

Cypress

Norrell Services
Whitlock Registry, The

Daly City

Manpower, Inc.

Delano

Delano Office Temporary Service

Diamond Bar

Cameron & Company

Downey

Adia Personnel Services
United Temporary Services, Inc.
Volt Temporary Services

Dublin

Office Specialists
Personnel Pool
Staff Builders

El Segundo

Volt Temporary Services

El Toro

Abigail Abbott Temporaries, Inc.

Encino

Adia Personnel Services
Bogard Temps, Inc.
Express Services, Inc.
United Temporary Services, Inc.

Escondido

Manpower, Inc.

Fair Oaks

Manpower, Inc.
Medtemp Personnel Services
Roberta's Temporary Service
Uniforce Temporary Services

Fairfield

Adia Personnel Services
Express Services, Inc.

Fontana

Volt Temporary Services

Fountain Valley

Courtesy Temporary Service, Inc.
Helpmates Personnel Services

Fremont

Adia Personnel Services
Manpower, Inc.
Office Specialists
Personnel Pool
Roberta's Temporary Service
Snelling Temporaries
Uniforce Temporary Services

Fresno

Adia Personnel Services
American Temporary Services
CDI Temporary Services, Inc. d/b/a
    Timesavers
Denham Temporary Services
Dunhill Temporary Systems
Manpower, Inc.
Personnel Pool
Professional Nurses Bureau

Snelling Temporaries
Volt Temporary Services

Garden Grove

Uniforce Temporary Services
Volt Temporary Services

Glendale

Adia Personnel Services
Bogard Temps
CDI Temporary Services, Inc.
Manpower, Inc.
Professional Nurses Bureau
United Temporary Services, Inc.
Valley Temps, Inc.

Glendora

Courtesy Temporary Service, Inc.

Hayward

Adia Personnel Services
Certified Personnel Service
Experienced Works
Manpower, Inc.
Personnel Pool
Snelling Temporaries
Staff Builders
Victor Interim Services
Volt Temporary Services

Hemet

Professional Nurses Bureau

Huntington Beach

Focus On Temps, Inc.
Manpower, Inc
Olsten Temporary Services

Irvine

Adia Personnel Services
Arhness Conventry, Inc.
Manpower, Inc.
Newport Temporaries, Inc.
Norrell Services
Temp Associates, Inc.
Vicki Heston Personnel Service

Jackson

Blue Ribbon Temporary

La Jolla

Manpower, Inc.
Westek Temporary Svcs.

La Mesa

Tempforce
Volt Temporary Services

Laguna Hills

Adia Personnel Services
Stivers Temporary Personnel
Talent Tree

Lakewood

Norrell Services
Talent Tree

Lawndale

Uniforce Temporary Services

Long Beach

Abigail Abbott Temporaries
Adia Personnel Services
Manpower, Inc.
Norrell Services
Professional Nurses Bureau
Staff Builders
Uniforce Temporary Services
United Temporary Services, Inc.
Victor Interim Services
Volt Temporary Services

Los Alamitos

Express Services, Inc.

Los Altos

CDI Temporary Services, Inc. d/b/a
Timesavers

Los Angeles

Accountants Overload
Adia Personnel Services
City Personnel Services, Inc.
Computemp of Los Angeles, Inc.
Express Services, Inc.
Manpower, Inc.
Metro Temporary Services
Norrell Services
PDQ Personnel Svcs., Inc.
Persona Personnel, Inc.
Personnel Pool

Primedica Healthcare Providers
Professional Nurses Bureau
Snelling Temporaries
Staff Builders
Stivers Temporary Personnel
Systemp
TRC Temporary Services, Inc.
Talent Tree
United Temporary Services, Inc.
Volt Temporary Services

Marina Del Rey

Talent Tree
Temp-Line Services

Menlo Park

Adia Personnel Services

Merced

Manpower, Inc.

Millbral

A & S Services

Milpitas

Manpower, Inc.

Mission Viejo

Manpower, Inc
United Temporary Services, Inc.
Volt Temporary Services

Modesto

Able 2 Staff
Adia Personnel Services
Manpower, Inc.
Personnel Pool
Professional Nurses Bureau

Montclair

PSI Personnel Services
Personnel Pool

Montebello

A & S Services

Monterey

Manpower, Inc.
Norrell Services

Mount Eden

Angus Nelson, Ltd.

Mountain View

Adia Personnel Services
Certified Personnel Service

Newhall

Santa Clarita Valley Temporaries, Inc.
Temporarily Yours

Newport Beach

Abigail Abbott Temporaries, Inc.
Adia Personnel Services
CDI Temporary Services, Inc. d/b/a
    Timesavers
Norrell Services
TRC Temporary Services, Inc.
United Temporary Services, Inc.

North Hollywood

Adia Personnel Services
Escrow Overload II

Northridge

Additional Tech Support, Inc.

Norwalk

Esp Personnel Services
Talent Tree

Oakland

Adia Personnel Services
Certified Personnel Service
Manpower, Inc.
Professional Nurses Bureau
Staff Builders
Systemp
Victor Interim Services
Volt Temporary Services

Oceanside

Professional Nurses Bureau
Staff Builders

Orange

Adia Personnel Services
Manpower, Inc.
Staff Builders
Victor Interim Services
Volt Temporary Services

Oxnard

Manpower, Inc.

Personnel Pool
Snelling Temporaries
Volt Temporary Services

Palm Desert

Norrell Services
Professional Nurses Bureau

Palm Springs

Southern Temporary Services

Palo Alto

Adia Personnel Services
Manpower, Inc.
Personnel Pool
Roberta Enterprises
Roberta's Temporary Service
Snelling Temporaries

Pasadena

Adia Personnel Services
Manpower, Inc.
Snelling Temporaries
Stivers Temporary Personnel
Talent Tree
Volt Temporary Services

Placentia

Norrell Services

Placerville

Blue Ribbon Temporary Personnel

Pleasant Hill

Adia Personnel Services

Pleasanton

CDI Temporary Services, Inc. d/b/a
   Timesavers
Manpower, Inc.
Snelling Temporaries
Volt Temporary Services

Rancho Cordova

Dunhill Temporary Systems

Rancho Cucamonga

Adia Personnel Services
CDI Temporary Services, Inc.
Courtesy Temporary Service, Inc.
United Temporary Services, Inc.

Redding

Express Services, Inc.
Norrell Services

Redlands

REA Temporary Services

Redondo Beach

Sawyer & Associates

Richmond

Manpower, Inc.

Ridgecrest

S.A.S.S.
T.O.S.S. Temporaries

Riverside

Adia Personnel Services
CDI Temporary Services, Inc.
Manpower, Inc.
Temporary Solutions, Inc.
Uniforce Temporary Services
Volt Temporary Services

Rolling Hills

Cameron & Company

Roseville

Dunhill Temporary Systems
Manpower, Inc.
Victor Interim Services

Sacramento

Able-Temps, Inc.
Action Temps, Inc.
Adia Personnel Services
CDI Temporary Services, Inc. d/b/a
   Timesavers
CalTemps
Cameron & Company
Certified Personnel Service
Express Services
Key Personnel
Manpower, Inc.
Norrell Services
Personnel Pool
Staff Builders
Tempeople, Inc.
Uniforce Temporary Services d/b/a
   Tempeople

Victor Interim Services
Volt Temporary Services

Salinas

Manpower, Inc.

San Bernadino

CDI Temporary Services, Inc. d/b/a
  Timesavers
Manpower, Inc.
Pay Plus Temporaries
Professional Nurses Bureau
Staff Builders

San Bruno

Adia Personnel Services
Manpower, Inc.
Personnel Pool
Uniforce Temporary Services

San Diego

Accountants, Inc.
Accountants Overload
Adia Personnel Services
Averest Service Corporation
CDI Temporary Services, Inc.
Dunhill Temporary Systems
Echales and Associates, Inc.
Georgia's Temporary Personnel
Lawton Company, Inc., The
Manpower, Inc.
Meridian Temporary Services
Norrell Services
Nurses Network, Inc.
Office Specialists
Physical Therapy Registry Network,
  Inc.
Pro Tem Legal Services
Professional Nurses Bureau
STAT Therapy
Snelling Temporaries
Staff Builders
TAD Temporaries
TOPS*
Talent Tree
Tempro Services
Uniforce Temporary Services
Victor Interim Services
Volt Temporary Services

San Dimas

Snelling Temporaries

San Francisco

Adia Personnel Services
Alan J. Blair Personnel
Alan Minton Personnel Services
American Staffing Company
CDI Temporary Services, Inc. d/b/a
  Timesavers
Certified Personnel Service
Dunhill Temporary Systems
Gallagher Staffing Associates
Leni Miller Temporary Services
Lona Jensen Temporary Services
Manpower, Inc.
Norrell Services
Office Specialists
People Connection, The
Personnel Pool
Professional Nurses Bureau
Proserv Temporary Service
Resource Temporary Service d/b/a
  RTS
Roberta's Temporary Service
Staff Builders
Talent Tree
TemPositions, Inc.
Temp-O-Rama/Input Temporary
Temporaries Network
TemPositions, Inc.
Uniforce Temporary Services
Victor Interim Services d/b/a Q Tech
Volt Temporary Services

San Gabriel

United Temporary Services, Inc.

San Jose

Adia Personnel Services
Base Line Temps
CDI Temporary Services, Inc. d/b/a
  Timesavers
Cameron & Company
Contemporaries of Santa Clara
Manpower, Inc.
Nurses Network, Inc.
Resource Personnel Services
Staff Builders
Victor Interim Services d/b/a Q Tech

San Juan Capistrano
Remedy Temporary Services

San Marcos
Adia Personnel Services
Dunhill Temporary Systems
Volt Temporary Services

San Mateo
Adia Personnel Services
Certified Personnel Service
Manpower, Inc.
Personnel Pool
Professional Nurses Bureau
Roberta's Temporary Service
Tempforce
Tod Temporary Services

San Rafael
Cameron & Company
Manpower, Inc.
Mary Bryon Associates Personnel Services, Inc.

San Ramon
Adia Personnel Services
Manpower, Inc.
Volt Temporary Services

Santa Ana
Adia Personnel Services
Helpmates Personnel Services
Norrell Services
Office Specialists
Professional Temporaries, Inc.
Stivers Temporary Personnel
TRC Temporary Services, Inc.
Volt Temporary Services

Santa Barbara
CDI Temporary Services, Inc.
Citywide Personnel Service
Manpower, Inc.
Snelling Temporaries
Staffamerica Temporary Svcs.
Volt Temporary Services

Santa Clara
Additional Tech Support, Inc.
Best Temporary Services
Golden West Temporary Services

Personnel Pool
Roberta's Temporary Service
Victor Interim Services d/b/a Q Tech

Santa Clarita
Express Services, Inc.
Manpower, Inc.

Santa Cruz
Manpower, Inc.

Santa Fe Springs
Helpmates Personnel Services

Santa Maria
Volt Temporary Services

Santa Monica
Manpower, Inc.
Stivers Temporary Personnel

Santa Rosa
Express Services, Inc.
Liberty Temporaries, Inc.
Manpower, Inc.
Norrell Services
Personnel Pool
Snelling Temporaries

Sherman Oaks
Manpower, Inc.
Norrell Services
Royal Personnel Services
Snelling Temporaries
Staff Builders
Stivers Temporary Personnel
Uniforce Temporary Services
Victor Interim Services

Simi Valley
CDI Temporary Services, Inc.
Volt Temporary Services

Sonoma
Nelson Personnel Services

South San Francisco
Volt Temporary Services

Stockton
Adia Personnel Services
Manpower, Inc.

Norrell Services
Personnel Pool
Stiles Temporary Services
Uniforce Temporary Services

Sunnyvale
Adia Personnel Services
CDI Temporary Services, Inc. d/b/a
  Timesavers
Manpower, Inc.

Sylmar
Victor Interim Services

Tarzana
Kimball Group Personnel Service
Tempforce
Talent Tree

Temple City
A & S Services

Thousand Oaks
Adia Personnel Services
Excel Personnel Services, Inc.
Manpower, Inc.
United Temporary Services, Inc.
Volt Temporary Services

Torrance
Abigail Abbott Temporaries, Inc.
Accountants Overload
Adia Personnel Services
CDI Temporary Services, Inc. d/b/a
  Timesavers
General Employment Temporaries
Helpmates Personnel Services
Manpower, Inc.
Norrell Services
Pat Services, Inc.
Talent Tree
United Temporary Service, Inc.
Volt Temporary Services

Turlock
Able 2 Staff

Tustin
Abigail Abbott Temporaries, Inc.
Personnel Pool
Snelling Temporaries

Talent Tree
United Temporary Services, Inc.

Upland
Manpower, Inc.
Snelling Temporaries
Talent Tree
Volt Temporary Services

Valencia
Sage Personnel Resources
United Temporary Services, Inc.

Van Nuys
Adia Personnel Services
Volt Temporary Services

Ventura
CDI Temporary Services, Inc.
Norrell Services
Staff Builders
Valley Temps, Inc.

Visalia
Adia Personnel Services
Automated Temporary Svc., Inc.
Manpower, Inc.
Personnel Pool
Professional Nurses Bureau

Vista
Snelling Temporaries

Walnut Creek
Adia Personnel Services
Dunhill Temporary Systems
Manpower, Inc.
Norrell Services
Personnel Pool
Prime Resources, Inc.
Snelling Temporaries
Staff Builders
Talent Tree
Victor Interim Services d/b/a
  Newton Associates
Volt Temporary Services

Weed
STEP FORWARD Temporary Service

West Covina

Courtesy Temporary Service, Inc.
Professional Nurses Bureau
United Temporary Services, Inc.

West Lake Village

Personnel Pool

West Los Angeles

TRC Temporary Services, Inc.

Westchester

Pat Services, Inc.

Westlake Village

CDI Temporary Services, Inc.
Royal Personnel Services

Westminster

Hospital Employee Labor Pool

Whittier

Crown Employment Agency, Inc.

Woodland

Adia Personnel Services

Woodland Hills

Accountants Overload
Adia Personnel Services
CDI Temporary Services, Inc.
Manpower, Inc.

Yuba City

Express Services, Inc.

COLORADO

Aurora

Express Services, Inc.
Norrell Services
Office Specialists

Boulder

Adia Personnel Services
Express Services, Inc.
Manpower, Inc.
Rocky Mountain Temporaries, Ltd.
Victor Interim Services d/b/a TOPS

Broomfield

Express Services, Inc.

Colorado Springs

Add Staff, Inc.
Adia Personnel Services
Express Services, Inc.
Manpower, Inc.
RUBICON
Snelling Temporaries
SOS Temporary Services
Stand-By Personnel
Trojan Engineering Company
Victor Interim Services d/b/a TOPS

Denver

Adia Personnel Services
Cameron & Company
Denver Temporary Svcs., Inc.
Ford Personnel Services
Goodwin Nelligan Temporary Svc.
J. Kent Temporaries
Manpower, Inc.
Norrell Services
Personnel Pool
Professional Respite Care, Inc.
Professional Nurses Bureau
SYSTEMP
Senior Skills
Stand-By Personnel
Stivers Temporary Personnel
Sunny Side/Temp Side, Inc.
Talent Tree
Tempforce
TOPS—Total Personnel Services
Uniforce Temporary Services
Victor Interim Services d/b/a TOPS
Volt Temporary Services

Englewood

Adia Personnel Services
CareerSearch, Inc.
Casey Services, Inc.
Denver Temporary Services, Inc.
Norrell Services
Peakload Services
Personnel Plus
SOS Temporary Services
Snelling Temporaries
Talent Tree
Volt Temporary Services

Fort Collins

Express Services, Inc.
Manpower, Inc.
Norrell Services

Glenwood Springs

Office Services Unlimited, Inc.

Golden

TAD Temporaries

Grand Junction

SOS Temporary Services

Greeley

Express Services, Inc.

Lakewood

Bank Temps, Inc.
Victor Interim Services

Longmont

Express Services, Inc.
Victor Interim Services

Loveland

Express Services, Inc.

Montrose

Chaffin Enterprises, Inc.

Northglenn

Victor Interim Services

Pueblo

At Your Service, Inc.
Express Services, Inc.
Manpower, Inc.
Tempforce

Westminster

Office Specialists

CONNECTICUT

Avon

Norrell Services

Bloomfield

Staff Builders

Bridgeport

BSI Temporaries, Inc.
CGS Temporary Services
Dunhill Temporary Systems
Manpower, Inc.
Victor Interim Services

Bristol

Manpower, Inc.

Colchester

Manpower, Inc.

Cos Cob

McIntyre Associates, Inc.

Danbury

BSI Temporaries, Inc.
Dunhill Temporary Systems
Manpower, Inc.
Snelling Temporaries
Temps, Inc.

Darien

Sound Temporaries

East Hartford

Dunhill Temporary Systems
Jobpro Temporary Services, Inc.
Manpower, Inc.

East Windsor

Dunhill Temporary Systems

Enfield

CGS Temporary Services
Elite Temporaries

Fairfield

Amtemp Temporary Services
Office Services of Ct, Inc.
Remedy Temporary Services d/b/a
    Thompson & Fields, Inc.

Farmington

Dunhill Temporary Systems

Glastonbury

BPA Temps
J. Morrisey & Company

Greenwich

Amtemp Temporary Services
Manpower, Inc.

Hamden

CGS Temporary Services
Norrell Services

Hampden

Manpower, Inc.

Hartford

Accounting Futures, Inc.
Adia Personnel Services
CDI Temporary Services, Inc.
CGS Temporary Services
Co-Opportunity Personnel Services
Exclusive Temporaries, Inc.
J. Morrissey & Company
Manpower, Inc.
Merry Employment Group, Inc.
Norrell Services
Options Unlimited Personnel Svc.
RJS Temps
Tempforce
Victor Interim Services

Manchester

Manpower, Inc.

Meridan

Uni/Temps, Inc.

Meriden

CGS Temporary Services
Manpower, Inc.

Middletown

Snelling Temporaries

Milford

Labor Force of America
Manpower, Inc.

Monroe

Resources Available, Inc.

New Britain

CGS Temporary Services
Manpower, Inc.

New Haven

Adia Personnel Services
Diversified Employment Service
Dunhill Temporary Systems
Jackie Matchett Temporary Svc.
Manpower, Inc.
Personnel Pool
Staff Builders

New London

Manpower, Inc.
Uniforce Temporary Services

Newington

Olsten Temporary Services

Norwalk

Amtemp Temporary Services
Manpower, Inc.
Snelling Temporaries

Norwich

Manpower, Inc.
Personnel Pool

Putnam

Talent Tree

Shelton

Diversified Employment Svcs.
Jackie Matchett Temporary Svcs.

Southbury

Resources Available, Inc.

Stamford

Adia Personnel Services
Advantage, Inc.
Amtemp Temporary Services
CDI Temporary Services, Inc.
Career Blazers Personnel Svcs.
Diana Office Temps
Human Resource Temps, Inc.
Manpower, Inc.
Norrell Services
Personnel Pool
Staff Builders
Systemp
Talent Tree
Tempforce
Uniforce Temporary Services

Victor Interim Services d/b/a
  Connecticut Temporaries

Stratford

Human Resource Temps
MK Temporary Services, Inc.
Office Services of Ct., Inc.
Staff Builders

Trumbull

Office Services of Ct.

Wallingford

Dunhill Temporary Systems
Manpower, Inc.

Waterburg

Dunhill Personnel of Middlesex

Waterbury

CGS Temporary Services
Jaci Carroll Personnel Service
Manpower, Inc.
Uni/Temps, Inc.

West Hartford

JBS, Inc.

Wilton

Pathfinder Group, Inc.
Wilton Personnel, Inc.

Windsor

Snelling Temporaries

Windsor Locks

Manpower, Inc.

DELAWARE

Dover

Manpower, Inc.

New Castle

CDI Temporary Services, Inc.
Snelling Temporaries

Newark

Caldwell Temporary Services
Manpower, Inc.
Norrell Services

Wilmington

BSI Temporaries
Caldwell Temporary Services
Careers USA, Inc.
Manpower, Inc.
Norrell Services
Personnel Pool
Staff Builders
Star Temporary Services
Victor Interim Services d/b/a CRT
  Interim Services

DISTRICT OF COLUMBIA

Washington

AIM Support Services
Adia Personnel Services
Advantage, Inc.
Aker Associates, Inc.
Alternative Resources Corp.
American Bus Careers Emp. Svcs.
Arrowood & Sano, Ltd.
Avalon & Company
Best Temporaries, Inc.
Career Blazers Personnel Svcs.
Careers USA, Inc.
CompeTemps By Dora, Inc.
Computer Temporaries, Inc.
Corporate Source, The
Don Richard Associates of D.C.
Durham Temporaries, Inc.
Exclusive Temporaries, Inc.
Florida Temporaries c/o Barry Wright
Enterprises
Graham, Incorporated
Ivy League Assistants, Inc.
Legal Assistants Corp
Manpower, Inc.
Norrell Services
Office Personnel Management
Office Specialists/Ingrid's
Personnel Pool
R. Duffy Wall & Associates
Staff Builders
Talent Tree
TeleSec Temporary Services
Temporary Resources
Temporary Staffing of Virginia
Tracy Temporaries, Inc.

Uniforce Temporary Services d/b/a
  T.P.I.
Volt Temporary Services
Walton-Thomas Placements, Inc.
Woodside Employment Consultants,
  Inc.

FLORIDA

Altamonte Springs

Careers USA
TRC Temporary Services, Inc.

Boca Raton

Manpower, Inc
Norrell Services
Office Specialists
Snelling Temporaries
Winston Personnel of Boca Raton

Boyton Beach

Norrell Services

Bradenton

T.O.P.S. Temps of Manatee
Your Staff Temporaries

Brandon

Action Temps, Inc.
Adia Personnel Services
Norrell Services

Clearwater

Ablest Services Corp
Action Temps, Inc.
Manpower, Inc.
Norrell Services
Staff Builders
Uniforce Temporary Services
Victor Interim Services

Coral Gables

Ad-Staff Temporary Svc., Inc.
Budget Temporary Services, Inc.

Daytona Beach

Manpower, Inc.
Norrell Services

Deerfield

Personnel Pool

Delray Beach

Adia Personnel Services
Personnel Pool

Fernandina Beach

JBS, Inc.

Fort Lauderdale

Atrium Personnel, Inc.
ATS Services, Inc.
Adia Personnel Services
Career Connection, Inc.
JBS, Inc.
Manpower, Inc.
Norrell Services
Office Specialists
Peakload Services
Personnel Pool
Personnel Pool of America, Inc.
Premier Services, Inc.
Snelling Temporaries
Staff Builders
Tracy Temporaries, Inc. d/b/a
  Tracy Labor
TRC Temporary Services, Inc.
Uniforce Temporary Services

Fort Myers

Adia Personnel Services
C.M. Temporary Services
Norrell Services
Personnel Pool
Remedy Temporary Services d/b/a
  Key Temps, Inc.
Snelling Temporaries
VIP Personnel Services

Fort Pierce

JBS, Inc.

Ft. Myers

Manpower, Inc.
Personnel Services of Ft. Myers

Ft. Pierce

Manpower, Inc.

Ft. Walton Beach

Manpower, Inc.

Gainesville

Dunhill Temporary Systems
Manpower, Inc.
Norrell Services
Personnel Pool
Tempforce

Gainsville

Manpower, Inc.

Gulf Breeze

Manpower, Inc.

Hialeah

Budget Temporary Services, Inc.
Office Specialists
Personally Yours Services, Inc.

Hobe Sound

Tempforce

Holly Hill

Adia Personnel Services
Tracy Temporaries, Inc.

Inverness

Personnel Pool

Jacksonville

ATS Services, Inc.
Ablest Services Corp.
Adia Personnel Services
Associated Temporary Staffing
CDI Temporary Services, Inc.
Express Services, Inc.
Florida Temporaries
JBS, Inc.
MSI International d/b/a Temps &
   Co.
Manpower, Inc.
Norrell Services
Personnel Pool
Remedy Temporary Services d/b/a
   Price Enterprises USA
Snelling Temporaries
TAD Temporaries
TRC Temporary Services, Inc.
Talent Tree
Todays Temporary
Tracy Temporaries, Inc. d/b/a
   Tracy Labor

Trend Temporary Services, Inc.
XLC Services

Jacksonville Beach

JBS, Inc.

Key West

Girl Friday of Florida Keys

Kissimmee

Personnel Pool

Lake Worth

Personnel Pool

Lakeland

Action Temps, Inc.
Manpower, Inc.
Norrell Services
Rita Temporaries

Largo

Epic Personnel Services, Inc.
Temp Careers
Victor Interim Services

Lauderhill

Careers USA, Inc.

Leesburg

Norrell Services
T.O.P.S. Temps

Lighthouse Point

Tracy Temporaries, Inc.

Maitland

Regency Temporaries, Inc.
Todays Temporary

Melbourne

Manpower, Inc.
Norrell Services

Miami

Adia Personnel Services
Budget Temporary Services, Inc.
Creative Staffing
I.M.S., Inc.
Linda Robins & Associates, Inc.
Manpower, Inc.
Norrell Services

Office Specialists
Olsten Temporary Services
Omnihelp, Inc.
Personnel Pool
Professional Resource Organization,
    Inc.
Snelling Temporaries
Staff Builders
Star Temps Star National, Inc.
TRC Temporary Services, Inc.
Tracy Temporaries, Inc.

Miami Beach

Budget Temporary Services, Inc.

Miami Lakes

Adia Personnel Services
Creative Staffing
Norrell Services
Staff Builders

Naples

Manpower, Inc
Personnel Pool

Newport-Richey

Staff Builders

North Miami

Adia Personnel Services
Office Specialists
SOC Temporary Services

Ocala

Manpower, Inc.
Norrell Services
Personnel Pool

Orange Park

Action Temps, Inc.

Orlando

Ablest Services Corp
Adia Personnel Services
ATS Services, Inc.
CDI Temporary Services, Inc.
Creative Staffing
Florida Temps, Inc.
JBS, Inc.
Manpower, Inc.
Norrell Services
Personnel Pool
Regency Temporaries, Inc.
Talent Tree
TopTalent, Inc.

Tracy Temporaries, Inc. d/b/a
    Tracy Labor
Transworld Temporaries
Victor Interim Services
Volt Temporary Services

Palm Beach Gardens

Quantum Resources Corporation

Palm Harbor

Adia Personnel Services

Panama City

Manpower, Inc.

Pembroke Pines

Star Temps (Star National, Inc.)

Pensacola

Keegan Temps, Inc.
Landrum Temporary Services
Manpower, Inc.
Personnel Pool

Perry

Manpower, Inc.

Pinellas Park

Action Temps, Inc.
Personnel Pool
Todays Temporary

Plant City

Manpower, Inc.

Plantation

Office Specialists
Snelling Temporaries

Pompano Beach

Tracy Temporaries
Xtra Helpers

Port Charlotte

Snelling Temporaries

Port St. Lucie

Craft Temporary Services, Inc.
Personnel Plus, Inc.
Staff Builders

Sarasota

Adia Personnel Services
Manpower, Inc.
Personnel Pool
Snelling & Snelling, Inc.
T.O.P.S. Temps
Victor Interim Services

St. Petersburg

Action Temps, Inc.
Adia Personnel Services
Computerpeople, Inc.
Florida Nursing Services
Gale Porter Temporary Services
Manpower, Inc.
Snelling Temporaries
Staff Builders
Victor Interim Services

Stuart

Manpower, Inc.

Sunrise

Norrell Services
Todays Temporary

Tallahassee

Manpower, Inc.
Norrell Services

Tampa

ATS Services, Inc.
Action Temps, Inc.
Adia Personnel Services
Express Services, Inc.
Florida Temps, Inc.
Gale Porter Temporary Service
Hallmark Temporaries, Inc.
Harris Services, Inc.
Manpower, Inc.
Norrell Services
Office Specialists
Personnel Pool
Snelling Temporaries
Staff Builders
Strictly of Counsel
System One Staffing, Inc.
TAD Temporaries
TRC Temporary Services, Inc.
Talent Tree
Temp Force d/b/a Talent Force

Tempworld Inc
Todays Temporary
Tracy Temporaries, Inc.
Transworld Temporaries
Victor Interim Services
Volt Temporary Services

Tavares

Personnel Pool

Tequesta

Adia Personnel Services

Venice

T.O.P.S. Temps of Venice

West Jacksonville

JBS, Inc.

West Palm Beach

Adia Personnel Services
CDI Temporary Services, Inc.
JBS, Inc.
Manpower, Inc.
NACORE
Personnel Pool
Preferred Temporary Services
Snelling Temporaries

Winter Haven

Manpower, Inc.

Winter Park

Norrell Services
Staff Builders
Talent Tree
Tempworld, Inc.
Trend Temporary Services
Victor Interim Services
Volt Temporary Services

GEORGIA

Albany

Manpower, Inc.
Temporary Advantage, Inc.

Athens

BOS Temporaries

Atlanta

A ONE SERVICE Personnel
ATS Services, Inc.
Action Temps, Inc.
Adia Personnel Services
Atlanta Personnel Services, Inc.
  d/b/a Atlanta Temps, Inc.
Careers USA, Inc.
Dunhill Temporary Systems
Durham Temporaries, Inc.
ETS Temporary Services
Exclusive Temporaries, Inc.
Georgia Temp, Inc.
International Insurance Person
LAWSTAF, INC.
MSI International d/b/a Preferred
  Temporary Svcs.
Manpower, Inc.
Maristaff, Inc.
Norrell Corporation
Peakload Services
Personnel Pool
Preferred Temporary Services
Premier Temps, Inc.
Sara Burden Temporary Staffing
Snelling Temporaries
Staff Builders
Systemp
TRC Temporary Services, Inc.
Talent Tree
Tanner Medical Placements
Temp Force
Temporaries Network
Temporary Staffing, Inc.
Tempworld Inc
Todays Temporary
Tracy Temporaries, Inc.
Turner Temporary Services
Victor Interim Services
Volt Temporary Services

Augusta

Career Personnel/Career Temps
Manpower, Inc.
Mr./Ms. Temps

Austell

Norrell Services

Calhoun

Temporary Placement

Cartersville

MSI International d/b/a Preferred
  Temporary Svcs.
Temporary Placement

Chamblee

Personnel Pool

College Park

Talent Tree
Temporary Specialties, Inc.

Columbus

Manpower, Inc.
Norrell Services
Victor Interim Services d/b/a
  Personnel Concepts

Conyers

Norrell Services
Talent Tree

Dalton

Temporary Placement Service

Decatur

Norrell Services

Duluth

Express Services
MSI International d/b/a Temps &
  Co.

Fulton

Personnel Pool

Gainesville

Etcon, Inc.

Jonesboro

TRC Temporary Services, Inc.
Tempworld, Inc.

La Grange

Manpower, Inc.

LaGrange

Victor Interim Services d/b/a
  Personnel Concepts

Lawrenceville

Norrell Services

Snelling Temporaries

Lilburn

Labor King Temporaries

Lithia Springs

TRC Temporary Services, Inc.

Macon

Employment Matchmakers, Inc.
MSI International d/b/a Temps &
  Co.
Manpower, Inc
Norrell Services

Marietta

Caldwell Temporary Svcs., Inc.
Durham Temporaries, Inc.
MSI International d/b/a Preferred
  Temporary Svcs.
Norrell Services
Premier Temps, Inc. div. The Lucas
  Group
Snelling Temporaries
TRC Temporary Services, Inc.
Volt Temporary Services

Martinez

Job Shop Temp
Norrell Services
Personnel Pool

Morrow

Personnel Pool
Snelling Temporaries
Temporaries Network

Newnan

Help Services, Inc.

Norcross

ATS Services, Inc.
Careers USA, Inc.
MSI International d/b/a Temps &
  Co.
Norrell Services
Snelling Temporaries
Staffing Resources
TRC Temporary Services, Inc.
Talent Tree
Volt Temporary Services

Peachtree City

Peachtree Temporaries, Inc.

Ringgold

Temporary Placement

Roswell

Dynamic Dental Services, Inc.
GES Temporaries
MSI International d/b/a Temps &
  Co.
Snelling Temporaries
TRC Temporary Services, Inc.
Talent Tree
Volt Temporary Services

Savannah

Exclusive Temporaries, Inc.
JBS, Inc.
Manpower, Inc.
Norrell Services
Personnel Pool
TRC Temporary Services, Inc.

Smyrna

MSI International d/b/a Temps &
  Co.
Snelling Temporaries
TRC Temporary Services, Inc.

St. Marys

Satilla Business Services, Inc.

Stockbridge

Express Services, Inc.

Stone Mountain

Atlanta Personnel Services, Inc.
  d/b/a Atlanta Temps, Inc.
Tempway, Inc.

Thomson

Mr./Ms. Temps

Tucker

CDI Temporary Services, Inc.
Durham Temporaries Inc
TRC Temporary Services, Inc.
Talent Tree

Valdosta
Team Temps, Inc.

Villa Rica
Norrell Services

Woodstock
Interstaff, Inc.

HAWAII

Hilo
Uniforce Temporary Services

Honolulu
Adia Personnel Services
Dunhill Temporary Systems
Kahu Malama Nurses, Inc.
Manpower, Inc.
Personnel Pool of America, Inc.
Snelling Temporaries
Strictly Professional
Uniforce Temporary Services

Kailua-Kona
Dunhill Temporary Systems
Uniforce Temporary Services

Kona
Personnel Pool

Lihue
Personnel Pool

Pearl City
Uniforce Temporary Services

IDAHO

Boise
Express Services, Inc.
Manpower, Inc.
Prostaff Temporary Services

Idaho Falls
Express Services, Inc.
Manpower, Inc.

Lewiston
Express Services, Inc.

Moscow
Express Services

ILLINOIS

Alton
Availability, Inc.

Arlington Heights
Adia Personnel Services
Professional Nurses Bureau
Tempstaff, Inc.

Aurora
Adia Personnel Services
Hipp Temporary Skills
Manpower, Inc.
Ready Men, Inc., d/b/a
Stivers Temporary Personnel

Barrington
Assured Staffing

Bensenville
BSI Temporaries
Crown Services, Inc.

Bloomington
CDI Temporary Services, Inc.
Manpower, Inc.

Buffalo Grove
AllStaff Services
Temp/Help Ltd.

Carbondale/Marion
Manpower, Inc.

Carol Stream
C. Berger And Company

Champaign
Manpower, Inc.
Norrell Services

Chicago
A-Pro Temporaries, Inc.
Adia Personnel Services
Alpha Personnel Services
Alternative Resources Corp.
Appropriate Temporary Svc.

BPS/Temps, Inc.
CDI Temporary Services, Inc.
Careers USA, Inc.
Casey Services, Inc.
The Choice For Temporaries
Debbie Temps, Inc.
Dunhill Temporary Systems
First Temporary Services, Inc.
Good Workers, Inc.
Gray Personnel Services
Grove Temporary Services
Helpmate Temporaries
LML Secretarial Services
Lasalle Services, Ltd.
Manpower, Inc.
Med-Call Corporation
N.J.W. Office Personnel
Norrell Services
O/E Management Services
Operation Able-Able's Pool of
   Temporaries
Page Business Services, Inc.
People Incorporated—Temporaries
Personnel Pool
Profile Personnel, Inc.
Ready-Men, Inc.
Salem Services
Staff Builders
Stivers Temporary Personnel
Systemp
Talent Tree Personnel Services
Thirty-Three Temporaries, Inc.
Transportation Help, Ltd.
Unique Office Services, Inc.
V.I.P., Inc., Very Important
   Personnel, Inc.
XLC Services

Collinsville

Temporary Team

Crystal Lake

Assured Staffing
Working World, Inc.

Danville

Manpower, Inc.

Decatur

Manpower, Inc.
Tempforce

Deerfield

Adia Personnel Services
Debbie Temps, Inc.
Stivers Temporary Personnel

Des Plaines

CDI Temporary Services, Inc.
Career Temporary Services
Casey Services, Inc.
Norrell Services
Ready Men, Inc., d/b/a
Staff Builders
Stivers Temporary Personnel
Todays Temporary

Downers Grove

Adia Personnel Services
Casey Services, Inc.
Grove Temporary Services

Edwardsville

Staff Builders

Elgin

Barr's Temporary Service, Inc.
Hipp Temporary Skills
Manpower, Inc.
Tempstaff, Inc.

Elk Grove Village

Uniforce Temporary Services

Elmhurst

Adia Personnel Services
Creative People, Inc.
Professional Nurses Bureau

Elmwood Park

Adia Personnel Services

Evanston

Stivers Temporary Personnel
Victor Interim Services

Evergreen Park

Manpower, Inc.

Fairview Heights

Adia Personnel Services
Tempforce

Franklin Park
Alpha Temporary Service

Freeport
Manpower, Inc.

Geneva
Barr's Temporary Service, Inc.
TAD Temporaries
Tempstaff, Inc.

Glendale Heights
Ann Lynne Temporaries, Inc.

Hazel Crest
Adia Personnel Services

Itasca
Manpower, Inc.

Joliet
Adia Personnel Services
Genie Temporary Services
Manpower, Inc.
Norrell Services
Temp/Help Ltd.

Kankakee
Manpower, Inc.

La Grange
Ready Men, Inc., d/b/a

LaSalle
Manpower, Inc.

Lake Bluff
Manpower, Inc.

Lansing
Manpower, Inc.

Libertyville
Adia Personnel Services

Lincolnshire
Alternative Resources
  Corporation

Lincolnwood
Personnel Pool

Lisle
Claimtemps, Inc.
Snelling Temporaries

Lombard
Dunhill Temporary Systems
TAD Temporaries

MacOmb
Adia Personnel Services

Matteson
Davis Temporaries, Inc.

Moline
Manpower, Inc.
Tempforce
Temporary Additions

Mt. Prospect
Manpower, Inc.
Ready Men, Inc.

Mt. Vernon
Manpower, Inc.

Mundelein
Manpower, Inc.

Naperville
Debbie Temps, Inc.
Manpower, Inc.
Norrell Services
Personnel Pool
Temp/Help Ltd.
Tempstaff, Inc.

Niles
Debbie Temps, Inc.

North Riverside
Manpower, Inc.

Northbrook
Manpower, Inc.
Professional Nurses Bureau
Victor Interim Services

Oak Brook
Personnel Pool
Salem Services, Inc.

Stivers Temporary Personnel

Oak Brook Terrace

Ready Men, Inc., d/b/a

Oak Lawn

Adia Personnel Services
Norrell Services

Oak Park

Adia Personnel Services

Oakbrook

Manpower, Inc.
Staff Builders
Victor Interim Services

Oakbrook Terrace

Adia Personnel Services
Norrell Services
Salem Services, Inc.
Snelling Temporaries
Talent Tree
Tempro Resources, Inc.

Palatine

Blair Business Services, Inc.
Manpower, Inc.

Peoria

CDI Temporary Services, Inc.
Express Services, Inc.
Manpower, Inc.
Norrell Services

Quincy

Adia Personnel Services
Manpower, Inc.

Rantoul

Manpower, Inc.

River Forest

Personnel Pool

Rochelle

Manpower, Inc.

Rockford

Dickey Temporaries
Employment Resources, Inc.
Furst Temporary Services

Gaffney Employment Services, Inc.
Manpower, Inc.
Norrell Services
Tempstaff, Inc.
Victor Interim Services d/b/a
  Selectability
The WORK Place

Rosemont

Talent Tree

Schaumburg

Adia Personnel Services
Career Temporary Services
Careers USA, Inc.
Debbie Temps, Inc.
Manpower, Inc.
Norrell Services
Personnel Pool
Salem Services
Snelling Temporaries
Stivers Temporary Personnel
Talent Tree
Temporaries Network
Todays Temporary

Skokie

Adia Personnel Services
Manpower, Inc.
Norrell Services
Ready-Men, Inc.
Salem Services

Springfield

Alice Campbell Temporaries
Express Services, Inc.
Manpower, Inc.
Norrell Services

St. Charles

Manpower, Inc.

Vernon Hills

Express Services, Inc.
Victor Interim Services d/b/a Victor
  Personnel Staffing

W. Dundee

T.H.E. Agency, Inc.

Wauconda
Manpower, Inc.

Waukegan
Manpower, Inc.
Matthews Professional Employment
Specialists, Inc.
Victor Interim Services

Westchester
CPS Temporary Services

Westmont
Norrell Services

Wheeling
Debbie Temps, Inc.

INDIANA

Angola
Manpower, Inc.
Time Services, Inc. d/b/a Time
Temporary Services

Auburn
Manpower, Inc.

Bloomington
Manpower, Inc.

Bluffton
Flexible Personnel

Columbus
Manpower, Inc.
Personnel Management, Inc.

Crawfordsville
Work Force

Crown Point
Staff Builders

Elkhart
Corporate Staffing Resources,
Manpower, Inc.
Personnel Pool

Evansville
Manpower, Inc.

Norrell Services
Temporaries Incorporated

Fort Wayne
Adia Personnel Services
Corporate Staffing Resources
Flexible Personnel
Manpower, Inc.
Norrell Services
Personnel Pool
Temp One, Inc.
Time Services, Inc. d/b/a Time
Temporary Services
Victor Interim Services

Frankfort
Manpower, Inc.

Goshen
Flexible Personnel
Quantum Resources Corporation

Grange
Time Services, Inc. d/b/a Time
Temporary Services

Hammond
Manpower, Inc.

Indianapolis
Adia Personnel Services
American Nursing Care, Inc.
Brooks Business Services
CDI Temporary Services, Inc.
Crown Services, Inc.
Datassistants
Dunhill Temporary Systems
Etc. Temporary Services, Inc.
Manpower, Inc.
Norrell Services
Personnel Management, Inc.
Personnel Pool
Snelling Temporaries
Staff Builders
Stivers Temporary Personnel
TRC Temporary Services, Inc.
Temporaries Incorporated
Tempro Resources, Inc.
Victor Interim Services
XLC Services

Kendallville

Flexible Personnel
Time Services, Inc. d/b/a Time
  Temporary Services

Kokomo

Manpower, Inc.
Time Services, Inc. d/b/a Time
  Temporary Services

LaPorte

Manpower, Inc.

Lafayette

Adia Personnel Services
Manpower, Inc.

Merrillville

Tempforce

Mooresville

Benefit Resources, Inc.

Muncie

Flexible Personnel
Manpower, Inc.

Plymouth

Manpower, Inc.

Richmond

American Nursing Care, Inc.
Manpower, Inc.

Shelbyville

Manpower, Inc.
Personnel Management, Inc.

South Bend

Manpower, Inc.
Norrell Services
Tempro Resources, Inc., div./CMS
  Management Svcs., Inc.

Terre Haute

Manpower, Inc.

Warsaw

Corporate Staffing Resources
Flexible Personnel
Manpower, Inc.

Time Services, Inc. d/b/a Time
  Temporary Services

IOWA

Ames

Manpower, Inc.
Staff Builders

Ankeny

Manpower, Inc.

Bettendorf

Norrell Services
Tempro Services

Burlington

Manpower, Inc.

Cedar Rapids

Manpower, Inc.
Norrell Services

Council Bluffs

Help, Inc.

Davenport

Chenhall's Temporary Help Svc.
Manpower, Inc.

Des Moines

Manpower, Inc.
Norrell Services
Personnel Pool

Dubuque

Manpower, Inc.

Iowa City

Manpower, Inc.

Keokuk

Help Temporary Placement
Taske Force

Marshalltown

Manpower, Inc.

Mason City

Express Services

Ottumwa
Manpower, Inc.

Sioux City
Manpower, Inc.

Waterloo
Manpower, Inc.

West Des Moines
CDI Temporary Services, Inc.
Staff-Temps

KANSAS

Atchison
Manpower, Inc.

Emporia
Manpower, Inc.

Hutchinson
Manpower, Inc.

Kansas City
Uniforce Temporary Services

Lawrence
Manpower, Inc.

Leawood
Penmac Personnel Services

Manhattan
Manpower, Inc.

Olathe
C&M Temporaries

Ottawa
Manpower, Inc.

Overland Park
Adia Personnel Services
CDI Temporary Services, Inc.
Personnel Pool
Snelling Temporaries
Staff Builders
Stivers Temporary Personnel
Uniforce Temporary Services
Victor Interim Services

Salina
Manpower, Inc.

Shawnee Mission
Tempforce

Topeka
Dunhill Temporary Systems
Express Services
Manpower, Inc.

Wichita
Dunhill Temporary Systems
Manpower, Inc.
Norrell Services
Personnel Pool

KENTUCKY

Ashland
Manpower, Inc.

Bowling Green
Manpower, Inc.

Carrollton
Garner-Scott Temporary Service

Crescent Springs
Personnel Pool

Elizabethtown
Manpower, Inc.

Florence
Adia Personnel Services
American Nursing Care, Inc.
Crown Services
Manpower, Inc.

Frankfort
Datassistants
Norrell Services

Georgetown
Norrell Services

Henderson
Norrell Services

Lexington

Adia Personnel Services
American Nursing Care, Inc.
CDI Temporary Services, Inc. d/b/a
    TopTalent, Inc.
C.M. Temporary Services
Dunhill Temporary Systems
JBS, Inc.
Manpower, Inc.
Norrell Services
Personnel Pool
Snelling Temporaries
Temps Employment, Inc.

London

The Job Shop Employment Service

Louisville

Adia Personnel Services
CDI Temporary Services, Inc. d/b/a
    TopTalent
Crown Services, Inc.
Datassistants
Employment Group, Inc.
Engineering Help, Inc.
Falls City Temporaries
Manpower, Inc.
Metro Temporaries, Inc.
Norrell Services
Paula York Personnel, Inc.
Personnel Pool
Staffmasters
Thoroughbred Temps, Inc.
Victor Interim Services

Paducah

People Lease, Inc.
Tempsplus of Paducah, Inc.

Richmond

Express Services, Inc.

Shelbyville

Manpower, Inc.

LOUISIANA

Baton Rouge

Manpower, Inc.
Norrell Services
Personnel Pool

Gretna

Norrell Services

La Place

Manpower, Inc.

Lafayette

Acadiana Temporary Service
Manpower, Inc.
Norrell Services

Lake Charles

Manpower, Inc.
Staff Builders

Laplace

Am-Pm Temporary Services

Luling

Am-Pm Temporary Services

Metairie

Adia Personnel Services
Manpower, Inc.
Norrell Services

Monroe

Manpower, Inc.

New Orleans

Exclusive Temporaries, Inc.
Manpower, Inc.
Norrell Services
Quixx Temporary Services, Inc.
Staff Builders
Tempforce
Workload Temporary Services

Shreveport

Manpower, Inc.
Snelling Temporaries

St. Rose

Norrell Services

MAINE

Augusta

Bridget Temporary Services
Manpower, Inc.

Bangor

Manpower, Inc.
Pagemployment

Biddeford

Manpower, Inc.

Lewiston

Manpower, Inc.

Portland

Bonney Temps div. of Bonney
  Personnel
Dunhill Temporary Systems
Manpower, Inc.
Nursing Network
Personnel Pool

Rockland

Ask, Inc.

MARYLAND

Annapolis

CDI Temporary Services, Inc.
Manpower, Inc.
Quality Temps, Inc.
TMG Personnel Services

Baltimore

Able Temporaries
Additional Tech Support, Inc.
Adia Personnel Services
Assured Medical Temps, Inc.
BF&M Temps, Inc.
BSI Temporaries, Inc.
CDI Temporary Services, Inc.
Careers USA, Inc.
Human Service Connection, Inc.
Manpower, Inc.
MHS, Inc.
Norrell Services
Personnel Pool
Primedica Healthcare Providers
S.E.S. Temps, Inc.
Staff Builders
Talent Tree
TeleSec Temporary Services
Tracy Temporaries, Inc.
Uniforce Temporary Services
Victor Interim Services

Bethesda

Manpower, Inc.
Social Work Temps
Sparks Personnel Services, Inc.

Bladensberg

Tracy Temporaries, Inc.

Calverton

Team Work, Inc.

Camp Springs

Manpower, Inc.

Chevy Chase

Dental Power

Cockeysville-Hunt Va

Uniforce Temporary Services

Columbia

CDI Temporary Services, Inc.
Manpower, Inc.
Snelling Temporaries
Staff Builders

Easton

Professional Temporaries

Edgewood

Uniforce Temporary Services

Ellicott City

TAD Temporaries

Fallston

Staff Builders

Frederick

Dunhill Temporary Systems
Manpower, Inc.
Sparks Personnel Services, Inc.

Gaithersburg

Adia Personnel Services
Manpower, Inc.
Plus Temps
Talent Tree
TeleSec Temporary Services

Germantown

S Corp.

Glen Burnie

Manpower, Inc.

Greenbelt

Advantage, Inc.
Manpower, Inc.
Quality Temps, Inc.
Talent Tree

Hagerstown

Manpower, Inc.
Staff Builders

Hyattsville

BSI Temporaries, Inc.
Rapid Writer Temporary Service
TeleSec Temporary Services
Trinity Temporaries & Business
  Services

Kensington

Monarch Temporary Services
PRSI/Denta-Pro
TeleSec Temporary Services

Landover

Adia Personnel Services
BSI Temporaries, Inc.
Exclusive Temporaries, Inc.
Norrell Services
Sparks Personnel Services, Inc.

Largo

Stat Medical Services, Inc. d/b/a
  Choice Professional Resources

Laurel

BSI Temporaries, Inc.
CDI Temporary Services, Inc.
Manpower, Inc.
TeleSec Temporary Services

Lexington Park

Personnel Resources

Linthicum

Staff Builders

Lutherville

Norrell Services

North Bethesda

Forbes Temporaries, Inc.

Prince Frederick

True Temps, Inc.

Rockville

Adia Personnel Services
Advantage, Inc.
Dunhill Temporary Systems
Eldertemps, Inc.
Manpower, Inc.
Monarch Temporary Services
Office Specialists
S Corp
Sparks Personnel Services, Inc.
Talent Tree
TeleSec Temporary Services
Temporaries One
Temporary Resources
Volt Temporary Services

Salisbury

Manpower, Inc.
Snelling Temporaries

Silver Spring

BSI Temporaries, Inc.
Barnett Temporaries Barnett Business
  Service, Inc.
Manpower, Inc.

Timonium

BSI Temporaries, Inc.
Snelling Temporaries
Staff Builders

Towson

Adia Personnel Services
Manpower, Inc.
Marge Fox Personnel Services
TAD Temporaries
Todays Temporary

Waldorf

Manpower, Inc.

Westminister

Carroll County Personnel Svcs.

Wheaton

Staff Builders
TeleSec Temporary Services

MASSACHUSETTS

Acton

Manpower, Inc.
Office Specialists

Attleboro

Adia Personnel Services

Boston

Adia Personnel Services
Alternative Resources Corp
Anodyne
Arbor Associates
Beacon Hill Professionals, Inc.
CDI Temporary Services, Inc.
Certified Lab Temps, Inc.
Cunney & Jospe', Inc.
Hoteltemps Corporation
John Leonard Personnel Association
KNF&T Temps
Manpower, Inc.
Massachusetts Legal Bureau a/k/a
    Personnel Resource Group
Medical Register/MRI Temps Div.
    Sullivan & Cogliano Cos.
New Boston Temps, Inc.
Office Specialists
Peakload Services
Personnel Pool
Preferred Temporaries, Inc.
R.A.D. Temporaries
Skill Bureau, The
Staff Builders
Sterling Office Services (Temploy-
    ment & Office Angels)
TAD Temporaries
Talent Tree
Uniforce Temporary Services
Victor Interim Services
Volt Temporary Services

Braintree

Manpower, Inc.
Volt Temporary Services

Brockton

Manpower, Inc.
Staff Builders

Brookline

Office Specialists

Burlington

EP Temps, Inc.
Manpower, Inc.
Norrell Services
Office Specialists
Oxford and Associates, Inc.
TAD Temporaries

Cambridge

Adia Personnel Services
Brattle Temps
MacTemps
Manpower, Inc.
New Boston Temps, Inc.
Norrell Services
Office Specialists
The Resource Group, Inc.
Staff Builders
Sterling Office Services (Temploy-
    ment & Office Angels)
TAD Temporaries

Chelmsford

Adia Personnel Services
Manpower, Inc.
Office Specialists
Snelling Temporaries
TAD Temporaries
Talent Tree
Volt Temporary Services

Chestnut Hill

Kelly-Luce Radiographers Ltd.

Dedham

Anodyne

Edison

Adia Personnel Services

Fairhaven

Snelling Temporaries

Fall River
Able Temps
Uniforce Temporary Services

Falmouth
Manpower, Inc.

Fitchburg
Manpower, Inc.

Framingham
Adia Personnel Services
JBS, Inc.
Manpower, Inc.
New England Temps, Inc.
Norrell Services
Office Specialists
Select Temporary Services, Inc.

Franklin
Action Personnel, Inc.

Gardner
Talent Tree

Gloucester
Aid Temporary Services

Greenfield
Harmon Temporary Service

Holyoke
Manpower, Inc.

Hudson
Talent Tree

Leominster
Talent Tree

Lexington
Adia Personnel Services
Manpower, Inc.

Livingston
Adia Personnel Services

Lynn
Tempforce

Malden
Manpower, Inc.

Office Specialists

Mansfield
TAD Temporaries

Marlboro
Manpower, Inc.

Marston Mills
Temporarily Yours

Methuen
Office Specialists

Methven
Aid Temporary Services

Milford
Manpower, Inc.
Office Specialists

Natick
Stivers Temporary Personnel

Needham
Adia Personnel Services
Career Center, Inc.
Manpower, Inc.

New Bedford
Manpower, Inc.

Newburyport
Key Personnel, Inc.

Newton Upper Falls
TAC/TEMPS, Inc.

North Andover
Manpower, Inc.

North Attelboro
Manpower, Inc.

North Dartmouth
Adia Personnel Services

North Quincy
New Boston Temps, Inc.
Staff Builders

Northboro

TAD Temporaries

Norwood

Buckingham Personnel Services
Manpower, Inc.

Peabody

Manpower, Inc.
Office Specialists

Pittsfield

Manpower, Inc.
Uniforce Temporary Services

Plymouth

Allied Personnel Services, Inc.

Quincy

Anodyne Corporation
Executemps, Inc.
Office Specialists
Sterling Office Services (Temploy-
    ment & Office Angels)
TAD Temporaries
Talent Tree

Revere Beach

Omnihelp, Inc.

Salem

Aid Temporary Services
Hawthorne Nursing Registry, Inc.

South Natick

Faith Casler Associates, Inc.

Springfield

CGS Temporary Services
Dunhill Temporary Systems
Manpower, Inc.
Prime Time Personnel, Inc.
United Temporaries of Mass.

Stoneham

Office Specialists

Stoughton

New Boston Temps, Inc.
Office Specialists

Stow

Tara Professionals, Inc.

Wakefield

Adia Personnel Services
Office Specialists

Waltham

Additional Technical Support
Anodyne
Office Specialists
S&C Office & Industrial Temps
Uniforce Temporary Services

Walthum

Adia Personnel Services

Wayland

TAD Temporaries

West Springfield

Management Search, Inc.
Personnel Pool

Westborough

Suburban Temporaries, Inc.
Talent Tree

Weymouth

Norrell Services

Woburn

Adia Personnel Services
Arivella Associates, Inc.
New Boston Temps, Inc.
Search Temps, Inc.
Staff Builders
Volt Temporary Services

Worcester

Manpower, Inc.
New Boston Temps, Inc.
New England Search Temporaries
Norrell Services
Personnel Pool of America, Inc.
Talent Tree
Temp Resources, Inc.

Worchester

Medical Business Service

MICHIGAN

Adrian
Adia Personnel Services
Manpower, Inc.

Allegan
Manpower, Inc.

Ann Arbor
Adia Personnel Services
Arbor Temporaries, Inc.
Associated Information Consult
Communitemps, Inc.
Manpower, Inc.
Norrell Services
Personnel Pool
Victor Interim Services

Auburn Hills
Adia Personnel Services

Battle Creek
Employment Group, Inc.
Manpower, Inc.
Norrell Services
Personnel Pool

Bay City
Manpower, Inc.

Benton Harbor
Manpower, Inc.

Big Rapids
Manpower, Inc.

Birmingham
Himelhoch Temporary Svcs., Inc.
Uniforce Temporary Services

Bloomfield Hills
Manpower, Inc.

Brighton
Adia Personnel Services

Brooklyn
Adia Personnel Services

Burton
Adia Personnel Services

Cadillac
Manpower, Inc.

Chelsea
Victor Interim Services

Clawson
Bloomfield Nursing Services

Coldwater
Manpower, Inc.
Personnel Pool

Dearborn
Adia Personnel Services
CDI Temporary Services, Inc.
Manpower, Inc.
Norrell Services

Dearborn Heights
Personnel Pool

Detroit
Adia Personnel Services
CDI Temporary Services, Inc.
Employers Temporary Service, Inc.
J.R. Temporary Labor Services
Manpower, Inc.
Snelling Temporaries
Victor Interim Services

East Detroit
Personnel Pool

East Lansing
Uniforce Temporary Services

Farmington Hills
Adia Personnel Services
Manpower, Inc.
Norrell Services
Temporary Resources, Inc.
Victor Interim Services

Fenton
Manpower, Inc.

Flint
Greater Flint Temporaries, Ltd.
Manpower, Inc.
Norrell Services

Trialon Corporation
Victor Interim Services

Fraser

Manpower, Inc.

Grand Blanc

Century Temporary Services, Inc.

Grand Haven

Manpower, Inc.

Grand Rapids

Adia Personnel Services
Advance Personnel Svcs., Inc.
Employment Group, Inc.
Hudson V.I.P.S.
Manpower, Inc.
Norrell Services
Peoplemark, Inc.
Personnel Pool
Snelling Temporaries
Staffing, Inc.
TRC Temporary Services, Inc.
Tempforce
Victor Interim Services

Grandville

Barman Select Temporary Svcs.

Greenville

Temporaries Unlimited, Inc.

Hillsdale

Adia Personnel Services
Manpower, Inc.

Holland

Manpower, Inc.

Jackson

Adia Personnel Services
Employment Group, Inc.
Manpower, Inc.
Victor Interim Services

Kalamazoo

Adia Personnel Services
Employment Group, Inc.
Manpower, Inc.
Personnel Pool
Snelling Temporaries

Lake Orion

Workforce, Inc.

Lansing

Adia Personnel Services
Employment Group, Inc.
Manpower, Inc.
Norrell Services
Victor Interim Services

Lapeer

Manpower, Inc.

Lathrup Village

Prince Holliday Enterprises, Inc.
  d/b/a Metrostaff Temporary
  Personnel

Livomiz

Prince Holliday Enterprise, Inc.

Livonia

AIM Labor
Acro Services Corporation
Adia Personnel Services
G-Tech Services, Inc.
Manpower, Inc.
Partners In Placement
Snelling Temporaries
Uniforce Temporary Services

Ludington

Manpower, Inc.

Madison Heights

Contempra Temporary Personnel

Manistee

Manpower, Inc.

Marshall

Manpower, Inc.

Menominee

Manpower, Inc.

Midland

Manpower, Inc.
Victor Interim Services

Milford
Manpower, Inc.

Monroe
Manpower, Inc.

Monroe
Staff Builders
Victor Interim Services

Mount Clemens
Workforce, Inc.

Mt. Clemens
Snelling Temporaries

Mt. Pleasant
PPI Ltd.

Muskegon
Manpower, Inc.

Oak Park
Renaissance Services, Inc.

Owosso
Manpower, Inc.

Petoskey
Manpower, Inc.

Plymouth
Arbor Temporaries, Inc.
Norrell Services

Pontiac
Manpower, Inc.
Personnel Pool
Workforce, Inc.

Port Huron
Manpower, Inc.

Portage
Manpower, Inc.

Rochester
Manpower, Inc.
Norrell Services

Rochester Hills
Snelling Temporaries

Saginaw
Manpower, Inc.
Norrell Services
Victor Interim Services

South Field
Sharan Corporation

Southfield
Accountants One, Inc.
Adia Personnel Services
Alternative Resources Corp.
CDI Temporary Services, Inc.
Davis-Smith Medical-Dental Emp.
IFS Corporation, d/b/a IFS Temps
Manpower, Inc.
Personnel Pool
Snelling Temporaries
Staff Builders
Temporary Professionals, Inc.
Trojan Engineering Co.
Uniforce Temporary Services

Southgate
ETD Temporary Service

St. Joseph
Beacon Services
Employment Group, Inc.
Scope Services, Inc.

Sterling Heights
Adia Personnel Services
CDI Temporary Services, Inc.
TRC Temporary Services, Inc.

Sturgis
Manpower, Inc.
Perry Personnel Plus, Inc.
Personnel Pool

Swartz Creek
Thomas Temporaries

Taylor
Manpower, Inc.

Three Rivers
Manpower, Inc.

Traverse City

Manpower, Inc.

Trenton

Snelling Temporaries

Troy

Ampro Services, Inc.
Entech Services, Ltd.
Express Services, Inc.
Kelly Services, Inc.
Manpower, Inc.
Norrell Services
O/E Management Services
Peak Services
Personnel Options
Snelling Temporaries

Utica

Manpower, Inc.

Warren

Benchmark Temporary Help
Norrell Services

Westland

ETD Temporary Service

Wyandotte

Adia Personnel Services

Ypsilanti

Adia Personnel Services
The Employment Connection

Zeeland

Manpower, Inc.

MINNESOTA

Bloomington

Alternative Staffing, Inc.
Alternative Resources Corp.
CDI Temporary Services, Inc.
Express Services
LawTemps
Quality Temp, Inc.
Uniforce Temporary Services

Brooklyn Center

CDI Temporary Services, Inc.

Personnel Pool

Burnsville

Manpower, Inc.

Chaska

Express Services, Inc.

Duluth

Manpower, Inc.

Edina

Adia Personnel Services
Jewell Personnel, Inc.
Norrell Services
Personnel Pool
Solmark Temporary Services
Victor Interim Services d/b/a
    Gordon-Victor

Fridley

Express Services, Inc.
Preferred Temporary Services

Mankato

Manpower, Inc.

Minneapolis

Adia Personnel Services
Crown Services, Inc.
Dobbs Temporary Services, Inc.
Manpower, Inc.
PC Temps
Staff Builders
Staff-Plus, Inc.
Stivers Temporary Personnel
Templeton & Associates
Temporarily Yours, Inc.
Uniforce Temporary Services
Victor Interim Services d/b/a
    Gordon-Victor

Monticello

Action-Plus Temporary Service

New Hope

Express Services, Inc.

North Mankato

Express Services, Inc.

Owatonna
Express Services, Inc.
Manpower, Inc.

Rochester
Express Services, Inc.
Manpower, Inc.

Rogers
Temporary Assets, Inc.

Roseville
CDI Temporary Services, Inc.

Saint Paul
Personnel Pool

Spring Lake Park
Temporary Assets, Inc.

St. Cloud
Express Services, Inc.
Manpower, Inc.   .

St. Louis Park
CDI Temporary Services, Inc.

St. Paul
Adia Personnel Services
Freelance Professionals, Inc.
Jeane Thorne Temporary Service
Manpower, Inc.
Norrell Services
Personnel Pool of America
Staff Builders

Winona
Manpower, Inc.

MISSISSIPPI

Greenville
Greenville Temps

Gulfport
Manpower, Inc.
Multi Temps

Hattiesburg
Manpower, Inc.

Jackson
Express Services, Inc.
Jackson Temporaries, Inc.
Manpower, Inc.
Norrell Services
Tempforce

Olive Branch
Norrell Services

Pascagoula
Manpower, Inc.

Vicksburg
Manpower, Inc.

MISSOURI

Affton
Adia Personnel Services

Camdenton
Jeanne's Professional Services

Chesterfield
Adia Personnel Services
B. Loehr Temporaries
CDI Temporary Services, Inc.

Clayton
Adia Personnel Services
CDI Temporary Services, Inc.
Manpower, Inc.
Snelling Temporaries
Staff Builders

Columbia
Express Services, Inc.
Manpower, Inc.

Creve Coeur
Adia Personnel Services
Remedy Temporary Services
    d/b/a Mid/America Placement
Snelling Temporaries

Gladstone
Adia Personnel Services .
Personnel Pool
Snelling Temporaries

Hannibal
Adia Personnel Services

Jefferson City
Manpower, Inc.

Joplin
Manpower, Inc.

Kansas City
Adia Personnel Services
Business Personnel Svcs., Inc.
CDI Temporary Services, Inc.
Crown Services, Inc.
Dunhill Temporary Systems
Express Services, Inc.
Legal Assistance/Grafton, Inc.
Manpower, Inc.
Norrell Services
Personnel Pool
Snelling Temporaries
Stivers Temporary Personnel
Uniforce Temporary Services

Kirkwood
Supplemental Medical Svcs., Inc.

Maryland Heights
CDI Temporary Services, Inc.

Rolla
Express Services, Inc.

Saint Joseph
Express Services, Inc.

Saint Louis
CDI Temporary Services, Inc.
Personnel Pool

Springfield
Manpower, Inc.
PenMac Personnel Services
Personnel Pool

St. Ann
B. Loehr Temporaries
Stivers Temporary Personnel

St. Joseph
Manpower, Inc.

St. Louis
ADIA Personnell Services
All Temps
B. Loehr Temporaries
Core Personnel Services, Inc.
Crown Services, Inc.
Dunhill Temporary Systems
JBS, Inc.
Manpower, Inc.
Norrell Services
Staff Builders
Stivers Temporary Personnel
Talent Tree
TRC Temporary Services, Inc.
Tempforce
Victor Interim Services

MONTANA

Billings
Express Services, Inc.
Manpower, Inc.
The Temporary Connection

Bozeman
Express Services, Inc.

Butte
Express Services, Inc.

Great Falls
Express Services, Inc.

Helena
Express Services, Inc.
Personnel Plus, Inc.

Kalispell
Express Services, Inc.
Labor Contractors

Missoula
Express Services, Inc.

NEBRASKA

Lincoln
CDI Temporary Services, Inc.
Express Services, Inc.
MSP Resources, Inc.

Manpower, Inc.
Norrell Services
Tempforce
Todays Temporary

Omaha

CBC Temporaries, Inc.
CDI Temporary Services, Inc.
Celebrity Services
Crown Services, Inc.
Help, Inc.
Manpower, Inc.
Norrell Services
Personnel Pool
Snelling Temporaries
Todays Temporary
Victor Interim Services

NEVADA

Carson City

Manpower, Inc.

Henderson

Manpower, Inc.

Las Vegas

Accountants Resource/Legal Plus
Adia Personnel Services
Allen Temporary Services
CDI Temporary Services, Inc.
Express Services, Inc.
Manpower, Inc.
The MedLaw Group, Inc.
Norrell Services
Staff Builders
Uniforce Temporary Services

Reno

Manpower, Inc.
Tempforce
Uniforce Temporary Services

Sparks

Manpower, Inc.
Personnel Services, Inc.

NEW HAMPSHIRE

Amherst

Office Resources

Bedford

Snelling Temporaries

Brookline

PPM Personnel

Concord

Manpower, Inc.
TPS, Inc. of Concord

Dover

Manpower, Inc.

Greenland

Uniforce Temporary Services

Hudson

Nursing Network

Keene

Tri-State Professionals, Inc.

Lebanon

Temporary Or Permanent (TOP)

Manchester

Manpower, Inc.
Office Specialists
Personnel Pool
Staff Builders

Merrimack

Additional Tech Support, Inc.

Nashua

Career Connections, Inc.
Key Personnel, Inc.
Manpower, Inc.
Norrell Services
PPM Personnel
Work Force, Inc.

North Hampton

Key Personnel, Inc.

Portsmouth

Manpower, Inc.
Med-Dent Office Professionals
Norrell Services
Staff Builders

Salem
Key Personnel, Inc.
Manpower, Inc.

South Hampton
CALL-A-TECH, INC.

West Lebanon
The Temporary Connection

NEW JERSEY

Atlantic City
Manpower, Inc.

Bayonne
A+ Temporary Services

Belle Mead
Professional Temps, Inc.

Berlin
Temp Source, Inc., The

Bloomfield
Talent Tree

Bridgewater
CDI Temporary Services, Inc.
Staff Builders

Cedar Knolls
Manpower, Inc.

Cherry Hill
Accu Temporary Services
Dunhill Temporary Systems
J & J Temporaries
Manpower, Inc.
National Recruiters, Inc.
Snelling Temporaries
TRC Temporary Services, Inc.
Victor Interim Service d/b/a CRT
    Interim Services

Clifton
Assurance Personnel Services
Manpower, Inc.
Uniforce Temporary Services

Clinton
Norrell Services

Cranford
Manpower, Inc.

Denville
Manpower, Inc.

East Brunswick
Applied Personnel, Inc.
CDI Temporary Services, Inc.
Manpower, Inc.
Snelling Temporaries
Todays Temporary

East Meadow
Uniforce Temporary Services

Eatontown
CDI Temporary Services, Inc.
Manpower, Inc.
Snelling Temporaries

Edison
Brickforce Temporaries, Inc.
Cittone Temps
Dunhill Temporary Systems
J & J Temporaries
Joule Data Temporaries
Metro Temp
Solution Temporary Services
Systemp
Todays Temporary
Transworld Temporaries
Victor Interim Services d/b/a
    ACCT Unlimited

Elizabeth
G-P Temps
Manpower, Inc.

Englewood Cliff
Brooks Temporary Services, Inc.

Florham Park
Victor Interim Services d/b/a
    ACCT Unlimited

Freehold
Omni Temps, Inc.

Sameday Temps
Transworld Temporaries

Ft. Lee
Todays Temporary

Hackensack
Manpower, Inc.
Norrell Services
Personnel Pool

Haddonfield
Careers USA, Inc.

Hamilton Square
Manpower, Inc.
Transworld Temporaries

Highland Park
Norrell Services

Hoboken
Manpower, Inc.

Holmdel
Adia Personnel Services

Iselin
Manpower, Inc.

Jersey City
Devon Temps
Ready Temps, Inc.

Landing
Busy Bee Temps, Inc.

Lawrenceville
CDI Temporary Services, Inc.
Munson Temporaries

Marlton
Adia Personnel Services
CDI Temporary Services, Inc.
Staff Builders

Matawan
Manpower, Inc.

Metuchen
Uniforce Temporary Services

Millburn
Clare, Inc.

Montclair
Devon Temps

Montvale
Manpower, Inc.

Morris Plains
AKP Associates, Inc.

Morristown
J. Davis Associates
Manpower, Inc.
Para-Temp Support Services, Inc.
Talent Tree

Mountainside
J. Davis Associates

Mt. Olive
Manpower, Inc.

Netcong
Top Temps Secretarial Svcs., Inc.

Newark
Busy Bee Temps, Inc.
Uniforce Temporary Services

North Brunswick
Staff Builders

Paramus
Adia Personnel Services
CDI Temporary Services, Inc.
Career Blazers Personnel Svcs.
Keyes Temps
Norrell Services
Remedy Temporary Services d/b/a
    Evergreen Consulting
Talent Tree
Todays Temporary
Uniforce Temporary Services

Parsippany
CDI Temporary Services, Inc.
Career Blazers Personnel Svcs.
Dial A Temporary
New Career Personnel Services

Norrell Services
Prime Time Personnel, Inc.

Paterson

Busy Bee Temps, Inc.
JBS, Inc.
Personnel Pool

Pennsauken

Norrell Services

Pennsville

Manpower, Inc.

Piscataway

Adia Personnel Services
Dial A Temporary

Plainsboro

Adia Personnel Services
Norrell Services

Point Pleasant Beach

Adia Personnel Services

Princeton

Caliper Assessment, Inc.
Future Temps div. Future Resource
  Systems
J & J Temporaries
Staff Builders

Racine

Excel/Temporaries, Inc.

Ramsey

Brooks Temporary Services, Inc.

Rutherford

CDI Temporary Services, Inc.
Uniforce Temporary Services

Scotch Plains

Apoxiforce

Secaucus

SYSTEMP
Victor Interim Services d/b/a
  ACCT Unlimited

Shrewsbury

Adia Personnel Services

Norrell Services

Somerset

J & J Temporaries
Personnel Pool

Somerville

Complete Personnel Services
Manpower, Inc.
On Call Personnel, Inc.
Snelling Temporaries

South Orange

Manpower, Inc.

Summit

Uniforce Temporary Services

Toms River

Adia Personnel Services
The Office Staff

Trenton

J & J Temporaries

Union

Talent Tree

Vineland

Manpower, Inc.
National Recruiters, Inc.

Voorhees Township

Manpower, Inc.

Washington Township

Staff Builders

Wayne

Manpower, Inc.
Personnel Pool
Transworld Temporaries

West Caldwell

Manpower, Inc.

NEW MEXICO

Albuquerque

Adia Personnel Services
Advantage Temporary Staffing
Express Services

Manpower, Inc.
Nick-Of-Time Temporary Service
Norrell Services
Personnel Pool
Snelling Temporaries
Uniforce Temporary Services
Volt Temporary Services

Farmington

Temporarily Yours, Inc.
Uniforce Temporary Services

Hobbs

Express Services, Inc.
Manpower, Inc.
Organization Plus

Las Cruces

Express Services
Manpower, Inc.

Roswell

Manpower, Inc.
Tempforce

Santa Fe

Manpower, Inc.
Santa Fe Services, Inc.
Snelling Temporaries

NEW YORK

Albany

Freedom Services
Manpower, Inc.
Norrell Services
Snelling Temporaries
Staff Builders
Uniforce Temporary Services

Amherst

Victor Interim Services

Auburn

Manpower, Inc.

Batavia

Staff Builders

Binghamton

J. Anthony Associates. Ltd. d/b/a
    Cosmopolitan Personnel S
Manpower, Inc.
Norrell Services

Brooklyn

Tempforce
Staff Builders

Buffalo

Ablest Services Corp.
Computerpeople
Dunhill Temporary Systems
Durham Temporaries, Inc.
Extra Help Employment Services
Manpower, Inc.
Norrell Services
Personnel Pool
Staff Builders
TAD Temporaries
Temp Careers, Inc.
Tempforce
Victor Interim Services

Cambria Heights

Tempforce

Central Islip

Norrell Services

Corning

Manpower, Inc.
Snelling Temporaries

Depew

Durham Temporaries, Inc.

East Meadow

Norrell Services
Talent Tree
Tempforce
Winston Temporaries

Elmhurst

Norrell Services
Staff Builders

Elmira

Manpower, Inc.

Fairport
Adia Personnel Services
Express Services, Inc.
TAD Temporaries
Victor Interim Services

Flushing
Snelling Temporaries

Forest Hills
Adia Personnel Services

Fulton
Manpower, Inc.

Garden City
Preferred Personnel Svcs., Inc.

Geneva
Manpower, Inc.

Glens Falls
Keena Temporary Services

Hartsdale
Talent Tree

Hauppauge
Staff Builders
Sterling Temporary Services

Henrietta
Manpower, Inc.

Hicksville
Manpower, Inc.
Staff Builders
Uniforce Temporary Services

Huntington Station
Winston Temporaries

Ithaca
J. Anthony Associates Ltd.
Manpower, Inc.
Norrell Services

Jamaica
Paramount Temporary People, Inc.

Jamestown
Manpower, Inc.

Staff Builders

Jericho
Adia Personnel Services

Lake Success
Manpower, Inc.
Staff Builders, Inc.

Latham
Manpower, Inc.

Levittown
Personnel Pool

Liverpool
Personnel Pool

Lockport
Staff Builders

Massapequa
Dunhill Temporary Systems

Melville
Career Blazers Personnel Svcs.
Manpower, Inc.
Norrell Services
Personnel Pool
TemPositions, Inc.
Uniforce Temporary Services

Middletown
Here's Help, Inc.

Mineola
Norrell Services
Snelling Temporaries

Nanuet
Hertz Temporary Services
Temporary Staffing Services

New City
Talent Tree

New Hartford
Norrell Services

New Hyde Park
Uniforce Temporary Services

New Rochelle

Tempforce

New York

ATS Services, Inc.
Accountancy Personnel, Inc.
Accountants & Auditors Temps
Adia Personnel Services
Advantage, Inc.
Alternate Resources
Alyson Taylor Temporary Svcs. of
   New York
American Business Careers Empl.
Beneficial Temporaries
Career Blazers Temporary Personnel
Connection Network, Inc. d/b/a
   Temporary Magic
Cross Temps
Dante Personnel Services, Inc.
Ecco Service Group, Inc.
Eden Temporary Services, Inc.
F.L.A.G. Services, Inc.
Gainor Temporary Services
Guidance Services, Inc.
Holiday Temporary Services, Inc.
Irene Cohen Temps, Inc.
Landmark Temporaries, Inc.
Legal Assistants Corp.
Legal Resources, Inc.
Madison Avenue Temporary Service
Manpower, Inc.
Norrell Services
Payson People, Inc.
Personnel Pool
Planned Staffing, Inc.
Powerforce
Pro Temps, Inc.
Sloan Temporary Service, Inc.
Staff Builders
Suzanne Davis Temporaries, Inc.
Swing Shift, Inc.
Systemp
TLI International
Talent Tree
Techlancers, Inc.
Tele-Temps, Inc.
Tempforce
TemPositions
Temporarily Yours Personnel
TemPositions

Tempsations
Uniforce Temporary Services
Victor Interim Services d/b/a Interim
   Systems
Winston Temporaries, Inc.
Word Processing Professionals

Newburgh

Manpower, Inc.

Niagara Falls

Durham Temporaries, Inc.
Staff Builders
Victor Interim Services

North Syracuse

Uniforce Temporary Services

North Tonawanda

Staff Builders

Norwich

Manpower, Inc.

Ossining

Crickett Personnel Services

Perinton

Manpower, Inc.

Plattsburgh

Temporary Assignments

Poughkeepsie

Dutchess Temps, Inc.
Manpower, Inc.
Norman Temporary Services, Inc.

Riverhead

Staff Builders

Rochester

Ablest Services Corp.
Adia Personnel Services
CDI Temporary Services, Inc.
Durham Temporaries, Inc.
Eagle Temporary Service, Inc.
Employee Relations Assoc., Inc.
   Extra Help Employment Services
Employment Store, Inc.
Manpower, Inc.
Med-Scribe, Inc.

Norrell Services
Personnel Pool
Scot Resources, Inc.
Snelling Temporaries
TAD Temporaries
Tempforce
Victor Interim Services

Saratoga Springs

Manpower, Inc.
Uniforce Temporary Services

Schenectady

Manpower, Inc.

Scotia

Omnihelp, Inc.

Smithtown

A.S.A.P. Temporaries
Uniforce Temporary Services

Spring Valley

Manpower, Inc.

Staten Island

Gerri G., Inc.

Syracuse

Ablest Services Corp.
Adia Personnel Services
CDI Temporary Services, Inc.
Ernestwell, Ltd.
Innovative Career Strategies d/b/a
  The Career Source
J. Anthony Associates Ltd.
Manpower, Inc.
Norrell Services
Personnel Pool
Staff Builders
TAD Temporaries
Uniforce Temporary Services
Victor Interim Services

Tonawanda

Durham Temporaries, Inc.

Troy

Manpower, Inc.

Uniondale

Manpower, Inc.

Utica

Manpower, Inc.
Tempforce

Wappingers Falls

EDC Temps, Inc.

West Seneca

Victor Interim Services

Westbury

The Olsten Corporation

White Plains

Career Blazers of White Plains
EDC Temps, Inc.
Irene Cohen Temps, Inc.
Manpower, Inc.
Norrell Services
Personnel Pool
Reinhard Temps, Ltd.
Snelling Temporaries
Staff Builders
Stivers Temporary Personnel
Talent Tree
Uniforce Temporary Services

Williamsville

Ablest Services Corp.
Norrell Services
Vestaff, Inc.

Woodbury

Dunhill Temporary Systems

Yorktown Heights

Career Blazers Personnel Svcs.
Uniforce Temporary Services

NORTH CAROLINA

Albemarle

ATI Temporary & Personnel Svcs.
Albemarle Temporaries, Inc.

Asheville

Adia Personnel Services
Friday Temporary Services, Inc.
Manpower, Inc.
Uniforce Temporary Services

Burlington

Blethen Temporaries, Inc.

Cary

Manpower, Inc.
Office Specialists

Chapel Hill

Delta Professional Services, Inc.
Monarch Temporary Services

Charlotte

Ablest Services Corp.
Accurate Personnel/Temps
Action Personnel Services
Adia Personnel Services
Associated Temp Staffing, Inc.
CDI Temporary Services, Inc.
Corporate Personnel Consultant and
   Temporaries, Inc.
Creative Temporaries Corp.
Executive Reflections
Express Services
Manpower, Inc.
Norrell Services
Office Specialists
Personnel Pool
Resources Employment Svcs., Inc.
S-H-S Temps of Charlotte
Staff-Additions, Inc.
Talent Tree
Temp Force d/b/a Talent Force
Tempo Temporaries
Temporary Advantage, Inc.
Tempworld, Inc.
Todays Temporary
Tracy Temporaries, Inc.
Victor Interim Service

Durham

Blethen Temporaries, Inc.
Elite Personnel Services, Inc.
Manpower, Inc.
Monarch Temporary Services
Personnel Pool
Tracy Temporaries, Inc.

Elkin

Temporary Resources Div. of Exec
   Resources, Inc.

Fayetteville

Manpower, Inc.
Mega Force Temporaries
Uniforce Temporary Services

Gastonia

Manpower, Inc.
Uniforce Temporary Services

Greensboro

Ablest Services Corp.
Adia Personnel Services
Becks Temporary Services, Inc.
Graham & Associates Temporaries
Griffin Temporaries
Manpower, Inc.
Norrell Services
Personnel Pool
Regency Temporaries, Inc.
TRC Temporary Services, Inc.
Tracy Temporaries, Inc.

Greenville

Manpower, Inc.
Victor Interim Services d/b/a Anne's
   Temporaries

Henderson

Blethen Temporaries, Inc.

Hendersonville

Manpower, Inc.

Hickory

Manpower, Inc.
Uniforce Temporary Services

High Point

Griffin Temporaries
Manpower, Inc.
Marlette Baker Temporaries, Inc.
Norrell Services
P.S. Temporaries

Jacksonville

Pro-Type Services

Kernersville

Griffin Temporaries
Manpower, Inc.
Todays Temporary

Kill Devil Hills

Tar Heel Temporary Service

Kinston

Manpower, Inc.
McCain Temporary Services
Victor Interim Services d/b/a Anne's
   Temporaries

Laurinburg

Manpower, Inc.
Mega Force Temporaries

Matthews

Corporate Personnel Consultant
   d/b/a A&J Industrial Labor
Uniforce Temporary Services

Mebane

Mebane Temporary Services

Mocksville

Gantt Personnel, Inc.

Monroe

TPS, Inc.

Mooresville

Foxcroft Temporary Svcs, Inc.

Morganton

Helping Hands Temporary Svcs.

Morgantown

Temporary Staffing Systems, Inc.

New Bern

Victor Interim Services d/b/a Anne's
   Temporaries

Newton

Manpower, Inc.

Oxford

Manpower, Inc.
Monarch Temporary Services

Raleigh

Ablest Services Corp.
Corporate Personnel Consultant and
   Temporaries, Inc.
Creative Temporaries Corp.

Elite Personnel Services, Inc.
Labor Resource, Inc.
Manpower, Inc.
Monarch Temporary Services
Norrell Services
Office Specialists
Personnel Pool
Tracy Temporaries, Inc.

Raleigh-Durham

Adia Personnel Services

Rockingham

Unifour Nursing Service, Inc.

Rocky Mount

Manpower, Inc.
Victor Interim Services d/b/a Anne's
   Temporaries

Sanford

Uniforce Temporary Services

Shelby

Manpower, Inc.
Personnel Services Unlimited
Uniforce Temporary Services

Smithfield

Taylor Temporary Services

Statesville

Carolina Health Professionals
Foxcroft Temporary Services, Inc.

Triangle Park

Labor Resource, Inc.

Washington

Victor Interim Services d/b/a Anne's
   Temporaries

Wilmington

MSI International d/b/a Temps &
   Co.
Manpower, Inc.
Norrell Services
Production Support Services

Wilson

Office Services Unlimited

Winston-Salem

CDI Temporary Services, Inc.
Employers' Relief, Inc.
Griffin Temporaries
Manpower, Inc.
Norrell Services
Personnel Solutions, Inc.
Temporary Resources
Todays Temporary
Uniforce Temporary Services

Yadkinville

Temporary Resources

NORTH DAKOTA

Fargo

Manpower, Inc.

OHIO

Akron

Flex-Team Professional Tempora
Lake Land Labor
Manpower, Inc.
Staff Builders
Victor Interim Services
Visiting Hours, Inc.
WEM

Beachwood

Adia Personnel Services
Ameritemps, Inc.
CDI Temporary Services, Inc.
Corporate Connection Temporary
Egar Employment, Inc.
Leader Personnel, Inc.
Visiting Hours, Inc.

Bedford

Archer Temporaries

Boardman

Victor Interim Services

Bryan

Flexible Personnel

Canton

Manpower, Inc.

Victor Interim Services

Chardon

Visiting Hours, Inc.

Chillicothe

Tempo Help

Cincinnati

Adia Personnel Services
Adow Personnel Services
ADOW Personnel Services of Cin.
American Nursing Care, Inc.
CBS Personnel Services, Inc.
C.M. Temporary Services
Crown Services, Inc.
Express Services, Inc.
Le-Gals, Inc./Tempstaff
Legal Plus, Inc.
Manpower, Inc.
Metro Temporaries, Inc.
Norrell Services
Personnel Pool
Preferred Temporary Services
Protemps, Inc.
Snelling Temporaries
Staff Builders
TRC Temporary Services, Inc.
Todays Temporary
Tri-Temps, Inc.
Victor Interim Services
XLC Services Temporaries

Circleville

Victor Interim Services

Cleveland

Adia Personnel Services
Alternative Resources Corp.
Area Temps
CDI Temporary Services, Inc.
Crown Services, Inc.
Flex-Force Employment Services
Flex-Temp Employment Svcs, Inc.
Le-Gals, Inc.
Manpower, Inc.
Norrell Services
PRN Staffing, Inc.
Progressive Systems
Rogell Temps
Snelling Temporaries

Staff Builders
TRC Temporary Services, Inc.
The Reserves Network, Inc.
Time Services, Inc. d/b/a Time
  Temporary Services
Victor Interim Services

Columbus

Act I Temporaries, Inc.
Adia Personnel Services
Buckeye Temporaries, Inc.
CDI Temporary Services, Inc.
Crown Services, Inc.
Flex-Temp Employment Svcs., Inc.
Manpower, Inc.
Norrell Services
Personnel Pool
PharMacy People
Snelling Temporaries
Staff Builders
TAD Temporaries
Time Services, Inc.
Victor Interim Services (Downtown)
XLC Services

Coshocton

Manpower, Inc.
Shannon Temporary Services, Inc.

Dayton

CBS Temporary Services
Express Services, Inc.
Extrahelp Temporary Services
MSI International d/b/a Preferred
Temporary Svcs.
Manpower, Inc.
Noble Temporarys, Inc.
Norrell Services
Personnel Pool
Snelling Temporaries
Staff Builders
Victor Interim Services
XLC Services

Defiance

Personnel Pool

Delaware

Adia Personnel Services

Dover

Manpower, Inc.

Dublin

Adia Personnel Services

Elyria

Staff Builders
Victor Interim Services

Euclid

The Reserves Network, Inc.

Fairfield

Manpower, Inc.

Findlay

Adia Personnel Services
Manpower, Inc.
Personnel Pool

Grove City

Shannon Temporary Services

Hamilton

Personnel Pool

Highland Heights

Highland Personnel Svcs.

Hudson

CDI Temporary Services, Inc.
Victor Interim Services

Independence

American Professional Temporaries
Remedy Temporary Services d/b/a
  Advantage Personnel
The Reserves Network, Inc.

Kettering

American Nursing Care, Inc.

Lakewood

Target Temporaries, Inc.

Lancaster

Interim Temporaries, Inc.

Lima

American Nursing Care, Inc.
Manpower, Inc.

Norrell Services
Personnel Pool

Lorain

CDI Temporary Services, Inc.

Mansfield

Manpower, Inc.
Snelling Temporaries
Tempforce
Victor Interim Services

Marion

American Nursing Care, Inc.
Manpower, Inc.

Marysville

Victor Interim Services

Maryville

Adia Personnel Services

Mason

Manpower, Inc.

Medina

Victor Interim Services
Visiting Hours, Inc.

Mentor

Staff Builders
Victor Interim Services

Middleburg Heights

CDI Temporary Services, Inc.
Staff Builders

Middletown

Manpower, Inc.
Palmer Temps, Inc.

Milford

PJC Temps & Services, Inc.

Newark

Manpower, Inc.
Norrell Services
Victor Interim Services

North Canton

Staff Builders

North Olmstead

Victor Interim Services

Parma Heights

Staff Builders
Victor Interim Services

Perrysburg

Norrell Services
Renhill Temporaries

Piqua

Brownlee Personnel Services, Inc.

Ravenna

Visiting Hours, Inc.

Rocky River

The Reserves Network, Inc.

Sandusky

Flex-Temp Employment Services
Manpower, Inc.

Shaker Heights

Victor Interim Services

Sidney

Adia Personnel Services

Springfield

American Nursing Care, Inc.
Express Services, Inc.
Manpower, Inc.
Norrell Services
Staff Builders

Strasburg

Victor Interim Services

Sylvania

Phoenix Temporary Svcs.
Temporary Staffing, Inc.

Toledo

Adia Personnel Services
Aim Temporaries div. of Aim
    Executives, Inc.
Flex-Temp Employment Svcs., Inc.
Manpower, Inc.
Network Staffing, Inc.

Norrell Services
Snelling Temporaries
Staff Builders
Victor Interim Services

Troy

Manpower, Inc.
Victor Interim Services

Warren

Flex-Temp Employment Svcs., Inc.
Western Reserve Personnel

Washington C.H.

Interim Temporaries, Inc.

West Chester

Quality Associates, Inc.
Tri-State Temporaries, Inc.

Westlake

CDI Temporary Services, Inc.

Wickliffe

TAD Temporaries

Willoughby

Progressive Personnel, Inc.

Wooster

Manpower, Inc.
Victor Interim Services
Visiting Hours, Inc.

Worthington

American Nursing Care, Inc.
Anne Jones Temporaries, Inc.
CDI Temporary Services, Inc.

Youngstown

Manpower, Inc.
Victor Interim Services

Zanesville

Darrow Temporaries
Manpower, Inc.

OKLAHOMA

Ada

Express Services, Inc.

Chickasha

Express Services, Inc.

Lawton

Express Services, Inc.

Midwest City

Genie Personnel Services, Inc.

Muskogee

Express Services, Inc.

Norman

Express Services, Inc.
PAB Personnel, Inc.

Oklahoma City

Adia Personnel Services
Avante, Ltd.
Dividend Personnel Services
Express Services, Inc.
Genie Personnel Services, Inc.
MTW Employment Agency
Manpower, Inc.
Norrell Services
Office Extras, Inc.
Pro-Temporaries
Professional Nurses Bureau
Sooner Temporary Services
TNT Temps
TRC Temporary Services, Inc.
Tempforce
Todays Temporary

Piedmont

Express Services, Inc.

Ponca City

Personnel Staffing, Inc.

Pryor

Express Services, Inc.

Salupa

Snelling Temporaries

Shawnee

Express Services, Inc.

Stillwater

Express Services, Inc.

Tulsa

Adia Personnel Services
Express Services, Inc.
Key Temporary Personnel, Inc.
Manpower, Inc.
Maxwell/Temps, Inc.
Norrell Services
Snelling Temporaries

Westville

Brewer Temporaries

OREGON

Beaverton

Cascade Temporary Staffing
Manpower, Inc.
Personnel Pool
Temp Technology, Inc.
Volt Temporary Services

Bend

Express Services

Canby

Temps 4 You, Inc.

Corvallis

McLellan Temporaries, Inc.

Eugene

Express Services, Inc.
Manpower, Inc.
Oregon Temporary Services, Inc.
Staff Management Associates

Medford

Express Services, Inc.

Milwaukie

Uniforce Temporary Services

Pendleton

Express Services, Inc.

Portland

Manpower, Inc.
Adia Personnel Services
CDI Temporary Services, Inc. d/b/a
  AAAA Temporary Services
Express Services

Job Shoppers, Inc.
Manpower, Inc.
Snelling Temporaries
Staff Builders
Uniforce Temporary Services
Volt Temporary Services

Roseburg

Express Services, Inc.

Salem

Express Services, Inc.
Manpower, Inc.
Staff Builders

Springfield

Norrell Services

PENNSYLVANIA

Allentown

Adia Personnel Services
Allied Temporary Services
CDI Temporary Services, Inc.
Manpower, Inc.
Norrell Services
Personnel Pool
Russoli Temps
Transworld Temporaries
Uniforce Temporary Services

Altoona

Manpower, Inc.

Bala Cynwyd

Adia Personnel Services
Norrell Services

Bedford

Thomas Temporary Personnel

Bethlehem

Manpower, Inc.

Blue Bell

CDI Temporary Services, Inc.
McCallion Staffing Specialists

Bristol

Uniforce Temporary Services

Camp Hill
The Byrnes Group

Carlisle
Adia Personnel Services

Carnegie
Tempforce

Chambersburg
Adia Personnel Services

Concordville
ADI Computer Services, Inc.

Coraopolis
Alzed Enterprises Ltd.

Danville
D.S.S. Temps

Doylestown
JRP Temps, Inc.
Personnel Services, Inc.

Easton
Adia Personnel Services
Manpower, Inc.

Erie
All Seasons Placement
Hartman Personnel Services
Manpower, Inc.
TAD Temporaries
Talented Temporaries, Inc.

Exton
Adia Personnel Services
Dayta Temporary Services, Inc.

Feasterville
Adia Personnel Services
American Temporary Services
Careers USA, Inc.
Dunhill Temporary Systems
Manpower, Inc.
Standby Temporary Service
Tempforce

Fort Washington
CDI Temporary Services, Inc.

Norrell Services

Franklin Center
Norrell Services

Freedom
Temporaries North

Greentree West
Adia Personnel Services

Hanover
Adia Personnel Services

Harrisburg
Adia Personnel Services
Manpower, Inc.
Personnel Pool

Hershey
Uni-Temp/Div of Just Temps, Inc.

Horsham
Adia Personnel Services
CDI Temporary Services, Inc.

Irwin
Temp Services, Inc.

Jenkintown
Metrix Temporaries, Inc.

Johnstown
Manpower, Inc.

King of Prussia
Adia Personnel Services
CDI Temporary Services, Inc.
Caldwell Temporary Services
Manpower, Inc.
Norrell Services
Todays Temporary
Uniforce Temporary Services
Victor Interim Services d/b/a CRT
    Interim Services

Kingston
Personnel Pool

Lafayette Hill
Peak Personnel, Inc.

Lancaster

Adia Personnel Services
CDI Temporary Services, Inc.
Computer PLUS Temporaries
Manpower, Inc.
Norrell Services
Personnel Pool
Snelling Temporaries
Temporary Resources div. Robscot, Inc.
The Byrnes Group
Uniforce Temporary Services

Langhorne

J & J Temporaries

Latrobe

PRS Consultants

Lebanon

Tempforce
Uni-Temp/Div. of Just Temps, Inc.

Lemoyne

Capital Area Temporary Service
Keystone Temporary Services
Norrell Services

Malvern

CDI Temporary Services, Inc.

Meadow Lands

Professionally Yours, Temporaries

Media

CDI Temporary Services, Inc.
Eagle Staffers & Placers
Manpower, Inc.
Norrell Services
Pyramid Temporary Services, Inc.

Melvern

McCallion Staffing Specialists

Monroeville

Adia Personnel Services
Alzed Enterprises Ltd.
Carol Harris Temporaries, Inc.

Montgomereyville

McCallion Staffing Specialists

Norristown

Careers USA, Inc.

Oil City

Manpower, Inc.

Paoli

LL Temporary Associates

Philadelphia

Adia Personnel Services
American Temporary Services
CDI Temporary Services, Inc.
Careers USA, Inc.
E.J. Bettinger Co.
Express Services, Inc.
KSI Temporary Services
LegalAssist of Philadelphia
Manpower, Inc.
Norrell Services
Personnel Pool
Rent A Temp, Inc.
The Resource Group, Inc.
Snelling Temporaries
Standby Temporary Services
Stivers Temporary Personnel
Systemp
TSI Personnel, Inc.
TeleSec Temporary Services
Temp Force
Victor Interim Services d/b/a CRT Interim Services

Pittsburgh

Abacus Personnel, Inc.
Adia Personnel Services
Admiral Temporary Services, Inc.
Allegheny Personnel Services
Allstaff Temporary Services
Alzed Enterprises Ltd.
Crown Services, Inc.
Daily Services, Inc.
The Employment Connection
Financial Temps
Law Skil
Legal Management Services, Inc.
Manpower, Inc.
Marsetta Lane Temp-Service, Inc.
Norrell Services
Pancoast Temporary Services, Inc.
Personnel Pool

Pittsburgh Temporaries, Inc.
Reflex Services, Inc.
Snelling Temporaries
Staff Builders
Stivers Temporary Personnel
TAD Temporaries
Temporary Accounting Personnel
TEMPS
Temporary Office & Personnel

Plymouth Meeting

Valleystaff Incorporated

Pottstown

Manpower, Inc.

Pottsville

Uni-Temp

Quakertown

Russoli Temps
Staff Builders

Reading

Manpower, Inc.
People Unlimited, Inc.
Personnel Pool

Scranton

CDI Temporary Services, Inc.
Manpower, Inc.
National Recruiters, Inc.
Norrell Services
Personnel Pool
Uniforce Temporary Services

Springfield

Careers USA, Inc.

State College

Manpower, Inc.

Stroudsburg

Manpower, Inc.
Russoli Temps

Swarthmore

Etc. Office Temporaries

Tarentum

Professionals Plus Temporary

Trevose

CDI Temporary Services, Inc.
Flextemps
Manpower, Inc.

Uniontown

Laurel Business Services

Warrington

Personnel Solutions, Inc.

Wayne

Bradley Temporaries, Inc.
Metro Temps
Norrell Services
Snelling Temporaries
Staff Builders Temp Personnel
Standby Temporary Service
Stivers Temporary Personnel

West Chester

Careers USA, Inc.
Manpower, Inc.
Victor Interim Services d/b/a CRT
    Interim Services

Westchester

Norrell Services

Wexford

Norrell Services

Wilkes-Barre

Horizon Personnel Svcs., Inc.
Manpower, Inc.
Norrell Services
Uniforce Temporary Services

Williamsport

Depasquale Temps
Hats-Howe About Temps
Uni-Temp/Div of Just Temps, Inc.

Willow Grove

Manpower, Inc.
Victor Interim Services d/b/a CRT
    Interim Services

Worminster

McCallion Staffing Specialists

Wyomissing

GWR Personnel Resources, Inc.
Gage Personnel Services

York

Adia Personnel Services
BSI Temporaries, Inc.
The Byrnes Group
CDI Temporary Services, Inc.
Employment East Temps
Manpower, Inc.
Norrell Services
Personnel Pool

PUERTO RICO

Hato Rey

Career Contract Services, Inc.
Personnel Pool

RHODE ISLAND

Lexington

Adia Personnel Services

Lincoln

Todays Temporary

Middletown

Aquidneck Employment Svcs., Inc.
Manpower, Inc.

Providence

Adia Personnel Services
Employment Usa, Inc.
Manpower, Inc.
Norrell Services
Office Specialists
Personnel Pool
Services Rendered, Inc.
Staff Builders

Warwick

Manpower, Inc.
Talent Tree
Todays Temporary

SOUTH CAROLINA

Aiken

Job Shop Temp
Manpower, Inc.
Mr./Ms. Temps
TRC Temporary Services, Inc.

Anderson

Hammett Temps Temporary
    Personnel
Manpower, Inc.

Barnwell

Manpower, Inc.

Charleston

Adia Personnel Services
Manpower, Inc.
Tempo, Inc.

Chester

Uniforce Temporary Services

Columbia

CDI Temporary Services, Inc.
Gallman Personnel Services
Manpower, Inc.
Nationwide Specialized Temporaries
Norrell Services
Personnel Pool
Quantum Resources Corporation
Roper Temporary Services
Snelling Temporaries
TRC Temporary Services, Inc.

Florence

MSI International d/b/a Temps &
    Co.
Manpower, Inc.
Quantum Resources Corporation

Greenville

CDI Temporary Services, Inc.
Dunhill Temporary Systems
MSI International d/b/a Temps &
    Co.
Manpower, Inc.
Norrell Services
Personnel Pool
Snelling Temporaries

Talent Tree
Total Recruiting Services, Inc.
Uniforce Temporary Services

Greenwood

Manpower, Inc.

Hartsville

Manpower, Inc.

Hilton Head Island

Tempo Personnel Services, Inc.

Lancaster

Uniforce Temporary Services

Myrtle Beach

Manpower, Inc.

North Charleston

Abacus Temporary Services
Exec-Aids DIV Charles Foster
  Company
Norrell Services
Personnel Pool

Orangeburg

Gallman Personnel Services

Rock Hill

CDI Temporary Services, Inc.
Uniforce Temporary Services

Spartanburg

Advantage Temporary Services
Manpower, Inc.
Talent Tree

Walterboro

Gallman Personnel Services

SOUTH DAKOTA

Aberdeen

Express Services, Inc.

Rapid City

Express Services, Inc.

Sioux Falls

Manpower, Inc.
Staff Pros

Victor Interim Services d/b/a Staff
  Pros

TENNESSEE

Alcoa

Evinco Employment Services

Athens

Preferred Temporary Services

Brentwood

CDI Temporary Services, Inc.
Dianne Holt Personnel, Inc.
Jane Jones Enterprises
Norrell Services, Inc.
Tom Bain Personnel, Inc.

Chattanooga

Carolyn's Temporary Service
Corporate Staffing Resources
MSI International d/b/a Temps &
  Co.
Manpower, Inc.
Tempforce

Clarksville

Tempforce

Cleveland

MSI International d/b/a Preferred
  Temporary Svcs.

Columbia

Human Resources Incorporated
Jane Jones Enterprises, Inc.

Cordova

CDI Temporary Services, Inc.

Dyersburg

Express Services
Manpower, Inc.

Franklin

Human Resources Incorporated

Germantown

Norrell Services

Goodlettsville

Jane Jones Enterprises, Inc.

Hendersonville

Exclusively Temporary Service

Jackson

Manpower, Inc.
Tempforce

Johnson City

Manpower, Inc.
Uniforce Temporary Services

Kingsport

Snelling Temporaries

Knoxville

Career Systems, Inc.
Cobble Personnel, Inc.
Evinco Professional
Manpower, Inc.
Personnel Pool
Professional Temporary Svcs.
Techs On Call
Temp Systems, Inc.

La Vergne

Human Resources Incorporated

Lawrenceburg

Varner Personnel, Inc.

Lenoir City

MSI International d/b/a Preferred
Temporary Svcs.

Martin

The Hamilton-Ryker Company

Maryville

Cobble Personnel, Inc.

McMinnville

New Horizons Services, Inc.

Memphis

Ablest Services Corp.
Accountants & Bookkeepers Pers.
Adia Personnel Services
Jane Jones Enterprises

Leased Labor, Inc.
Manpower, Inc.
Norrell Services
Peoplemark, Inc.
Personnel Pool
Snelling Temporaries
Staff Builders
Temp Force d/b/a Talent Force
TopTalent, Inc.

Morristown

Manpower, Inc.

Murfreesboro

Human Resources Incorporated

Nashille

Human Resources Incorporated c/o
    Lovell Communications

Nashville

Ablest Services Corp.
Adia Personnel Services
Amtemps, Inc.
Cobble Personnel, Inc.
Human Resources Incorporated
Jane Jones Enterprises, Inc.
Manpower, Inc.
Multi Service Systems
Norrell Services
Personnel Pool
TRC Temporary Services, Inc.
Tennessee Temporary Service
Todays Temporary
Tracy Temporaries, Inc.
Victor Interim Services

Oak Ridge

Cobble Personnel, Inc.

Shelbyville

New Horizons Services, Inc.

Smyrna

Jane Jones Enterprises

Tiney Flats

Eastern Services, Inc.

Tullahoma

Human Resources Incorporated
New Horizons Services, Inc.

TEXAS

Abilene

Manpower, Inc.

Addison

Manpower, Inc.
Personnel Pool

Amarillo

Manpower, Inc.

Arlington

Adia Personnel Services
Manpower, Inc.
Norrell Services
Personnel Pool
Talent Tree
Victor Interim Services

Austin

Adia Personnel Services
Austin Temporary Services
Burnett Personnel Services
CDI Temporary Services, Inc.
Dunhill Temporary Systems
Durham Temporaries, Inc.
Express Services, Inc.
Manpower, Inc.
Norrell Services
Office Specialists
Personnel Pool
Secretaries Plus, Inc.
Talent Tree
Todays Temporary
Victor Interim Services
Volt Temporary Services

Barker

Peakload Services

Beaumont

Manpower, Inc.
Personnel Source, The

Bedford

Dividend Personnel Services

Manpower, Inc.

Brenham

Norrell Services

Brownsville

Manpower, Inc.

Bryan-College Station

Manpower, Inc.

Carrollton

Adia Personnel Services
MSI International d/b/a Temps &
   Co.
Manpower, Inc.
Snelling Temporaries
TRC Temporary Services, Inc.
Volt Temporary Services

Corpus Christi

Anne Wilson Temporary Personnel
Express Services, Inc.
Madden Temporary Services, Inc.
Manpower, Inc.
Snelling Temporaries
Uniforce Temporary Services

Dallas

Absolutely Professional Temps
Adia Personnel Services
Alternative Resources Corp.
CDI Temporary Services, Inc.
Computemp of Dallas, Inc.
Durham Temporaries, Inc.
MSI International d/b/a Temps &
   Co.
Manpower, Inc.
Mortgage Banker Consultants
Norrell Services
ODESCO Temporaries
Peakload Services
Personnel Pool
Power Temps, Inc.
Secretaries Plus, Inc.
Select Temporaries, Inc.
Staff Builders
TRC Temporary Services, Inc.
Talent Tree
Temporaries Network
Todays Temporary

Victor Interim Services
Volt Temporary Services
Wordtemps, Inc.

Denton

Express Services, Inc.
Manpower, Inc.

El Paso

Gail Darling Temporaries
Manpower, Inc.
TRC Temporary Services, Inc.
Tempforce

Fort Worth

Adia Personnel Services
Dunhill Temporary Systems
Gail Darling Temporaries
Manpower, Inc.
Norrell Services
Peakload Services
Personnel Pool
Todays Temporary
Uniforce Temporary Services
Volt Temporary Services

Garland

Manpower, Inc.

Graham

Express Services

Harlingen

Manpower, Inc.

Houston

ADDTEMPS/AMERICA
Adia Personnel Services
Burnett Personnel Services
CDI Temporary Services, Inc.
Computemp of Houston, Inc.
Core Personnel Services-Texas
Demos & Expos By Jeanie, Inc.
Enterprise Personnel Services
Houston Temporaries, Inc.
Legal Temp Company, The
Link American Services
MSI International d/b/a Temps &
   Co.
Management Agency Exchange, Inc.
   d/b/a Max Temps

Manpower, Inc.
Norrell Services
Nortek Services Company
Peakload Services
Personnel Pool
Quest Temporaries, Inc.
Skilled Contract Services, Inc.
Skillmaster Temporary Services
Snelling Temporaries
Staff Builders
Steitz & Corbett Personnel Gro
Systemp
Talent Tree
Temp-Plus, Inc.
Temporaries Network
Temporary Help Serv Assn of Tx
Tracy Temporaries, Inc. d/b/a
   S.B. Tracy & Associates
Victor Interim Services

Houston Heights

Personnel Pool

Irving

Adia Personnel Services
CDI Temporary Services, Inc.
Dunhill Temporary Systems
Express Services, Inc.
MSI International d/b/a Temps &
   Co.
Manpower, Inc.
Norrell Services
Personnel Pool
Select Temporaries, Inc.
TRC Temporary Services, Inc.
Talent Tree
Temporaries Network
Todays Temporary
Volt Temporary Services

Jacksonville

Norrell Services

Killeen

Express Services, Inc.

Longview

Manpower, Inc.
Snelling Temporaries

Lubbock

Manpower, Inc.
Snelling Temporaries

Lufkin

Manpower, Inc.

McAllen

Manpower, Inc.

Mesquite

TRC Temporary Services, Inc.

Midland

Adia Personnel Services
Manpower, Inc.
Temp Time
Temporary Resources, Inc.
V.I.P. Limited

New Braunfels

Professional Nurses Bureau

Odessa

Adia Personnel Services
Manpower, Inc.

Pasadena

Burnett Personnel Services
Certified Temporary Services

Plano

CDI Temporary Services, Inc.
Manpower, Inc.
Todays Temporary
Volt Temporary Services

Richardson

Adia Personnel Services
TDY Temporaries
TRC Temporary Services, Inc.
Todays Temporary

San Angelo

Manpower, Inc.

San Antonio

Adia Personnel Services
CDI Temporary Services, Inc.
Dunhill Temporary Systems
Durham Temporaries, Inc.

Express Services, Inc.
Manpower, Inc.
Peakload Services
Personnel Pool
Professional Nurses Bureau
Select Temporaries, Inc.
Talent Tree, Inc.
Todays Temporary
Victor Interim Services
Wise & Associates, Inc.

Sherman

Express Services, Inc.
Manpower, Inc.

Temple

Express Services, Inc.
Manpower, Inc.
Personnel Pool

Texarkana

Exxtra Help, Inc.

Tyler

Manpower, Inc.

Waco

Express Services, Inc.
Manpower, Inc.
Norrell Services

Wichita Falls

Care Team Management Services
Express Services, Inc.
Manpower, Inc.

UTAH

Murray

SOS Temporary Services

Ogden

Manpower, Inc.
SOS Temporary Services

Orem

Manpower, Inc.
SOS Temporary Services

Salt Lake City

Express Services, Inc.

Manpower, Inc.
SOS Temporary Services
Tempforce
Victor Interim Services
Volt Temporary Services

Sandy
Adia Personnel Services

VERMONT

Arlington
Heritage Personnel Services

Brattleboro
Harmon Temporary Service

Burlington
Manpower, Inc.
The 500 Recruiters

S. Burlington
Norrell Services

Williston
Triad Temporary Services, Inc.

VIRGINIA

Alexandria
Adia Personnel Services
BSI Temporaries, Inc.
Best Temporaries, Inc., Federal
  Systems Division
Editorial Experts, Inc.
Manpower, Inc.
Norrell Services
Tracy Temporaries, Inc.
Volt Temporary Services

Annandale
Forbes Temporaries, Inc.

Arlington
BSI Temporaries, Inc.
Careers USA, Inc.
Manpower, Inc.
Med-Force, Inc.
Personnel Pool
Talent Tree

Aylett
All American Professional Serv.

Baileys Crossroads
Temporary Resources

Blacksburg
Norrell Services

Charlottesville
Manpower, Inc.
Snelling Temporaries

Chesapeake
Manpower, Inc.
Reliance Temporary Services

Danville
Ameristaff Companies, Inc.

Fairfax
Action People, Inc.
Manpower, Inc.
Talent Tree
TeleSec Temporary Services

Falls Church
Adia Personnel Services
Advantage Temporary Services
Manpower, Inc.
Norrell Services
Talent Tree
TeleSec Temporary Services

Hampton
CDI Temporary Services, Inc.
Select Temporary Services

Harrisonburg
Manpower, Inc.

Herndon
Adia Personnel Services
Manpower, Inc.
Volt Temporary Services

Hillsville
Surry Temporary Services, Inc.

Lexington
Jobshop, Inc.

Luray

Jobshop, Inc.

Lynchburg

Manpower, Inc.

Manassas

Temporary Solutions, Inc.
Tracy Temporaries, Inc.
Volt Temporary Services

Martinsville

Ameristaff Companies, Inc.

McLean

Contemporary Nursing, Inc.
Don Richard Associates of DC
Manpower, Inc.
Monarch Temporary Services
Sparks Personnel Services, Inc.
Uniforce Temporary Services

New Market

Jobshop, Inc.

Newport News

Adia Personnel Services
Lee Temps Associates, Inc.
Manpower, Inc.
Norrell Services
Reliance Temporary Services
Uniforce Temporary Services

Norfolk

CDI Temporary Services, Inc.
Gress Associates, Inc. T/A Don
Manpower, Inc.
Norrell Services
SOS Temporary Services, Inc.
Select Temporary Services
Snelling Temporaries
Sunbelt Temporaries
Todays Temporary
Tracy Temporaries, Inc.

Petersburg

Manpower, Inc.

Reston

CDI Temporary Services, Inc.
Forbes Temporaries, Inc.

Manpower, Inc.
Norrell Services
Select Temporary Services
Sparks Personnel Services, Inc.
TAD Temporaries
Talent Tree
Temporary Exchange, Inc.

Richmond

Abacus Temporary Services
Adia Personnel Services
All American Professional Svcs.
Battelle Temps, Inc.
CDI Temporary Services, Inc.
Dunhill Temporary Systems
Legal Temporaries
Manpower, Inc.
Norrell Services
The Personal Secretary, Inc.
Personnel Pool
Quantum Resources Corporation
Remedy Temporary Services
Select Temporary Services
Snelling Temporaries
Staff Builders
Temporary Resources
Tracy Temporaries, Inc.
Workforce, Inc.

Roanoke

Adia Personnel Services
Manpower, Inc.
Norrell Services

Rosslyn

Key Accounting Temporaries, Inc.

South Boston

Ameristaff Companies, Inc.
Paper Tigers, Inc.

Springfield

Manpower, Inc.
Talent Tree

Staunton

Jobshop, Inc.
Manpower, Inc.

Strasburg

Jobshop, Inc.

Stuarts Draft
Jobshop, Inc.

Tappahannock
Jobshop, Inc.

Tysons Corners
Manpower, Inc.

Vienna
Adia Personnel Services
BSI Temporaries, Inc.
CORE Personnel, Inc.
PRN Nursing Temps, Inc.
Remedy Temporary Services d/b/a
   ZIA, Inc.
Temporaries Network
Temporary Help Experts and The
   Accounting Temporaries
Temporary Resources
Volt Temporary Services
WN Hunter & Associates
Woodside Employment Consultants,
   Inc.

Virginia Beach
Abacus Services, Inc.
Adia Personnel Services
All American Professional
Manpower, Inc.
P.C. Employment Services, Inc.
Protemps Temporary Services
Remedy Temporary Services d/b/a
   Skill Dynamics Corp.
Uniforce Temporary Services

Waynesboro
Express Services

Williamsburg
Production Support Services

Winchester
AES Corporate Services, Inc.
Adia Personnel Services
Manpower, Inc.

WASHINGTON

Anacortes
Apex Technical Services, Inc.

Belleview
Uniforce Temporary Services

Bellevue
Express Services, Inc.
MSI International d/b/a Temps &
   Co.
Remedy Temporary Services d/b/a
Glen Oaks Enterprises
Volt Temporary Services

Bothell
Uniforce Temporary Services

Bremerton
Express Services, Inc.

Chehalis
Express Services, Inc.

Everett
Express Services, Inc.

Federal Way
Personnel Pool
Volt Temporary Services

Kennewick
Express Services, Inc.

Kent
Dunhill Temporary Systems
Express Services, Inc.

Lacey
Employment Northwest, Inc. Temp

Lynnwood
Express Services, Inc.
Norrell Services
Volt Temporary Services

Olympia
Express Services, Inc.
Manpower, Inc.

Port Angeles
Angeles Temporary Services

Redmond
Express Services, Inc.
Personnel Pool

Renton
Volt Temporary Services

Seattle
Accounting Force, Inc.
Adia Personnel Services
Bostwick Temporary Services
Dunhill Temporary Systems
Manpower, Inc.
Manus Temporary Services
Norrell Services
Personnel Pool
Professional Resource Group
Snelling Temporaries
Staff Builders
Techstaff, Inc.
Todays Temporary
United Temporary Services, Inc.
Volt Temporary Services

Spokane
Express Services, Inc.
Manpower, Inc.

Tacoma
Adia Personnel Services
Express Services, Inc.
Manpower, Inc.
Norrell Services
Personnel Pool

Tukwila
Volt Temporary Services d/b/a Volt
    Technical Svcs.

Vancouver
Express Services, Inc.
K-M Services
Manpower, Inc.
Personnel Pool
Volt Temporary Services

Walla Walla
Express Services, Inc.

Wenatchee
Express Services, Inc.

Yakima
ADD Temporary Help Service, Inc.
Express Services, Inc.

WEST VIRGINIA

Bluefield
Saunders Temporary Services

Charleston
Manpower, Inc.

Charlestown
United Talent

Clarksburg
Manpower, Inc.

Huntington
Manpower, Inc.

Inwood
Plaza Personnel & Reporting Svce.

Martinsburg
Manpower, Inc.

Morgantown
Manpower, Inc.

Parkersburg
Norrell Services
Quantum Resources Corporation
X-Tras

Wheeling
Manpower, Inc.

WISCONSIN

Appleton
Flex-Staff Temporary Services
Landmark Temporary Services
Manpower, Inc.
Norrell Services

Beaver Dam
Boyd-Hunter, Inc.

Beloit
Manpower, Inc.
Victor Interim Services d/b/a
    Dependability

Brookfield

Adia Personnel Services
Manpower, Inc.
TAD Temporaries

Brown Deer

Norrell Services

Eau Claire

Manpower, Inc.

Elkhorn

Manpower, Inc.

Fond du Lac

Manpower, Inc.

Ft. Atkinson

Terra Temporary Personnel

Grafton

Manpower, Inc.
SEEK, Incorporated

Green Bay

Employment Specialists
Manpower, Inc.
Norrell Services
Snelling Temporaries

Hartford

Boyd-Hunter, Inc.
SEEK, Incorporated

Horicon

Manpower, Inc.

Janesville

Manpower, Inc.

Kenosha

Merrick Temporary Services

La Crosse

Manpower, Inc.

Madison

American Business Resource Corp.
Manpower, Inc.
Norrell Services

Manitowoc

American Business Resource
Manpower, Inc.

Menomonee Falls

Manpower, Inc.

Menomonie

Manpower, Inc.

Mequon

SEEK, Incorporated

Milwaukee

Adia Personnel Services
Bluearrow/Flex-Force Services
Consulting Lab Services, Inc.
Crown Services, Inc.
Dunhill Temporary Systems
Hatch Temporary Services
Manpower, Inc.
Personal Services, Inc.
Personnel Pool
Personnel World, Inc.
SEEK, Incorporated
Snelling Temporaries
Spectrum Temporary Services
Stivers Temporary Personnel
Systemp
TAD Temporaries
Tempforce
Uniforce Temporary Services

Monroe

Manpower, Inc.

Neenah

Career Options, Inc.

Oshkosh

Manpower, Inc.

Racine

Manpower, Inc.

Reedsburg

Tempo, Inc.

River Falls

S.M.G. Personnel Services

Sheboygan

American Business Resource
Manpower, Inc.
SEEK, Incorporated

Stevens Point

American Business Resource

Sturgeon Bany

American Business Resource

Two Rivers

Engstrom Enterprises

Waukesha

Manpower, Inc.

Wausau

Manpower, Inc.

Wauwatosa

Adia Personnel Services
Dunhill Temporary Systems
Norrell Services
Staff Builders

West Allis

Celebrity Services

West Bend

SEEK, Incorporated

WYOMING

Casper

Express Services, Inc.
Manpower, Inc.

Cheyenne

Express Services, Inc.
Manpower, Inc.

Glossary

agency   An employment agency. *See* **employment agency.**

applicant   An individual seeking temporary employment with a temporary help company. In the employment agency business, *applicant* means a person seeking to be permanently placed.

assign   The act of sending a temporary employee to work on the premises of a customer of the temporary help company. "Assign" is different from a "referral," which describes the employment agency practice of sending an applicant to a prospective employer for an interview. "Refer," or "referral," does not apply to the act of assigning temporary employees.

assignment   The period of time during which a temporary employee is working on a customer's premises.

commingling   See joint operations.

contingent worker*   A worker with no attachment to any one employer.

Reprinted with permission from *Lexicon of Terms*, a publication of the National Association of Temporary Services (with additions).
* Not part of the NATS *Lexicon of Terms*.

coordinator   The staff employee of a temporary help company who assigns temporary employees to work on the customer's premises.

counselor   An employment agency employee who refers or places applicants for employment with employers. The term does not apply to a staff employee of a temporary help company. Many state employment agency laws require that counselors be licensed.

customer   The person, organization, or business that uses the services of a temporary help company.

dispatch   This term is generally used to refer to the act of assigning industrial temporary employees to report for work on a customer's premises.

employee leasing   An arrangement whereby a business transfers its employees to the payroll of a "leasing organization", after which the employees are leased back to their original employer where they continue working in the same capacity as before in an ongoing, permanent relationship.

fee   The amount charged by an employment agency for placing job seekers in permanent positions. The term does not refer to a temporary help company's gross profit or liquidated damages charge. *See* **liquidated damages.**

general employer   An employer who has the right to hire and fire an employee, is responsible for the employee's wages and benefits, and exercises ultimate supervision, discipline, and control over the employee. Temporary help companies are the general employers of their temporary employees. *See* **special employer.**

in-house temporary   An individual hired directly by a nontemporary help company as a permanent employee to perform various temporary assignments within that company.

independent contractor   A person, not an employee, who performs work for another. Unlike employees, independent contractors (1) are not subject to the control, and supervision of the person using the services regarding the details of how the work is to be performed, (2) generally have specialized training or education, and (3) supply all necessary tools, supplies, or equipment necessary to perform the work.

job order   *See* **work order.**

job shop   A colloquial term generally used to refer to businesses that supply longer term employees on a contract basis in technical or specialized areas such as engineering, drafting, and so forth.

joint operations   The operation of both a temporary help company and an employment agency by the same company. Problems arise when these fundamentally different operations are conducted with the same personnel, forms, and procedures, so that the two businesses are not easily distinguished by job applicants and customers. Such commingling leads to public confusion about the nature of the temporary help business and could subject the industry to employment agency regulation. To avoid customer confusion, NATS has developed guidelines to help NATS members keep the two businesses separate.

liquidated damages   Liquidated damages are monies paid by temporary help customers under agreements in which the customer agrees not to hire the temporary employee within some specified period of time and to pay damages for breach of that promise in the agreed upon, that is, liquidated, amount.

part-time   A work period less than the full work day or full work week. Part-time employees are not temporary employees because, unlike temporary employees, they work a regular schedule for their employer on an ongoing, indefinite basis. *See* **temporary employee.**

payrolling   A colloquial term in the temporary help industry that describes a situation whereby the customer, rather than the temporary help firm, recruits an individual and asks the temporary help firm to consider employing the individual and assigning him or her to the customer on a temporary basis. Once hired by the temporary help firm, the payrolled employees's employment relationship with the temporary help firm is the same as any other temporary employee.

placement   An employment agency term describing the act of suc-

cessfully placing a job seeker in a permanent position with an
employer.

refer* To send or direct an applicant to a client company for
consideration for permanent employment. (Not commonly used
in reference to temporary help.)

referral* The applicant referred by a permanent placement service
for consideration for permanent employment. (Not a term commonly used to denote a temporary applicant.)

special employer A term referring to a customer's legal relationship
to the temporary employees assigned to them. The relationship
is based on the customer's right to direct and control the specific
details of the work to be performed. As special employers,
customers have certain legal rights and obligations regarding
temporary employees. For example, because workers compensation insurance (which temporary help companies provide for
their employees) is the exclusive relief available to employees
against employers for work-related injuries, a temporary employee generally cannot sue his or her special employer (the
customer) for negligence. Hence, the customer's special employer
status insulates it from such liability. On the other hand, as
special employers, customers may also have certain obligations
to temporary employees, for example, not to discriminate against
them in violation of the civil rights laws. *See* **general employer.**

supplemental staffing The term is generally used to refer to the
practice of supplementing the permanent staff of hospitals and
nursing homes with nurses and other health-care personnel
employed by temporary help companies.

telecommuter* A staff employee who works either from home or
from a satellite office or "home base."

temp-to-perm Also referred to as "try before you hire." The practice
of sending temporary help employees on an assignment for the
express purpose of ultimately placing them in a permanent
position with the customer. This is an employment agency activity
that may subject a temporary help company to regulation under

---

* Not part of the NATS *Lexicon of Terms.*

state employment agency laws. Temp-to-perm practices include but are not limited to:

- Advertising temp-to-perm positions to attract workers seeking permanent jobs
- Suggesting or recommending to customers that they use temporary employees on a temp-to-perm basis
- Agreeing to customers' requests to send temporary employees on a temp-to-perm basis
- Sending temporary employees to customers to be interviewed for the purpose of determining who will be assigned to the customer on a temp-to-perm basis

temporary employee   An employee who does not make a commitment to an employer to work on a regular, ongoing basis but instead is free to accept (or reject) assignments at such times and for such lengths of time as the employee may choose. A temporary employee is obligated only to complete a particular assignment once one is accepted, but has no obligation to accept further assignments. *See* **part-time employee.**

temporary help service or firm   An organization engaged in the service business of furnishing its own employees (temporaries) to handle customers' temporary-staffing needs and special projects.

try before you hire   *See* **temp-to-perm.**

work order   An order received from a customer for a temporary help company's services. In the employment agency industry, the term job order refers to a request from a prospective employer authorizing the employment agency to find an appropriate prospective employee.

INDEX